Verification
and Arms Control

Published under the auspices of the Center for International
and Strategic Affairs, University of California, Los Angeles

A list of other Center publications appears
at the back of this book.

Verification and Arms Control

Edited by

William C. Potter
University of California,
Los Angeles

Lexington Books
D.C. Heath and Company/Lexington, Massachusetts/Toronto

Library of Congress Cataloging in Publication Data

Main entry under title:

Verification and arms control.

   Published for the Center for International and Strategic Affairs, University of California, Los Angeles.
   Includes bibliographical references and index.
   1. Nuclear arms control—Addresses, essays, lectures.   I. Potter, William C.   II. University of California. Los Angeles. Center for International and Strategic Affairs.
JX1974.7.V42   1985   327.1'74   84-48508
ISBN 0-669-09554-0 (alk. paper)

Published simultaneously in Canada
Printed in the United States of America on acid-free paper
International Standard Book Number: 0-669-09554-0
Library of Congress Catalog Card Number: 84-48508

Contents

Tables

Preface

This book is the product of a conference, "Verification and Arms Control," held at the University of California, Los Angeles, on January 25–26, 1984. The conference was sponsored by the UCLA Center for International and Strategic Affairs with the support of the UCLA Center for Russian and East European Studies and the Ploughshares Fund.

I wish to thank Michael Intriligator, Gerri Page, Leslie Rollins, and Daniel Skubik for their help in organizing the conference. I am also grateful to Richard Bitzinger for his assistance in preparing the manuscript for publication.

This book is dedicated to my 1984 UCLA student arms control negotiators who, in their simulation of U.S.–Soviet negotiations, demonstrated that verification and arms control need not be incompatible.

Abbreviations

ABM antiballistic missile

ACDA Arms Control and Disarmament Agency

ACOUSTINT acoustic intelligence

AEC Atomic Energy Commission

AEDS Atomic Energy Detection System

ALCM air-launched cruise missile

ARIA Advanced Range Instrumentation Aircraft

ARIS Advanced Range Instrumentation Ship

ASAT antisatellite

ASW antisubmarine warfare

BMD ballistic missile defense

BMEWS Ballistic Missile Early Warning System

BWC Biological Weapons Convention

C³ communication, command, and control

CBW chemical and biological weapons

CCD Conference of the Committee on Disarmament

CD Committee on Disarmament

COMINT communications intelligence

CTBT Comprehensive Test Ban Treaty

CWFZE chemical weapon free zone in Europe

DMSP Defense Meteorological Satellite Program

DSAT   satellite defense

ECM   electronic countermeasure

EHF   extremely high frequency

ELINT   electronic intelligence

EMP   electromagnetic pulse

ENDC   Eighteen-Nation Disarmament Committee

EOD   externally observable difference

EORSAT   electronic ocean reconnaissance satellite

FISINT   foreign instrumentation signals intelligence

FOB   fractional orbital bombardment

FROD   functionally related observable difference

GEODSS   Ground-based Electro-Optical Deep Space Surveillance

GLCM   ground-launched cruise missile

GPS   Global Positioning System

HF   high frequency

ICBM   intercontinental ballistic missile

INF   Intermediate Nuclear Force

JCC   Joint Consultative Commission

LF   low frequency

LTBT   Limited Test Ban Treaty

MIRV   multiple independently targeted reentry vehicle

MPS   Multiple Protective Shelter

NAVSPASUR   Naval Space Surveillance

NSS   national seismic station

NTM   national technical means

OSI   on-site inspection

PNET   Peaceful Nuclear Explosions Treaty

RADINT   radar intelligence

RORSAT   radar ocean reconnaissance satellite

RSTN   Regional Seismic Test Network

RV   reentry vehicle

SAC   Strategic Air Command

SAINT   satellite inspector system

SALT   Strategic Arms Limitations Talks

SCARS   System Control and Receiving Station

SCC   Standing Consultative Commission

SDS   Satellite Data System

SHF   super high frequency

SIGINT   signals intelligence

SLBM   submarine-launched ballistic missile

SLCM   submarine-launched cruise missile

SOSUS   Sound Surveillance System

SPADATS   Space Detection and Tracking System

SSBN   subsurface ballistic nuclear

SSN   subsurface nuclear

START   Strategic Arms Reduction Talks

TAV   transatmospheric vehicle

TEL   transporter-erector-launcher

TELINT   telemetry intelligence

TERCOM   terrain contour matching

TNF   theater nuclear forces

TTBT   Threshold Test Ban Treaty

UHF   ultra high frequency

VHF   very high frequency

VLF   very low frequency

Verification
and Arms Control

1
Introduction

William C. Potter

T he history of arms control negotiations since World War II is a continuous record of controversy over verification issues. The debate over verification, however, has recently entered a new phase in which the issue of Soviet noncompliance and U.S. responsiveness (or lack thereof) has become a political issue of first magnitude. Indeed, one can argue that in the Reagan administration, verification has become the most important standard against which arms control agreements—both past and prospective—are measured.

Unfortunately, the rise in public awareness of the issue of verification has not been matched by informed debate about the subject. This book is intended to facilitate such debate by presenting a variety of perspectives on the political and technical requisites of verification in a number of past, present, and potential arms control negotiating forums. It departs from most other treatments of the subject in its attentiveness to the political dimension of verification and to both Soviet and U.S. perspectives.

Major Issues in the Debate over Verification

The development in the 1960s of improved national technical means (NTM) of monitoring the military activities of other countries, especially satellite photo-reconnaissance, usually is credited with making progress in arms control possible. The United States' confidence in its ability to monitor Soviet weapons systems, for example, was a crucial factor in the U.S. decision in SALT I to abandon its long-standing demand for on-site inspection. NTM also provided the primary means by which the verification requirements for SALT II were met. Reliance on NTM, however, has come under increasing attack by critics of SALT, who argue that verification should be tailored to the needs of arms control rather than vice versa. Cooperative measures, they argue, especially intrusive forms of inspection, should be the preferred means to verify treaty compliance.

The necessity and effectiveness of cooperative measures of verification is the focus of chapter 2, by James Schear. In a careful examination of passive and active forms of cooperation, he demonstrates that they are not the magical solution to the problems of verification, as is often implied by their proponents.

Especially significant is his finding that on-site inspection is unlikely to provide greater confidence in the monitoring of many aspects of treaty compliance than that obtainable by passive measures and NTM.

An important aspect of verification that has received little scrutiny, at least in the public domain, is Soviet views on treaty compliance. Allan Krass's chapter makes a significant contribution to the study of these Soviet perspectives. As Krass points out, Soviet attitudes toward verification, while often at odds with those of the United States, do have a logic and coherence and may be less incompatible with U.S. interests than is usually assumed. Particularly noteworthy—and controversial—are his conclusions that the Soviets may be correct in their recognition of the advantages of agreeing in principle before haggling over details, in their understanding of the need for some a priori assumption of trust, and in their skepticism about the utility of on-site inspection.

Warren Heckrotte's chapter, "Verification of Test Ban Treaties," provides a useful case study in which to test a number of the propositions raised by Schear and Krass. Based in large part on his own extensive experience negotiating with the Soviets, Heckrotte corroborates a number of the principles of Soviet verification behavior noted by Krass. He finds, for example, that one principle governing the Soviet position at the test ban negotiations in the 1970s was that monitoring requirements had to be justified for the purpose of verification. When they were justified, the Soviets were prepared to accept some measure of intrusive inspection in order to reach agreement on the Peaceful Nuclear Explosion and Comprehensive Test Ban treaties. Like Schear, however, Heckrotte notes the limited technical effectiveness of on-site inspection. His analysis of the test ban treaties is also important for its finding that the Soviet approach to verification underwent a major transformation during the course of the negotiations.

The test ban treaties represent the arms control area in which the most progress has been made toward overcoming the technical obstacles to verification. Among the areas in which technical difficulties are most acute are antisatellite weapons, cruise missiles and bombers, and biological and chemical weapons. These are the topics addressed in the chapters by William Durch, Dean Wilkening, and F.R. Cleminson.

In his chapter, Durch examines the verification requirements of three alternative approaches to limiting antisatellite weapons: a "zero-zero" agreement, requiring the dismantling of all existing direct-attack ASAT systems; a "zero development and testing" agreement; and a "one-each" agreement, allowing both parties one type of direct-attack ASAT. He concludes that of the three approaches, the most desirable in terms of the trade-off between uncertainty and risk is an indefinite test ban on both kinetic and beam ASAT weapons, accompanied by a "rules-of-the-road" agreement delimiting permissible types of behavior in space.

The picture Wilkening presents of the prospects for monitoring cruise missile and bomber limitations by NTM is a gloomy one—particularly for cruise missiles, because of their small size, variable range, dual (conventional/ nuclear) warhead capability, and compatibility with multiple launch platforms. At best, according to Wilkening, NTM can monitor cruise missile characteristics and activities with moderate levels of confidence; that confidence drops to a low level if an effort is made at deliberate concealment. Also disturbing is his conclusion about the limited utility of functionally related observable differences (FRODs) as a verification aid, a measure relied upon to count "heavy bombers" and air-launched cruise missiles in SALT II.

Unlike the bilateral negotiations to limit nuclear weapons, efforts to ban biological and chemical weapons have been concentrated in the multinational Conference of the Committee on Disarmament. F.R. Cleminson's chapter provides a Canadian perspective on negotiations over the issue of verification in that forum. Although not optimistic about the prospects for major progress, he is encouraged by the January 1984 Soviet proposal on a chemical weapon-free zone in Europe and by the April 1984 U.S. draft convention on the prohibition of chemical weapons.

The chapter by Michael Krepon and the one by Mark Lowenthal and Joel Wit focus explicitly on the often neglected political dimension of verification. Although the authors disagree in their interpretation of the adequacy of prior verification procedures, they share the concern that, at present, verification is being asked to bear too great a burden. As Lowenthal and Wit point out, although verification was once seen as a means to build public support for arms control, it has now become a political instrument for its obstruction. This is due in part, Krepon suggests, to the successful efforts of critics of SALT I and SALT II to redefine the generally accepted standard of verification from "adequate" to "effective," without specifying what constitutes effective verification. Particularly disturbing to Lowenthal and Wit is the virtual absence in the current politics of verification of any middle ground between those who are persuaded that the Soviets are "cheating" and insist that arms control agreements must await improved means of verification and those who are willing to take substantial verification risks for the sake of achieving arms control. The key to correcting this situation and depoliticizing verification, Lowenthal and Wit maintain, is to provide Congress and the public with more information about the compliance process.

One of the impediments to more informed debate over verification has been the inaccessibility of much relevant information on U.S. capabilities for monitoring Soviet strategic weapons developments. The product of Jeffrey Richelson's thorough survey of the open literature is the most complete public account of current U.S. monitoring systems. Richelson's chapter also has the virtue of calling attention to the value of technical collection capabilities, not only for verifying treaty compliance but also for providing much of the information upon which arms control negotiating positions are built and Soviet proposals are assessed.

The architects of the 1972 SALT accords were aware that questions would arise regarding treaty compliance, and they provided for the creation of the Standing Consultative Commission (SCC) to deal with such questions. Dan Caldwell's concluding chapter examines the operation of the SCC since its founding and evaluates its performance. He concludes that although the current status and future of the SCC are in doubt, the body has operated effectively for over a decade in resolving compliance-related questions.

The Future of Verification and Arms Control

Five years ago, when the companion volume to this study went to press,[1] verification was a contentious issue in the arms control debate, but it was not the decisive one. Today, this situation has changed, and verification stands as the litmus test by which arms control proposals are assessed. Moreover, there is little doubt that the political basis for verification has seriously eroded in the United States at the same time that the technical requirements for verification have become more demanding. This development is apparent in the two major reports on Soviet treaty compliance released by the White House in 1984: "The President's Report to Congress on Soviet Noncompliance with Arms Control Agreements," and the General Advisory Committee on Arms Control and Disarmament report, "A Quarter Century of Soviet Compliance Practices Under Arms Control Commitments, 1958–1983." (See appendixes A and B for the texts of the reports.) According to the testimony of one of the contributors to the October 1984 General Advisory Committee report, "no one who saw the complete technical evidence advanced could doubt that the violations are so significant as to call into question the very notion that the superpowers retain enough common interest in arms control to warrant continuing negotiations."[2] To be sure, the Reagan administration has not publicly advanced that conclusion and indeed has sought at the end of its first term to revive arms control negotiations with the Soviets. Verification, however, is likely to serve as the preferred political means by which opponents to arms control—both within and outside the administration—justify their attack.

The contributions to this volume indicate the formidable verification difficulties that confront arms control today. The more certainty of treaty compliance verification is asked to provide, the greater the difficulty. The uncertainties in potential agreements, however, must be balanced against the risks posed by an unconstrained arms race. When viewed in these terms, verification and arms control may yet have a future.

Notes

1. William C. Potter, ed., *Verification and SALT: The Challenge of Strategic Deception* (Boulder, Colo.: Westview Press, 1980).
2. Colin S. Gray, "Moscow Is Cheating," *Foreign Policy,* Fall 1984, p. 141.

2

Cooperative Measures of Verification: How Necessary? How Effective?

James A. Schear

"Cooperative verification"—the practice of using voluntary or negotiated measures to enhance the verifiability of arms control agreements—has become a fashionable concept in recent years. At their 1979 summit meeting in Vienna, Presidents Carter and Brezhnev endorsed the use of cooperative measures in the verification of future strategic arms agreements. Likewise, in its 1982 report, the Palme Commission on Disarmament and Security Issues stressed the possibility of taking steps beyond national technical means (NTM) of verification, including on-site inspection, to satisfy the monitoring requirements of various types of agreements. And in their early statements on policy, aides to President Reagan observed that a willingness on the part of the Soviet Union to accept such measures would be seen as a "litmus test" of its commitment to negotiated arms restraint.[1]

Any concept that commands such broad allegiance ought to be treated with caution. Cooperative measures mean different things to different people; and disagreements regarding their design, intrusiveness, and implementation often stem from more general disputes over the aims and substance of arms control. For example, the Strategic Arms Limitation Talks (SALT) exemplified the view that agreed measures for verification could be worked out on a step-by-step basis. At the outset, the parties could agree on little more than to confine themselves to negotiating limitations that each would verify with unilateral monitoring methods. This, of course, was "cooperation" in its most elementary form. In SALT I, the United States gave up its long-standing demand for on-site inspection rights, while the Soviet Union conceded its equally insistent position that American intelligence-gathering systems could have no legitimate use. In SALT II, where verification requirements were more demanding, both

The author wishes to thank Albert Carnesale, Michael Krepon, Mark M. Lowenthal, Steven Miller, and Walter Slocombe, who offered helpful comments and suggestions on an earlier version of this chapter. He is also grateful for financial support provided by the Joseph Rowntree Charitable Trust.

worked out additional arrangements to streamline monitoring tasks (for example, through "type" counting rules), to strengthen the effectiveness of NTM capabilities (for example, by extending the ban on deliberate concealment to include testing activities), and to tackle particular monitoring problems with collateral measures (for example, by proscribing the production, testing, and deployment of the Soviet SS-16 ICBM). Again, the general rule of thumb was to negotiate solutions to verification problems in a seriatim fashion and to address compliance ambiguities in a private diplomatic channel—the Standing Consultative Commission (SCC)—which had been established under SALT I. But reliance on NTM, at least for the United States, remained preeminent.

Not everyone was satisfied with this approach. Certain critics of SALT argued that cooperative measures—especially intrusive forms of inspection—should be the preferred instrument of treaty verification. There were frequent complaints throughout the 1970s that SALT's focus on "verifiable" indicators of strategic capability ignored many important aspects of the arms race; that joint verification arrangements in SALT were not strong enough to prevent Soviet deception; and that successive U.S. administrations were slow to challenge suspicious Soviet behavior or actually covered up violations. According to some critics (especially, but not always, conservative ones), it was not sensible policy to tailor arms control provisions to NTM capabilities; instead, it was argued, verification should be tailored to the needs of arms control. Thus, if useful limits could not be monitored to desired levels of confidence unilaterally, the data necessary to meet verification requirements would have to be obtained through cooperative measures, which NTM would largely supplement.

Given these differences of view expressed during SALT, widespread agreement about the desirability of cooperative measures is deceptive; it is less a clear guide to policy than an invitation to further controversy. Indeed, the very concerns that make verification a divisive issue—the fears of undetected strategic threats—also make cooperative measures extremely difficult to negotiate. Questions regarding Soviet compliance with the 1972 Antiballistic Missile (ABM) Treaty and other agreements and American unwillingness to implement SALT II have heightened mutual suspicions and narrowed the possibilities for serious bargaining. In addition, the growing link between the mobility and survivability of nuclear weapons will increase the sensitivity of each side to any measure that makes the basing modes of weapons more transparent. For these reasons, the task of developing new cooperative measures that are both realistic and useful is likely to be a demanding one. The place to start is by asking the basic questions: First, what sorts of monitoring requirements in the Strategic Arms Reduction Talks (START) and the Intermediate Nuclear Forces (INF) talks might require cooperative verification arrangements? Second, how will they affect (or be affected by) the negotiating process—that is, what interests would each side seek to advance or protect in talks on cooperative measures? Third, what kinds of measures would actually improve verification?

Verification Issues in START and INF

Soviet-American diplomatic exchanges during 1981 set the stage for discussions about verification but did little to foreshadow precisely what types of cooperative measures would be considered at the START and INF talks. On August 21, in a demarche delivered to Soviet officials in Washington, the Reagan administration spelled out its view that cooperative measures would be a necessary element in the verification of future agreements and invited the Soviet government to discuss the matter either in a separate diplomatic channel or at the negotiations themselves.[2] While administration officials denied press reports that they were making Soviet acceptance of on-site inspection a precondition for new talks, the president himself stressed the need for a departure from past practices. The new U.S. approach, he said, would emphasize "openness and creativity—rather than the secrecy and suspicion which has undermined confidence in arms control in the past."[3] As the former director of the Arms Control and Disarmament Agency, Eugene V. Rostow, later explained:

> The new and creative ideas will be means of cooperation that go beyond NTM. Maybe on-site inspections; maybe television cameras. There may be challenge inspections, that you would have a right to ask, "We want to go and inspect the plant at such-and-such a place."[4]

For their part, the Soviets did not balk at the idea of discussing the issue but expressed the view that discussions of verification should take place in the context of specific negotiations. Then, in a highly publicized November 1981 interview with the German weekly *Der Spiegel*, Brezhnev alluded to the possibility that the Soviet Union might be willing to accept "other forms of inspection, given confidence."[5] Although American officials took this to be a positive sign, statements by Brezhnev and others appeared to be qualified in two important ways. First, progress on cooperative measures, the Soviets maintained, could only come about in an atmosphere of more cordial political relations, as was the case in the 1970s. As one Soviet academic observed:

> Detente contributed toward greater confidence in relations between states thus creating additional possibilities for the solution of concrete verification problems in keeping with the interests of states without jeopardizing their security.[6]

Second, Soviet statements reflected far greater stress on the continued ability of NTM to meet major verification requirements. In the Soviet view, cooperative efforts would aim to supplement, not supplant, reliance on unilateral monitoring methods. In other words, there was nothing to indicate that the Soviets were contemplating commitments on verification any more extensive or binding than what they pledged to accept in SALT II's Declaration of Principles.

How, then, will cooperative measures factor into the negotiations? Despite the intermittent probing of 1981, neither side was willing or able to move the Geneva talks toward a detailed discussion of the issue before the end of 1983, when the Soviets walked out. The Soviet delegation reportedly insisted that verification issues should be deferred pending progress on certain questions of scope (for example, the inclusion of aircraft in the INF talks), while American efforts to develop a negotiating package for both START and INF were hampered by bureaucratic bickering in Washington.[7] Moreover, at first glance, a review of the administration's substantive positions over this period does not immediately reveal that its proposals would have necessarily complicated existing verification tasks. The aggregate limitations proposed for START and INF were (and remain) denominated largely in terms of warheads and delivery systems and could be verified through the use of indirect measures (for example, counting launchers) and the application of SALT-type counting rules. Limits on missile throw-weight, or other more esoteric and difficult-to-verify constraints, have played a less visible role in U.S. proposals, despite early indications to the contrary.[8] Even the more ambitious zero-option proposal of 1981—to cancel deployments of Pershing 2 and ground-launched cruise missiles (GLCMs) in return for the dismantling of the Soviet Union's entire inventory of intermediate-range missiles—was in fact not seen to pose an overwhelming verification challenge. Indeed, as Rostow argued, "Basing our proposal on a ban should ease verification in any INF agreement."[9]

A closer inspection, however, reveals a somewhat different picture. First, a number of the definitions contained in U.S. proposals would substantially broaden the present array of treaty monitoring requirements. For example, the United States has dropped SALT's primary unit of limitation—launchers of ballistic and cruise missiles—in favor of "deployed" warheads on missiles. In SALT, "deployed" missiles were accounted for by virtue of their direct correspondence with an operational launcher—that is, a fixed silo launcher, a ballistic missile submarine (SSBN) tube, or (for air-launched cruise missiles) a long-range bomber. However, the administration prefers a definition of deployed weapons that would cover the reload and spare missiles located at or near Soviet launch sites, as well as those missiles on deployed launchers. The Soviets typically have not stored excess missiles at their ICBM launch complexes and agreed not to do so under SALT II. However, the transporter-erector-launchers (TELs) for SS-20 squadrons are normally deployed with reload missiles at main operating bases, and the Soviet Union may elect to follow the same pattern with its new mobile intercontinental ballistic missile (ICBM), the SS-X-25.[10]

Definitional questions affecting verification are also reflected in the administration's approach to cruise missile limitation. The Carter administration sought to limit long-range cruise missiles as a generic type on the grounds that distinctions between conventional and nuclear-armed cruise missiles were difficult to make (or keep, given the fungible nature of cruise missiles generally).

However, present U.S. policy addresses only the long-range and nuclear-armed versions, since the Reagan administration wishes to protect its option to deploy large numbers of conventional ground-, sea-, and air-launched cruise missiles. Thus, compared with SALT monitoring activities, the Reagan administration's approach imposes some wholly new requirements—to determine the location, numbers, and readiness of weapon systems other than those deployed on launchers and to distinguish between cruise missiles on the basis of mission rather than the external features of their launch platforms.

A second complication has emerged in the form of the collateral restrictions the United States wishes to place on nondeployed systems. Except for its provisions on rapid reload systems, SALT II did not address the possibility of a Soviet covert deployment involving the "reconstitution" of deactivated missiles. During the SALT II ratification hearings, Carter administration officials argued that there was no evidence to suggest that types of stockpiled Soviet ICBMs—the SS-7s, SS-8s, SS-9s, and older SS-11s—were being serviced as an operationally ready force. They also maintained that newer missiles were not being produced in numbers exceeding normal testing and replacement requirements.[11] The Reagan administration, however, appears to regard this cheating scenario as more plausible. It wants to place limits on numbers of weapons at storage, servicing, and test facilities—limits that would certainly require, for verification, the sort of information about overall inventories that cannot be obtained with NTM—and to establish more extensive dismantling procedures to include missile components along with launchers and associated equipment now covered by SALT.[12]

A third element of change in U.S. verification policies has been foreshadowed by the administration's desire to reduce the discretionary aspects of verification cooperation, especially relating to concealment practices. For example, SALT II's provisions on the encryption of telemetry were attacked by critics on the grounds that they would allow the Soviets too much leeway to determine for themselves what sort of information was necessary for verification, making future acrimony in the SCC a virtual certainty. As Rostow remarked:

> We told the Soviet Union that there will have to be a radical improvement in their willingness to provide data. It is time in our view to end the old cat and mouse game which has resulted in nothing but grief for both sides and to implement procedures of sustained cooperation which could lead to better things.[13]

As part of their new emphasis, Reagan administration officials have sought (despite some resistance from the Pentagon) a complete ban on the encryption of telemetry broadcasts, as well as more ambitious requirements to furnish data on inventory stockpiles and advance notification of all ballistic missile flight tests.

Finally, there appears to be a new, more skeptical attitude about the role of the SCC in verification. A number of officials in Washington appear less inclined to relegate certain technical tasks to the SCC as a matter of routine. One indication of this was seen in the INF talks, where American negotiators have insisted that dismantling procedures for weapons would have to be spelled out in the treaty text and not in SCC protocols. Whereas many policymakers in the 1970s saw the SCC as a productive channel for dealing with sub rosa issues that might bog down more freewheeling (and politicized) negotiations, a prominent view in the present administration holds that SCC consultations often provide a means for the Soviet Union to evade or obfuscate issues of overriding importance to the United States.[14]

Whether these elements of the Reagan administration's approach to verification are really necessary or practical—even if they are desirable on their own merits—is an open question. Certain proposals, such as prior notification of all missile tests, are well established in the negotiating history of SALT; other proposals, such as collateral limits on nondeployed systems, are new and more radical. Certain adjustments in the counting and limitation of nuclear forces are inevitable, given the direction of military research and development, and have little to do with political shifts in Washington. No doubt, SALT III negotiators would have found it vexing to shape constraints around new generations of ground-mobile ballistic missiles and cruise missiles (to which the Carter administration was committed), not to mention the numerous INF systems already in place. But other changes in policy (for example, those relating to SCC operations), appear to spring from an especially malign view of Soviet behavior and intentions, which is characteristic of, if not unique to, the Reagan administration. In sum, changes in the pattern of both politics and technology have conspired to reshape nuclear arms control priorities in ways that will make agreements intrinsically less verifiable through national methods of monitoring alone.

Negotiating Cooperative Measures

If the trends favoring greater reliance on cooperative measures appear immutable, what does this portend for the negotiations? Historically, it has been commonplace in the West to view any negotiation about verification essentially as a struggle pitting the Soviet mania for secrecy against U.S. desires for greater openness. In a general sense, of course, this states the obvious. The Soviet Union resists openness for its own sake, while we in the West have a hard time keeping secrets. Nevertheless, it is also a caricature of the bargaining process and therefore distorts the significance we may attach to its outcomes. For example, if the United States gives ground on an issue (such as telemetry), this is often portrayed as a fatal concession; at the same time, if the Soviet Union shows some flexibility (for example, on a database), this is sometimes seen to represent hints of a sea change in Soviet attitudes. It is no wonder, then, that bargaining activity—which perforce involves mutual compromise—is so prone to hyperbole and bitter dispute.

Reality is more complex. On the one hand, the Soviets have never been completely closed to the idea of verification. To be sure, there are always strict limits on Soviet flexibility. No negotiating strategy, however subtle, is going to change the hearts and minds of Soviet leaders on the question of secrecy, which is inherent in their society, in their government, and in the organization of their military-industrial production.[15] But there is also strong evidence to suggest that Soviet leaders were willing at times during the 1970s to make significant (and internally divisive) concessions on verification to achieve agreements.[16] On the other hand, Americans have never been as "open" about verification as the rhetoric from Washington would suggest. Even though U.S. leaders occasionally find it tempting to flag verification issues as a way to dramatize the closed nature of the Soviet Union, they, too, are aware of certain risks in advocating openness for its own sake. It is probably fair to say, then, that each side operates within certain constraints and that these constraints will complicate the negotiations in a variety of ways.

The first problem is basically political. It is rarely, if ever, the case that cooperative measures can be negotiated on the basis of balanced compromises. The United States requires NTM to substantiate claims of Soviet compliance; the Soviet Union has a multitude of open sources to utilize for intelligence purposes and does not rely on verification to the same extent. Thus, as Walter Slocombe has written:

> For all practical purposes, the Russians rightly understand every verification provision that gets into a treaty to be a concession that they are making to us. That makes such provisions extraordinarily difficult to negotiate.... [E]very stage is a significant negotiating effort—which the Soviets expect to be a two way process, with Soviet concessions on verification (both monitoring and precision) compensated by U.S. agreement on points of concern to the USSR.[17]

This raises a basic dilemma. While Soviet officials may find it difficult to accept (or to justify) concessions to the United States on verification, Western officials find it equally difficult to acquiesce to the use of verification as a Soviet bargaining chip. In the Comprehensive Test Ban (CTB) talks, for example, Soviet willingness to accept the installation of seismic monitoring stations on their territory was reportedly tied to British and American willingness to accept other Soviet positions, including the number of such stations that would be deployed in the West and other issues.[18] Likewise, in SALT, the Soviet Union's acceptance of counting rules for multiple independently targeted reentry vehicle (MIRV) systems was gained as part of a larger deal in which the United States agreed to drop demands for reductions of Soviet "heavy"

ICBMs, which alarmed domestic critics of the Carter administration. In sum, the practice of attempting to obtain Soviet agreement on cooperative measures with concessions on substance risks either stalling the negotiations or producing controversial agreements. As one Reagan administration official remarked: "We believe verification ought to be neutral and not require us to concede anything."[19]

Second, neither side will want to draw up or implement cooperative measures in ways that risk the loss of sensitive intelligence information. Traditionally, this has been the complaint of Soviet negotiators—that agreement to give the United States the right to inspect weapons systems or activities would ultimately be abused for espionage purposes. Despite their stonewalling in SALT I, the Soviets eventually accepted during the SALT II negotiations the necessity of being willing to confirm or modify U.S. estimates of Soviet force levels derived from NTM. But for more complex monitoring tasks, in which data could not otherwise be obtained remotely, it has been a common Soviet practice to negotiate strict limits on the location and timing of inspections and on the equipment specifications and the general activities of personnel engaged in the collection of data.

Collateral intelligence problems are not only a Soviet concern, however. In certain types of verification activity, such as the monitoring of telemetry broadcasts during Soviet missile flight tests, American officials have refused to give precise indications of what information was necessary, since this would expose U.S. intelligence sources and methods of data gathering and analysis, which the Soviets conceivably could exploit. Moreover, American declarations regarding the need for intrusive forms of inspection have not always reflected the fact that such measures might prove objectionable to certain quarters within the U.S. defense establishment. As one Pentagon official observed: "Not only do you need to know what cooperative measures can do for you, you have to understand what they may do *to* you."[20]

Third, both sides normally proceed on the understanding that there may be certain legal or political considerations that will tend to restrict each side's room for maneuver. Clearly, the United States can neither propose nor accept inspection measures that would run counter to U.S. domestic law or that would be applied to the territories of third parties (that is, NATO allies) without their consent. U.S. policymakers face the problem that if they proposed a regime of on-site inspections that permitted investigation of ambiguous activities in areas outside government-owned production or basing facilities, Soviet inspections might be contested in U.S. courts by private citizens as a breach of constitutional guarantees against unwarranted search and seizure. Although this might not be an obstacle at plants of companies doing work under government contract, the Soviets would no doubt regard any delay as a provocation worthy of retaliation.[21] Also, in INF negotiations, there would be the problem of gaining West German agreement to allow Soviet inspection of Bundeswehr facilities (for example, caserns housing deployments of the Pershing 1A SRBM), which

Bonn is likely to resist (as it did in the MBFR discussion of associated measures) in the absence of any corresponding right to undertake inspections on Soviet territory.

The Soviets do not face these sorts of concerns, but they have been sensitive to the possibility that any arrangement drawn up with the United States might set undesirable precedents vis-à-vis third parties. During the trilateral negotiations on CBT, there was general agreement on the idea of a two-tier verification system, which would include a general provision for on-site inspections on a "challenge" basis for all parties as well as a separate protocol for the nuclear-weapon state parties, spelling out detailed procedures for inspection and the rights and functions of the personnel carrying out the inspection.[22] This approach met American and British concerns for a certain measure of specificity in verification commitments and at the same time reduced what certain observers perceived to be Soviet anxiety that such procedures might ultimately be exploited by certain third parties (for example, the Israelis) for provocative purposes.

A final consideration regarding cooperative measures—one that is seldom appreciated outside the negotiations—is that, in the final analysis, they will not always be truly "cooperative"; that is, they will not improve the verifiability of an agreement if they rely on a division of labor between the parties in the collection or transfer of monitoring data. Indeed, both sides are likely to be suspicious of any data obtained through cooperative procedures that vary sharply with data available from unilateral intelligence sources.

Formal data exchanges exemplify this point. Although it is helpful to have on record a party's statement of its own force levels or the size of its nuclear test explosions, data that cannot be authenticated by the receiving party will not augment its knowledge per se. Walter Slocombe notes:

> For example, the Russians at a certain point in SALT I duly told us that they had exactly 1,398 ICBM launchers. After they told us that, we did not know anything more than we knew before, because 1,398 was the number we thought they had (counting their way). Given the openness of our system, we can never tell when they give us a piece of data whether it is the *correct* number, or whether they know we think it's the correct number, or whether it is merely the number *they wish us to think* is correct.[23]

Nor would cooperation work to the benefit of verification if it were injected into inspection practices. During the negotiations on the 1976 Peaceful Nuclear Explosions Treaty (PNET), the Soviet Union proposed arrangements that would have entailed Soviet and American personnel working together in carrying out certain monitoring procedures, ostensibly to control any abuse of the activities for unauthorized intelligence collection. However, while U.S. negotiators agreed on certain forms of cooperation during the inspections, they stoutly resisted any provisions that might raise questions about the integrity of

purposes only). START and INF will push this concept further: both sides will have to designate deployment areas (DDAs) for their ground-mobile missiles.[25] This would involve declaring the location of main operating bases, (MOBs), which include the servicing and garaging facilities for the missiles, their TELs, and mobile command units. Then, each side could designate an operational deployment area either by drawing a radius from the MOB out to an agreed distance—possibly 100 or 200 kilometers—or by designating geographical coordinates to avoid the overlapping of other DDAs or major metropolitan areas. Preventing overlap is thought to be a particular problem with deployments of Pershing 2 and GLCM.

If production limits on mobile missile launchers or missiles are agreed upon, each side would also declare its facilities for final assembly, servicing, and storage. The construction of new production facilities or DDAs could be permitted with notification in the consultative channel (as long as this did not violate other limitations); but absent any notification, the detection of deployment activities outside designated areas would be subject to challenge as a breach of an agreement.

Transparency Measures

While designation measures help to focus the work of NTM, the counting of weapons at the production or deployment stages of their life cycle, or the evaluation of their flight testing, may well depend on passive measures taken to increase their visibility (see table 2–2). In the area of test monitoring, the extension of SALT prenotification obligations to all systems whose testing is inherently difficult to track, such as cruise missiles and ballistic missiles that do not overfly international waters, would improve qualitative assessments. The suggestion has also been made that missile test ranges could be shifted to coastal areas (for cruise missiles, at least), and that the testing and the type of missile could be announced in advance.[26] All this, however, would require a change in emphasis from SALT, which linked notification procedures more to confidence building against surprise attack (for example, in the case of multiple ICBM launches) than to verification per se. Making this linkage more explicit would also require more specific commitments not to deny substantial portions of telemetry during flight testing. No single cooperative action, in the view of some observers, would do more to increase confidence in verification than to restore the degree of transparency of missile tests that existed before the Soviets began to encrypt their telemetry transmission.[27]

At the production and deployment stages, cooperation in the first instance could take the form of voluntary measures to assure a certain degree of transparency in the design of final assembly and basing facilities for mobile systems. The United States attempted to set such a precedent with the now-discarded Multiple Protective Shelter (MPS) basing scheme for the MX missile, which

Table 2-2
Transparency Measures

Measure	Application	Purpose	Precedents	Considerations
1. Obligation to display systems production phase)	Construction halls; final assembly areas for mobile ballistic and cruise missiles and launchers	To ease the counting of permitted systems	No (although practices that have had the effect of concealing the construction of SSBN and conversion of silo launchers were protested by both sides under SALT I, IAOW, Art. V)[a]	Some "current practices" in the production of mobile systems might have to be altered
2. Display systems (testing phase)	All test ranges for ballistic and cruise missiles	To help in determining the association between missiles and launchers	Yes (SALT II, Art. XV)	
3. Prenotification of flight testing	All tests of missiles that are subject to limitation	To improve assessments of performance parameters limited by an agreement	Partial (SALT II, Art. XVI, provides for notification of multiple ICBM launchers and flight tests that are designed to extend beyond national territories)	Both sides must agree in principle that advance notification is required for verification, in addition to reducing fears of surprise attack.
4. Obligation to broadcast relevant telemetry unencrypted	See tests of missiles that are subject to limitation	To improve assessments of performance parameters limited by an agreement	Yes (SALT II, Art. XV)	Present provisions are adequate but are not in force and are not being observed by the Soviet Union
5. Agreed criteria for layout of main operating bases (MOBs)	All DDAs of ground-mobile missile systems	To ease counting of systems in deployment; to deter covert deployment of excess systems in DDAs	No	Will require agreement on significant criteria (for example, size of buildings) and accord on the location and number of entry and exit points

Table 2–2 continued

Measure	Application	Purpose	Precedents	Considerations
6. Limit on squadron rotations	All systems at DDAs and designated storage or servicing areas	To improve count of systems passing through entry and exit points; to hedge against covert deployments in DDAs	No	Both sides will resist limits that hamper field exercises or alert procedures
7. Obligation to display dismantling of systems	All systems subject to limitation	To improve the counting of systems being removed from aggregate limits	Yes (in SCC protocols)	Present procedures apply only to launchers; if new agreements limit missiles and/or mobile launchers, a more explicit commitment to displaying systems would be required.

[a]IAOW = Interim Agreement on Offensive Weapons

included provisions for the final assembly of the missile and its associated launcher in open construction halls (to facilitate overhead monitoring) and for confinement of the deployed missiles to a DDA with controlled entry and exit points.[28] On the Soviet side, the basing scheme for the SS-20 missile facilitates the detection and counting of systems by virtue of the distinctive layout of its MOBs, the separate storage of missiles and TELs, and the size and appearance of the TEL garaging buildings.[29] Whether by accident or design, it is a basing scheme that, as one U.S. diplomat observed, "we would not want to modify even if we had a right to do so."

Negotiated measures may help formalize the transparency of production in a variety of ways. At the stage of final assembly, the counting of systems could be improved by a commitment to display weapons systems before their deployment. Since this is, in effect, the standard practice with SSBN and aircraft production, and with the removal of systems from operational service, it would be less difficult to negotiate than other types of measures. Even so, if it were agreed that the counting of overall inventories was necessary in START and INF, both sides could agree to a certain standard and verifiable rate of production so deviations from the norm would be subject to challenge. (The rates themselves could be declared and exchanged as part of the procedures for maintaining a database.)

At the deployment stage, transparency measures would be more difficult to introduce without interfering with the tactical deception that is essential to the survival of mobile systems in wartime. Nonetheless, short of exposing actual squadron rotations, there are a number of steps that could ease the task of keeping accurate count of permitted deployments. For example, both sides could agree on criteria for the basic layout of MOBs for their mobile missiles or GLCM deployments, possibly following the SS-20 analogy, and then commit themselves not to alter the pattern. Although this would not remove all doubt about the possibility of covertly introducing excess missiles into a DDA, it would certainly make it far more difficult to exploit construction activities as a route for evasion. Specifically, it would enable the United States to challenge the construction of facilities whose purpose was not immediately clear (and whose size gave rise to concern), just as the Soviet Union challenged the use of environmental protective shelters for personnel servicing Minuteman silo launchers.[30]

Another, more ambitious measure would be to work out an upper limit on the number of systems, cast in percentage terms, that could operate out of garrison (but within the DDA) at any one time. The limitations of such a measure are obvious: neither side would be ready to accept any interference with its forces on peacetime alert, and both sides would claim certain exemptions to allow for field exercises. But it would provide analysts with a formal standard against which to measure incoming data; it would establish a legal basis for questioning unexplained alterations in deployment routine; and it would, under certain conditions, provide a measure of strategic warning in crises.[31]

A final activity in which transparency measures may be helpful is with the dismantling or conversion of weapons. During the early 1970s, the SCC drew up detailed dismantling procedures that established an important precedent—that dismantling should be undertaken in such a way as to preclude the reassembly of systems in less time than it would take to build new ones.[32] With missile launchers, for example, this involves cutting off all connections with available power sources, removing the wires and cables, destroying the silo, and filling it in with dirt.[33] In agreements limiting missiles, rather than solely launchers, the requirements for displaying deactivation or conversion procedures would need to be more rigorous and open, especially since certain characteristics of Soviet fourth-generation ICBMs are not well known in the West.[34]

Collateral Measures

Designation and transparency measures help ease the task of counting or evaluating forces that are permitted and thus raise the potential risks of cheating. Collateral measures, in contrast, are intended to cut off the most likely routes to evasion and to prevent legal activity from threatening the intent of a treaty. In START and INF, the most plausible cheating scenarios might involve the production of mobile ballistic or cruise missiles at a clandestine plant and their transfer to covert locations within DDAs or onto weapons platforms (for example, surface ships) in large numbers. The detection of surreptitious production activity would almost entirely depend on NTM capabilities; collateral constraints could not help in such cases. However, certain provisions could be negotiated to make the movement of excess systems difficult.

One obvious (and legal) source of excess systems is storage areas. Thus, both sides may have to agree that storage areas would not be located at or near DDAs or naval bases. Fortunately, existing storage sites on both sides are reported to be few in number, are routinely monitored by NTM, and, with a few exceptions, would conform to a ban on colocation with deployed systems without much adjustment.[35] Another method of controlling access into the DDAs would be to limit the construction of airfields close to or within DDAs. In practice, this might require more flexibility on the Western side, since American INF forces rely more on air-transport than do Soviet INF. Still another, more ambitious measure would be to impose certain constraints on the size of floor space of buildings permitted within the operating area of the DDA—to require, for example, that the only structures large enough to house mobile launchers would be the garages designed to contain these launchers.[36] How negotiable these measures would be would depend in part on the specific circumvention problems, if any, raised at particular locations and on whether adopting these measures is seen by the Soviets as an alternative to more intrusive inspection methods. Their goal, after all, is mainly to boost confidence in NTM, not to generate data independently.

Clarifications and Counting Aids

Although passive cooperative measures may generally be useful in helping to put together an accurate picture of regulated military activities or weapon systems, there may also be cases in which disputes arise over data that are genuinely ambiguous or in which the two sides disagree about how certain activities—even unambiguous ones—ought to be measured against treaty limitations that are intrinsically difficult to define clearly (for example, on rapid-reload systems). To meet this challenge, one side may choose to set forth its view of precisely what sorts of ambiguities would give rise to problems or, alternatively, both sides may work to establish an agreed baseline for determining compliance or noncompliance with treaty provisions.

Efforts to clarify thresholds of acceptable behavior are not oriented toward improving verification in the sense of aiding NTM. Rather, they are tactics to be employed to influence the compliance behavior of the other side in particular circumstances. On occasion, the United States has taken steps—both in its own defense programs and in the negotiating setting—to anticipate and avoid verification and compliance problems. For example, with the MPS basing scheme for the MX missile, officials of the Carter administration were in effect attempting to set certain standards of verifiability that Moscow would have to take into account while moving forward with its own mobile ICBM program. In SALT II, the United States made it clear that certain specific test activities within the gray area, such as the simulation of reentry vehicle (RV) dispensing during missile flight tests without changing the position or velocity of the postboost vehicle, would be subject to challenge in the SCC.[37] Another example (albeit unrelated to verification) was seen in the Carter administration's clarification in the negotiating record that SALT II's noncircumvention clause (Article XII) would not affect existing patterns of cooperation with allies or preclude modernization.[38] In each case, the United States sought to ensure that there would be no misunderstanding on the part of the Soviets or others regarding how the United States would act or how it expected the Soviet Union to act under the restrictions of the agreement.

Unilateral steps of this kind have distinct risks. Neither side, of course, can anticipate in advance all the problems that might give rise to disagreements over compliance. Nor can these steps be viewed or justified as having a constraining effect on the actions of the other side, especially when unsuccessful efforts have already been made to arrive at agreed language.[39] Nonetheless, even in the absence of clear agreement, the act of clarifying one's position prior to taking a specific step will make it more difficult for the other side to complain that a violation has taken place (or that it was deceived during the negotiations). Correspondingly, unilateral clarifications may also provide a stronger basis for protesting actions of the other side—for example, RV dispensing simulations—and thus may raise the political costs of taking the step in the first place.

Measures to reduce the potential for compliance disputes are not solely unilateral, however. Both sides agreed in SALT II to a number of "counting rules" as a way, among other things, to avoid disagreements over how many warheads to attribute to certain types of systems; these rules could be carried over to future agreements. The expansion of the existing database is another important element in compliance cooperation. SALT II included agreed data on ten categories of offensive strategic arms, denominated primarily in terms of launchers, which would be updated periodically by both sides. In START and INF, the scope of the data would expand to encompass new categories of launch platforms (for example, nuclear-powered submarines (SSNs) carrying cruise missiles) and missiles that are declared to be operationally ready and deployed at the DDAs for reload purposes. Although the United States might consider proposing that both sides declare their total missile inventories, this would be of little value unless the numbers could be verified independently.

As suggested earlier, a database is not a substitute for NTM. As Walter Slocombe has observed, its purpose is to provide an "ostensible count" to compare with data collected from other sources and to expose differences of view during the negotiations regarding the status and function of certain systems. The object here is to avoid a situation in which one side suspects that the other is gaining advantage by juggling weapons categories or by claiming that newly detected weapons were "already there" at the time an agreement was reached.[40]

Active Measures: The Roles and Limits of OSI

No discussion of cooperative measures can overlook the role of on-site inspection (OSI)—the active measure that some observers regard as essential to the verification of future agreements. Prior to the early 1970s, OSI was a basic feature of every U.S. proposal for nuclear arms control. From a technical standpoint, there seemed to be no useful alternative to OSI. Politically, it united two important (if extreme) schools of thought in the spectrum of opinion on American foreign policy: those who wanted absolute guarantees of Soviet compliance with treaties and those who wanted to roll back the frontiers of state sovereignty and create world grovernment.[41]

Much has been made about Soviet resistance to OSI. As this chapter has already suggested, the Soviet Union's attitudes have likely been conditioned in part by the fact that verification is difficult to negotiate without the appearance of conceding points to the Americans. Perhaps NTM has always been preferable to Soviet leaders because it required only that they accept the existing situation of satellite reconnaissance—a "breach" of sovereignty they helped legitimize with the first Sputnik orbit over U.S. territory. By contrast, any decision about verification requiring positive action on their part—whether to restrict concealment practices or to allow in foreign personnel—has always been extraordinarily difficult to achieve. The Soviet Union is party to two multilateral conventions—the 1959 Antarctic Treaty and the Seabed Treaty of 1971—which proscribe, inter alia, deployments of nuclear weapons and which also include expansive provisions for close-in inspections.[42] However, their relevance for START and INF is diminished by the fact that their limits apply only to international territories or the high seas and cover hypothetical military activities. Agreements that allow access to Soviet territory have properly attracted more attention.

The 1976 PNET was the first agreement in which the United States and the Soviet Union worked out cooperative verification arrangements for actual nuclear programs—in this case, to ascertain the purpose and yield of certain types of nuclear explosions. Under PNET provisions, U.S. personnel would be permitted on-site to monitor group explosions with an estimated aggregate yield of over 150 kilotons. Then, in the CTB negotiations, agreement in principle was reached on the installation of national seismic stations (NSS) on the territories of the nuclear weapon states and on a U.S. initiative for on-site inspections on a voluntary or "challenge" basis. While the NSS were designed to be capable of transmitting authenticated seismic data to the other parties, OSI arrangements were intended to spell out the technical evidence necessary to support a request for (or refusal of) an inspection, as well as the rights and functions of designated personnel and the role to be played by the host country.[43]

In these and other cases, Soviet negotiating behavior has offered some useful clues to the logic behind their positions. In the PNET, for example, Soviet readiness to accept U.S. personnel was heavily influenced by strong American resistance to allowing group explosions as part of a PNET regime. As Warren Heckrotte has pointed out, once the Soviet Union had persuaded the United States to allow such explosions if there were some means to verify the size and purpose of individual yields, they then (and only then) proposed a monitoring technique to measure these yields and suggested that U.S. experts could be on-site to make the measurements. It was, in effect, their proposal. It was based on a calculation that the economic benefits of group explosions would outweigh the security risks of U.S. inspections, and it was qualified by the fact that the Soviets would retain control over the timing and location of such inspections (which, for "peaceful" explosions, meant no intrusions onto Soviet military reservations). Even with these caveats, Soviet acceptance was contingent on mutual agreement regarding the methods of inspection and on having a degree of access to monitoring equipment and data.[44]

The CTB experience was rather different. As with the PNET, design specifications for the NSS were made subject to mutual agreement, and the Soviets insisted on having access to the data being collected and transmitted to the other parties from their territory. Unlike the PNET, however, their support for OSI was much more tentative. Since the timing and location of an OSI would be dictated by ambiguous seismic events, not by Soviet decision making, the Soviets resisted any suggestion that the United States should have a guaranteed right to inspect. The American decision to propose challenge OSIs was made after it was concluded "that 'voluntary' OSI could serve as an equal deterrent [to cheating] if the rejection of a request could be established as a serious matter that in effect differed little from thwarting a guaranteed OSI."[45]

Nonetheless, the delegations remained far apart on the key questions of what methods or equipment would be used. While the Soviets indicated some willingness to discuss procedures to check for traces of radiation or engineering activity that might provide clues of testing, they apparently would not consider the use of certain types of seismic detection equipment that the United States deemed to be critical. Moreover, the Soviets wanted to discuss equipment issues in a consultative channel, rather than to work them out in the actual negotiation, as had been the case in the PNET talks. In short, the Soviets had agreed, as a U.S. diplomat said, "to a lot in principle but little in practice."

This does not mean that the Soviets have refused to consider binding obligations to accept an intermittent foreign presence for arms control purposes. In connection with arrangements for the purchase of high-speed computers during the 1970s, the Soviets expressed willingness to allow American personnel to monitor the use of these systems on a virtually continuous basis. Whether or not this was proposed merely to provide servicing expertise that the Soviets could not secure for themselves, it was potentially an important precedent in the transfer of technologies with dual uses.[46] In general, though, the record shows that the Soviet Union is far less likely to agree to OSI arrangements that focus on military activities when the decision making on the timing and geographical scope of an OSI is not in Soviet hands and, perhaps most of all, when the explicit purpose of the OSI is to investigate suspicious events rather than to confirm the nature of routine and permitted activity.

Of what relevance, then, is this experience for START and INF? If both sides discuss OSI, as seems likely in future negotiating rounds, they will probably devote their attention to two different types of inspection. First, there would be OSIs to monitor activities at designated areas; we will call these *first-order* OSI measures. Then, there might be proposals to check into ambiguous activities, possibly at designated areas but also (and most likely) at military-industrial facilities elsewhere; we will call these *second-order* measures. First- and second-order measures would differ considerably in terms of their prospective negotiability, their technical requirements (for example, equipment), their implementation, and their contribution to verification.

First-Order OSI Measures

First-order inspection measures are intended to augment NTM by obtaining data on permitted activities that cannot be done easily with the application of transparency measures. One kind of activity would be the movement of systems between final-assembly plants and DDAs, where monitoring techniques would measure the number of systems in transit and confirm the absence of unauthorized entry or exit of systems into or out of designated areas. Another type of activity would be one-time events, such as the closing down of a production facility or the dismantling of weapons. These are not highly dynamic activities, but they may require more continuous observation than could be provided by overhead reconnaissance systems. In either case, the implementation of such measures would depend on mutual agreement regarding the specific information required for verification, the specifications of the monitoring equipment, and the role of each side's personnel in the scheme.

The data required for verification are always the most critical and contentious issue. Choices concerning data collection are driven very much by the "need-to-know" principle. Production-oriented monitoring implies a treaty requirement to count total inventories of missiles and launchers (much as SSBNs and bombers are now counted). Deployment monitoring, especially focused on the movement of TELs and missiles at the DDAs, implies a lesser commitment to count only deployed systems. Yet the latter may involve *more* extensive collateral constraints if the size, readiness, and location of the overall inventory is not known. The paradox of START and INF verification, then, is that in choosing to shape an agreement around a more ambitious limit—that is, total inventory rather than deployed missiles or warheads—both sides may find it less necessary to impose restrictions at the operational level over the long term.[47]

What about the conditions of access and timing? Since first-order OSIs would be aimed only at keeping track of permitted activities, monitoring procedures are in effect set by Soviet (or American) production and deployment schedules, not by contentious evidence of cheating. It would therefore be important to establish first-order measures as both binding and routine (rather than ad hoc); and so long as access to equipment and data is not completely forfeited by the host country, OSIs of this type might be negotiable. Of course, even guaranteed OSIs would not exclude the possibility of covert attempts to "spoof" U.S. equipment or procedures. But preventive action could be taken to reduce this risk substantially, and evidence indicating willful interference would be a sufficiently grave matter to call the treaty into question in any case.

All this raises questions regarding the rights and functions of inspectors (or designated personnel), equipment specifications, and data security. It is reasonable to expect that both sides would want to negotiate limits on the number of personnel and the time they would have to perform their tasks; they would also demand that only equipment of agreed specifications be used, that they inspect it before use, and that they be supplied with a readout of the collected data. From the U.S. standpoint, there would also be concern to ensure that Soviet access to equipment would not defeat the effectiveness of the instruments or the authenticity of the data.[48]

In theory, there are ways to address these different concerns. One general approach would be to substitute sensors for personnel wherever possible in the conduct of monitoring activities. Passive data collectors—including optical, acoustic, and weight sensors—may be applicable to a variety of monitoring tasks, as in the area of nuclear nonproliferation. Their major task would be to characterize the tempo of activities within a designated area (for example, a final-assembly plant) without actually collecting information that would compromise technologies and designs embodied in the production process. This would be easiest in situations where whole plants were being shut down. Monitors would simply confirm the absence of large-scale production and track the average rate of activity required for maintenance. Otherwise, the effectiveness of on-site sensors would vary widely, depending on the type of weapon. To verify the output of an assembly plant where individual units are large, it might be necessary only to monitor certain "choke points" with a sensor array. To count smaller units (for example, cruise missiles) where production and exit rates are more difficult to monitor, it might also be necessary to keep track of certain inputs (for example, steel, electricity, or water) to detect variations in production activity or movement at exit points.

These are hardly trivial negotiating issues, but they may appeal to certain incentives on each side. In placing reliance on technical collection systems, both sides would be able to minimize human intrusions into the facilities under surveillance; to collect near-real-time data on a continuous basis; and to lessen mutual anxieties that designated personnel themselves might be engaged in espionage activities with agents on the inside. Even if both sides were able in the end to agree to only an extremely limited array of first-order OSI tasks, this would reduce fears regarding certain types of evasions (for example, at designated facilities) and would help establish a certain degree of mutual confidence.

Second-Order OSI Measures

The monitoring of permitted activities at designated facilities is only part of the problem, however. Even with the application of first-order OSI measures, treaty compliance could be called into question if NTM-detected signals suggesting the covert production and deployment of restricted systems elsewhere. The potential scenarios are not difficult to predict; they range from the deployment of excess numbers of short-range tactical nuclear forces (TNF) to circumvent INF limits, to covert production of ballistic missiles, to the deployment of long-range cruise missiles on new (undesignated) launch plat-forms. Passive cooperative measures might make significant violations more difficult to conceal, but it might still be difficult to make an accurate assessment of activities that were considered ambiguous. For this reason, certain analysts—including some officials in the Reagan administration—argue that provisions for OSI in future agreements must also include a guaranteed right to investi-gate possible violations at any place where they are likely to occur.

Few would dispute that second-order OSIs are unlikely to be viewed sympathetically by the Soviets; no doubt, some see this as their basic virtue. But would they be acceptable to the United States? As a practical matter, neither side is likely to delegate to the other an exclusive right to conduct OSIs at a time or place of its own choosing. Otherwise, as Wolfgang Panofsky, has pointed out:

> The presumption would be made, and possibly correctly, that the time and place for such searches would not be determined by the likelihood of an alleged violation . . . but by the desire of the intelligence apparatus of either side to take a closer look at certain installations.[49]

What this means is that both sides would have to agree in advance on the hypothetical cases in which OSI might be required and on the evidence neces-sary to establish the need of one, even before the hoary issues of designated personnel, equipment design, data security, and facilities to be declared off limits (for example, CIA headquarters) are discussed. Even then—assuming complete agreement on all these issues—neither side will want to forfeit politi-cal control over any procedure that results in the arrival of foreign inspectors on national territory. It is, in short, difficult to imagine any circumstances in which second-order OSIs would be an "automatic" process. The notion that inspectors could arrive on-site, at *any* site, within hours or days of a U.S. (or Soviet) decision to request an inspection is completely unreal, given reasonable security concerns on both sides.

Once it is clear that inspections could never be an open-ended invitation to the other side's intelligence personnel, second-order OSI begins to lose its attractiveness, even as a deterrent. First, there is virtually no aspect of nuclear arms control—especially with weapons that already present verification problems —in which the problem of substitution is not a real one. Cruise missiles are fungible systems—as, potentially, are MIRVed warheads. With the warning time that would inevitably come from a discussion of the evidence, OSI would be of little value if systems could be altered, exchanged, or removed before (or after) an inspection.[50] Nuclear weapons testing is often held up as an example of a situation in which OSI might make a difference, but the characteristics of seismic verification lend themselves to OSI in unique ways; the relevant evi-dence can be agreed to in advance more easily, while seismic signals also help localize the source of concern and thus the area of inspection, and the incriminating evidence (for example, radioactivity or aftershocks) may be difficult to conceal.[51] In no other area of arms control are these conditions so easily duplicated.

Second, the risks involved for the party in a position of having to make a "go/no-go" decision are frequently overlooked. To announce a request for an inspection (and thus to furnish the evidence) would immediately lift the veil from intelligence sources and methods that presumably would not be so effective again. Indeed, if NTM were good enough to build a case that something illegal was happening, one would expect that the extra weight of the evidence provided by OSI might not be worth the risk of exposing NTM capabilities. Beyond this, however, if a government thought it had enough evidence to warrant an OSI and then found nothing (or only ancillary traces of additional evidence), it could risk a possible loss of political credibility; it would spark a retaliatory OSI; and it might be inhibited from making the same decision the next time. The real or apparent deterrent value of the instrument would then be lost.

Finally, is there any reason to suspect that the Soviet Union would cooperate in demonstrating its own culpability? If the United States thought there was compelling evidence of a violation, Soviet willingness to permit an OSI would justifiably raise suspicions that the activity in question had been successfully covered up. More likely, however, the Soviets would find some pretext to stonewall even a guaranteed OSI. They would marshal their own "evidence" or charge that the OSI was a smokescreen for American intelligence gathering. Whatever the circumstances, if there ever really was a "smoking gun," an OSI would not find it. As the Carnegie experts concluded: "Essentially, 'rights' to OSI would at best provide a source of suspicion arising from a refusal to consent to an inspection to which the other side had a right."[52]

Conclusions

When all the issues surrounding cooperative measures are examined, it rapidly becomes clear that they are not a magical solution to the thorny problems of verification and compliance. Many in the West regard them as intrinsically valuable because they may inspire greater confidence, even trust, between the superpowers. To some extent this may be true, given incentives on both sides to negotiate such measures; but there are risks in pushing the concept too far. The Soviet penchant for secrecy can probably be affected only at the margins; it would be expecting too much of cooperative measures to suppose that they could transcend the deep-set sources of tension in the East–West relationship. Moreover, both sides are constrained, albeit in different ways, in terms of the sorts of measures they can propose or accept. Perhaps, then, it is best to view the value of cooperative measures in instrumental terms—as a way to achieve verifiable arms control—not as an end in themselves.

What can cooperative measures accomplish? Clearly, there are ways in which passive cooperative measures can help make NTM more effective. Building some transparency into the production and basing of weapons and designating areas where they can be produced or deployed would enable NTM to detect, to count, and to measure qualitative changes in the performance of weapons more effectively; collateral constraints could ease fears about surreptitious activities in and around designated areas; and clarifications or other counting aids could help reduce misunderstandings and lessen the gray areas of treaty provisions into which either side might probe.

Taking a realistic view, however, it is difficult to see how active cooperative measures could accomplish much more than this. In START and INF, the only potentially useful types of OSI are first-order measures—those that would function in circumstances in which there was no presumption that a party's compliance was in question. The object here would be simply to ensure that permitted activities conform to expected standards. Moreover, in the final analysis, after all the possible sources of ambiguity or false alarms are accounted for in the monitoring systems and procedures, U.S. officials may well decide that even first-order OSI would provide no greater confidence in monitoring than could be obtained with the expeditious use of passive measures (for example, displaying assembled systems) or periodic visits of designated personnel at prearranged times. The major calculation here is that deterrence to cheating at designated areas would always be substantial, while the chances of detecting illegal activity elsewhere ultimately would depend on the effectiveness of NTM and other sources of information.

Any other types of OSI measures immediately beg the question of diminishing returns. They would place tremendous pressures on the bargaining process—consuming, in effect, the sort of mutual confidence they are designed to enhance—and they might not be worth the small amount of additional information gained about compliance. Indeed, there is no logical reason to believe that OSI per se should represent a litmus test of successful arms control. As this analysis suggests, neither side is likely to grant the other the flexibility of action to make OSI a truly effective instrument for detecting violations—even if the right to inspect were in some sense guaranteed. Therefore, beyond reducing the likelihood of ambiguous situations that raise questions about compliance, the best cooperative measures can probably do is to reinforce mutual expectations that any activity that complicates or impedes verification, regardless of intent, is a proper concern for both sides and would be challenged. Given the present state of disarray in arms control, however, that would be no small step.

Notes

1. "Joint Statement of Principles and Basic Guidelines for Subsequent Negotiations on the Limitation of Strategic Arms," in U.S. Department of State, *The SALT II Agreement*, Selected Docs. No. 12B, (Washington, D.C.: U.S. Government Printing Office, July 1979), p. 58; Report of the Independent Commission on Disarmament and Security Issues, *Common Security: A Programme for Survival* (London: Pan Books, 1982); Eugene V. Rostow, Statement before the Committee on Armed Services, U.S. Senate, July 24, 1983.

2. Leslie H. Gelb, "U.S. Tells Soviet That Any Arms Pact Must Include On-Site Verification," *New York Times*, September 9, 1981; Eugene V. Rostow, Statement before the Armed Services Committee, House of Representatives, November 16, 1981.

3. President Ronald Reagan, Speech before the National Press Club, November 18, 1981.

4. U.S. Congress, House Committee on Foreign Affairs, *Review of Administration Initiatives on Strategic, Theater, and Conventional Arms Control*, 97th Cong., 1st sess. (Washington, D.C.: U.S. Government Printing Office, 1982), p.9.

5. Interview with President Leonid Brezhnev, *Der Spiegel*, November 2, 1981, reprinted in *Survival* 24 (January–February 1982): 37.

6. R. Zheleznov, "Monitoring Arms Limitation Measures," *International Affairs* (Moscow), July 1982, p. 78.

7. John Barry, "The Shadow Over Geneva," *The Times* (London), September 22, 1983, p. 10.

8. Proposals for throw-weight limits, however, have not been entirely absent. In its July 1983 START proposals, the United States withdrew its initiative for a limit of 850 on ballistic missiles but offered the Soviet side the choice of discussing overall aggregate limits in terms of warheads or throw-weight.

9. U.S. Congress, House Committee on Foreign Affairs, Subcommittee on International Security and Scientific Affairs, *Overview of Nuclear Arms Control and Defense Strategy in NATO*, 97th Cong., 2d sess. (Washington, D.C.: U.S. Government Printing Office, 1982), p. 12.

10. N.F. Wikner, "A Balance of Theater Nuclear Forces: Can We Count? Where Are the Reloads?" *Armed Forces Journal International*, May 1983, p. 92. Although Wikner claims that each SS-20 TEL is supplied with a reload missile, others suggest that there may be only five to six per squadron of nine TELs. See, for example, Barry, "Shadow Over Geneva."

11. See "Administration Comment" in U.S. Congress, Senate Committee on Foreign Relations, *The SALT II Treaty*, Part 6 (Mark-Up), 96th Cong., 1st sess. (Washington, D.C.: U.S. Government Printing Office, 1979), p. 574.

12. The administration's concerns in this area were foreshadowed in criticisms of the SALT II agreement made by individuals who are now part of the executive branch. See Richard N. Perle, "What Is Adequate Verification?" in *SALT II and American Security*, (Cambridge, Mass.: Institute for Foreign Policy Analysis, 1980), p. 54; and Lt. General Rowny, "Comment," in Senate Committee on Foreign Relations, *The SALT II Treaty*, p. 574.

13. Rostow, Statement before the Armed Services Committee, November 16, 1981.

14. For an exposition of this view, see Richard N. Perle, "A Broken Trail of Paper Promises," *Defense 84,* May 1984, p. 20.

15. For one view of why secrecy is crucial in the organization of the Soviet defense-industrial sector, see David Holloway, *The Soviet Union and the Arms Race* (London: Yale University Press, 1983), pp. 126–127.

16. During the Comprehensive Test Ban (CTB) talks, for example, U.S. officials were aware that the Soviet decision to accept national seismic stations (NSS) monitoring was an extremely contentious one that divided officials at the highest levels of the Soviet government. One account of the episode is found in Dale Van Atta, "Inside a U.S.–Soviet Arms Negotiation," *Nation,* December 19, 1981, p. 688. See also comments by Alan Neidle on the CTB talks in Alan F. Neidle, ed., *Nuclear Negotiations: Reassessing Arms Control Goals in U.S.–Soviet Relations* (Austin: University of Texas, 1982), p. 77.

17. Walter Slocombe, "Verification and Negotiation," in *The Nuclear Weapons Freeze and Arms Control,* (Cambridge, Mass.: Harvard University, Center for Science and International Affairs, 1983), p. 87.

18. Jimmy Carter, *Keeping Faith* (New York: Bantam Books, 1982), p. 229.

19. Walter Pincus, "U.S. Devising New Verification Terms for Talks on Missiles," *International Herald Tribune,* July 28, 1983, p. 2.

20. This point was made in the SALT II hearings; see Senate Committee on Foreign Relations, *The SALT II Treaty,* p. 563.

21. By the same token, the presumption must be that both sides already will have had extensive discussions on precisely how requests for inspections would be handled and how much time would be needed to process them.

22. Progress report on the CTB talks presented by the United States, the Soviet Union, and the United Kingdom to the Committee on Disarmament, July 31, 1980.

23. Slocombe, "Verification and Negotiation," p. 85.

24. Warren Heckrotte, "Negotiating with the Soviets," *Energy and Technology Review,* May 1983, p. 14.

25. For a brief discussion of the concept, see U.S. Congress, *Fiscal Year 1981 Arms Control Impact Statements,* (Washington, D.C.: U.S. Government Printing Office, 1980), pp. 61–63.

26. Richard Garwin, correspondence in *Scientific American,* June 1977, p. 6.

27. Carnegie Endowment for International Peace (CEIP), *Challenges for U.S. National Security: The Soviet Approach to Arms Control; Verification; Problems and Prospects; Conclusions* (Washington, D.C.: CEIP, 1983), p. 47.

28. Office of Technology Assessment, *MX Missile Basing* (Washington, D.C.: U.S. Government Printing Office, 1981), p. 317.

29. Details of the SS-20 system and its deployment mode are described in U.S. Congress, Subcommittee on Strategic and Theater Nuclear Forces, Senate Committee on Armed Services, *Strategic Forces Modernization Programs,* 97th Cong., 1st sess. (Washington, D.C.: U.S. Government Printing Office, 1981), p. 16.; Barry, "Shadow Over Geneva"; and Harry Sauerwein, "Mobile ICBM and Arms Control," *Survival* 23 (September–October 1981): 220.

30. Subsequently, the United States agreed to ban the emplacement of shelters over ICBM silos in the SALT II agreement (Art. XV, para. 3) and so helped set a precedent against similar Soviet activities, whose effect would be to impede treaty verification.

31. Thought has also been given to the idea of requiring that future garaging facilities have removable covers or hatches to facilitate counting by NTM. SS-20 garages are configured in this way, but there are apparently no plans to do so with Pershing 2 and GLCM deployments.

32. Personal interview with Sidney Graybeal, former U.S. Commissioner to the SCC, July 11, 1983.

33. Mark Lowenthal, "The START Proposal: Verification Issues" (Washington, D.C.: Congressional Research Service, 1982), p. 14.

34. Conversion practices for missiles, rather than launchers, will be further complicated if the United States wishes to reserve some portion of its missile stocks for space launch purposes—as, for example, the Scowcroft Commission recommended for the MX. Both sides would have to work out an exemption for systems removed from the aggregate limits but converted to this mission.

35. Systems configured for mobile deployment would have to conform to an additional provision—that launchers designed for a particular system be stored separately from the missiles. This would preclude a recurrence of the ambiguities that figure prominently, for example, in the dispute over the status of the surplus SS-16s stored at the missile test facility at Plesetsk.

36. See the analysis by Louis Finch (Congressional Research Service), "Verification of Ground-Mobile ICBM," in *Congressional Record,* April 7, 1983.

37. See Secretary of State Cyrus Vance's analysis of SALT II provisions in U.S. Department of State, *The SALT II Agreement,* p. 27.

38. See Senate Committee on Foreign Relations, *The SALT II Treaty,* pp. 235–236.

39. In SALT I, there were two instances—one regarding the construction of an ABM radar on the Kamchatka peninsula and one regarding the deployment of the SS-19—in which the Soviet Union ignored U.S. statements made during the talks and introduced into the negotiating record that set forth positions on compliance matters to which the Soviet delegation had not agreed. Criticism in the United States was sparked by the fact that these statements conveyed the impression of mutual accord, which was manifestly not the case.

40. Slocombe, "Verification and Negotiation," pp. 85–86. An example of data exchange helping to expose a problem in counting before an agreement was signed was the counting of the eighteen fractional orbital bombardment missiles (FOBs) that the Soviet Union maintained at Tyra-Tam, a missile testing facility. Initially, the Soviets resisted the idea of counting them in the aggregate but eventually agreed to dismantle twelve and convert six to test launchers after the United States argued that they would otherwise have to be counted as operational launchers.

41. Abram Chayes, "An Inquiry into the Workings of Arms Control Agreements," *Harvard Law Review* 85 (March 1972): 945.

42. The Antarctic Treaty (Art. VII, para. 3) provides that "all stations...shall be open at all times to inspection," while the Seabed Treaty (Art. III, para. 1) provides that states parties shall have the right to "verify through observation the activities of other states...provided that observation does not interfere with such activities."

43. Much of this was drawn from the PNET precedent; see Heckrotte, "Negotiating with the Soviets," pp. 14–15.

44. Ibid., p. 13.

45. Ibid., p. 17.

46. Personal interview with Wolfgang Panofsky, Director, Stanford Linear Accelerator Center, July 5, 1983.

47. This is not to say, however, that no restrictions on deployment would be necessary. Otherwise, the Soviets could claim that unexpected increases in the number of their deployed systems were due to a drawing down of stocks.

48. For example, the performance specifications of the NSS include "data authentication" equipment to detect efforts to tamper with data collection and transmission. See Paul A. Stokes, *The National Seismic Station,* Sandia Report 81–2134 (Albuquerque: Sandia National Laboratories, June 1982), pp. 11–12.

49. Wolfgang K. H. Panofsky, "On-Site Inspection: Cliché or Reality?" Loeb Lectures No. 3, Harvard University, March 1983.

50. The argument has been made that NTM could work in conjunction with an OSI request to spot alterations in activity at suspected missile production facilities, launch sites, or other areas, but such an approach has to consider the likelihood that the Soviets would have covered this possibility in their evasion planning.

51. See Panofsky, "On-Site Inspection." Even here, as Panofsky notes, it may be extremely difficult to detect evidence of a covert underground nuclear test.

52. CEIP, *Challenges for U.S. National Security,* p. 46.

3
The Soviet View of Verification

Allan S. Krass

I t is often pointed out that verification is "for all practical purposes
...strictly an American concern."[1] One analyst of Soviet attitudes toward
SALT devotes less than one page of his 110-page study to Soviet views on
verification and concludes that "verification is primarily an American problem
and thus not likely to be of much concern to members of the Soviet ruling
elite."[2]

Are these statements true? They certainly cannot be true in the sense that
Soviet leaders require no reassurance in the form of hard evidence that the
United States is living up to its obligations. Soviet leaders harbor at least as
much mistrust of U.S. intentions as the Americans do of the Soviets, and the
historical record of arms control negotiations reveals that Soviet leaders have
understood the need for appropriate (by their definition) verification and control virtually from the beginning. As early as 1946, the Soviet Union presented
an elaborate proposal for monitoring and controlling a ban on nuclear weapon
production, including the creation of an international control commission with
extensive powers of inspection and analysis.[3] However, because this control
machinery was not to be created and set in motion until the United States had
destroyed all its nuclear weapons, the plan was unacceptable to the United
States.

Since that time, Soviet negotiators have continued to offer verification
proposals in various negotiations, but the great majority of these have been
unacceptable to the U.S. side, just as the vast majority of U.S. verification
proposals have been unacceptable to the Soviet side. Therefore, it is incorrect
to assert that verification is not a Soviet concern—only that they approach the
problem of verification in very different ways than the United States.

This chapter will attempt to describe the Soviet approach to verification in
a systematic way and to see whether it is possible to form a coherent and
plausible explanation for the Soviet approach. Such an explanation cannot be
conclusive; it can only be a hypothesis to be tested for its validity against actual
behavior. There has been far too much neglect, oversimplification, and distortion of Soviet positions in the United States; if serious progress toward arms
control is to occur, this carelessness and superficiality must be overcome.

We begin with the basic assumption that the premises and logic of Soviet
attitudes toward verification can be discovered by observing Soviet actions in

arms control negotiations. Of course, it is possible that Soviet actions are totally opportunistic, cynical, and capricious. If this is so, however, then that, too, ought to be demonstrable by systematic comparison of Soviet words with Soviet actions. On the other hand, if Soviet attitudes do have a logic and coherence, it is essential to understand them if attempts at arms control are to have some hope of success. There have been surprisingly few serious attempts at such understanding among U.S. students of arms control.

Basic Principles

Soviet attitudes toward treaties in general and toward arms control treaties in particular have been described as "strict constructionist,"[4] suggesting that it would be worthwhile at the outset to define some important terms very carefully. The most important of these terms are *verification, intelligence,* and *espionage,* among which there is good reason to believe that Soviet decision makers and negotiators draw very sharp distinctions.

The word *intelligence* applies to the full range of activities engaged in by states to learn about the capabilities and intentions of other states. Intelligence gathering ranges all the way from reading the newspapers published in another state to infiltrating secret agents into its most sensitive military and political policymaking structures. *Espionage* occurs when these methods go beyond those sanctioned by "generally recognized principles of international law." I have placed this phrase in quotation marks because it has become a standard feature of the verification provisions of arms control treaties. It is used to distinguish those activities of such remote sensing devices as photographic satellites or radio antennas that qualify as national technical means (NTM) of verification from those that constitute illegal or improper intelligence gathering. Most recent arms control treaties contain provisions that prohibit any party from interfering, either actively or passively, with the national technical means of the other parties. These provisions create the legal basis for the legitimacy of NTM.

A clear definition of verification can now be constructed. Verification comprises those legal and proper intelligence activities that are carried out by a state for the exclusive purpose of satisfying itself that other states are in compliance with existing treaties and agreements. This clearly separates verification from both espionage, which is by definition illegal, and routine intelligence gathering, which is carried out whether or not a treaty exists.

This exercise in careful definition is important for clarifying the following analysis, but it should not be taken as an accurate reflection of the much more complex relationship among verification, intelligence, and espionage. In the real world of military and political competition, all information is potentially valuable, and it is rare that evidence for a possible violation of a treaty comes only from devices or mechanisms that are devoted specifically to verification. Conversely, it is virtually impossible to design a device for monitoring compliance with a treaty that does not also pick up other information (usually called collateral information) as well. Moreover, there is no question that espionage activity can be very helpful in the verification process, and vice versa.

Despite these overlaps and ambiguities, it is the essence of a strict constructionist approach to attempt to maintain as much precision as possible in the definitions of these terms. To the Soviet Union, this appears to mean attaching as narrow and precise a definition as possible to verification, thereby minimizing opportunities for the collection of collateral information.

With the meanings of the most important words understood, the next step is to establish a set of fundamental principles that define the Soviet approach to verification. Probably the clearest and most useful set was offered by Viktor Israelyan, the Soviet ambassador to the Conference on Disarmament in Geneva. According to Israelyan, the Soviet Union subscribes to the following "basic principles":

> 1. The conduct of verification should in no way prejudice the sovereign rights of states or permit interference in their internal affairs.
> 2. Verification cannot exist without disarmament measures for the limitation of armaments and for disarmament.
> 3. The scope and forms of verification should be commensurate with the character and scope of the specific obligations established.
> 4. The detailed elaboration of the verification provisions is possible only after an agreement on the scope of the prohibition has been mapped out.
> 5. We proceed from the assumption that a State becomes a party to a convention not in order to violate it but in order to abide strictly by the obligations it has assumed under it, and therefore that verification should not be built upon the principle of total distrust by States of one another.
> 6. International forms of verification should be limited.
> 7. . . . in the conditions of the present-day development of science and technology, any fairly less serious violation of an agreement in the field of disarmament. . . has no chance of remaining undetected for very long.[5]

If such basic principles are to be useful, they must have both permanence and flexibility. Flexibility is essential to allow the creation of verification arrangements that conform to the widely varying technological and political demands of different agreements. For all their flexibility in detailed application, however, the principles, if they are indeed principles, should remain identifiable in a wide variety of applications. The following section examines a number of historical and current arms control experiences to see if this is true.

The Basic Principles Applied

Clausewitz observed that "everything takes a different shape when we pass from abstraction to reality";[6] although he is certainly not the only person to have recognized this fact, it seems particularly appropriate to quote him in the present context. Every real arms control issue is characterized by particular military, technological, and political constraints that strongly affect the shape of the verification mechanism to be associated with it. To some extent, this can be an objective process in which the best possible fit between abstract principles and practical constraints is determined. But to an even greater extent, when the negotiating states operate from different sets of basic principles, it must be an exercise in political compromise involving concessions on the principles themselves. This is very difficult to do, of course—as the history of U.S.-Soviet arms control negotiations has amply demonstrated from the historical record.

This section will examine a number of generic issues in verification to see how Soviet principles have been applied and compromised in past negotiations and agreements. The first issue can be called the "agreement in principle" demand—that is, the Soviet requirement that agreement on the scope of the treaty must precede detailed discussion of verification provisions. Second is the question of "adequacy"—that is, how much verification is enough. Third is the problem of legitimacy—that is, what monitoring activities constitute legitimate verification techniques and where the boundary is between verification and espionage. Finally, what is the role of trust among states in the verification and compliance process?

Agreement in Principle

Principles 2, 3, and 4—taken together—constitute the basis for the Soviet position that attempts to implement or even to discuss verification schemes without first agreeing on the scope of a treaty are both pointless and counterproductive. The rational basis for this position lies in the desire to minimize the overlap between verification activities and other forms of military intelligence gathering, a motivation that can clearly be discerned in the following statement by Deputy Foreign Minister V. Zorin in 1961 regarding the Soviet position on verification of general and complete disarmament:

> The Soviet Union favors the most thorough and strict international control over the measures of general and complete disarmament,... [it] is at the same time resolutely opposed to the establishment of *control over armaments*.[7]

"Control over armaments" implies the carrying out of monitoring and inspection activities even as military competition continues, a situation that, according to a more recent Soviet commentator, can lead to "the kind of control that is designed not for effective disarmament, but for very different purposes"[8]—that is, espionage. The Soviet position is that verification without disarmament is illogical and potentially dangerous. It must be granted that there is a compelling logic behind this assertion, especially if the states involved do not possess nearly equal military strength.

The problem is well illustrated by the example of the "open skies" proposal made by the United States in 1955.[9] This proposal was ostensibly made to reduce "the fears and dangers of surprise attack" and would have involved complete freedom for reconnaissance aircraft of each country to survey the territory of the other as well as an exchange of "complete blueprints of our military establishments."[10]

There is now solid documentary evidence that fears of a surprise Soviet attack were seriously held at the highest levels of the U.S. government in the 1950s.[11] From this point of view, the "open skies" proposal reflected a genuine desire to reduce the suspicion and tension resulting from this concern. If this had been the only consideration, then "open skies" ought to have qualified as a legitimate arms control verification measure, even though it was not tied to any specific arms control or disarmament treaty.

However, the same collection of evidence shows that, in 1955, the United States possessed all the necessary weapons for a massive counterforce nuclear attack against the Soviet Union. The U.S. Air Force lacked only the accurate targeting data necessary to guarantee the success of such an attack.[12] In this context, the "open skies" plan can be seen as a military intelligence measure of the highest importance—one that would strengthen the weakest link in U.S. nuclear war-fighting plans.

The "open skies" plan was, of course, unacceptable to the Soviet Union, mainly for this latter reason. It was not simply obstructionism or some irrational penchant for secrecy that caused this rejection, any more than it was a pure desire by the United States to carry out espionage that prompted the proposal in the first place. But given the relative military weakness of the Soviet Union at the time and the consequent high value of the collateral information that would have been gained over and above that needed to reassure that no surprise attack was in preparation, it is hardly surprising that the plan was rejected. Indeed, many believe that the plan was offered in the full expectation that it would be rejeced.[13]

This example illustrates very clearly the rational basis of Soviet strict constructionism as applied to verification. Acceptance of the "open skies" plan without first agreeing to and implementing disarmament would be "control over armaments" as opposed to "control of disarmament." The former is, in principle, unacceptable, while the latter is something that the Soviets have always said they would accept.

The Soviet concept of prior agreement in principle was engagingly articulated in 1958 by S.K. Tsarapkin, the chief Soviet representative at the nuclear test ban negotiations. Tsarapkin summed up the U.S.-Soviet divergence of views with the following analogy:

> It is as though we started to argue here on how to preserve a bearskin when the bear itself was still in the woods. We would be arguing about whether to put the bearskin in the refrigerator or to pack it in mothballs in a trunk at home. In

the end, we would disagree with you on which brand of mothballs to buy and from which firm. The bear would be in the woods, alive and well, and we would have fallen out among ourselves over mothballs.[14]

Tsarapkin's imagery is highly illuminating but it does not do full justice to the U.S. position. He sees the United States as wanting to argue only about which method is best for preserving a bearskin, whereas a U.S. delegate would say that the problem is more fundamental—that is, whether *any* satisfactory method exists to preserve the bearskin. If the two sides agree to go out and shoot the bear before assuring themselves that the skin is indeed preservable, they will have wasted their time and the bear's life. So it is prudent to first make certain that adequate bearskin preservatives exist and are obtainable. One might imagine, for example, the two sides agreeing to collaborate on the construction of a perpetual motion machine. While the development of such a device would indeed be highly beneficial to both sides, there is every reason to expect that, despite the best efforts of their scientists, the "details" of the implementation would prove insurmountable.

The U.S. argument is eminently reasonable, but if the U.S. approach is taken and the parties negotiate first on preservation methods, the question immediately arises as to *how effectively* the bearskin would be preserved—that is, what constitutes "adequate preservation"? In this discussion, there is indeed a possibility, even a high probability, for all kinds of disagreement and endless wrangling over details and subtle value judgments. Here the Soviet approach seems to offer real advantages. If both sides can first agree in principle to shoot the bear and take the skin, then this agreement in itself ought to be sufficient to overcome smaller disagreements over details and justify a common search for the best feasible preservation method. Once the skin has been taken, it becomes imperative to preserve it in the best possible way, and it is in the interests of both parties to collaborate in the preservation. It is better to have the bearskin—which is presumably valuable to both parties—and to do the best one can with preservation, rather than to let the bear get away while the parties conduct an endless search for the perfect preservation method.

The contradiction between what appear to be two valid approaches must be resolved if arms control is to be achieved. If the resolution is to be achieved on a basis of equality (another often articulated Soviet principle), then the resolution must involve some compromise of principle on both sides. The fact that a number of arms control agreements have been reached and that these agreements contain verification provisions satisfactory to both sides (at least at the time the treaties were signed) shows that such compromise is possible. It is important to study these compromises to learn what degree of flexibility exists in each side's basic principles. However, because this chapter deals with Soviet attitudes, it will focus only on Soviet compromises; a more symmetrical view is presented elsewhere.[15]

The first significant concessions made by the Soviet Union took place in 1954–1955, following the death of Joseph Stalin. This is best illustrated by a sequence of events in the spring of 1955, in meetings of the United Nations Disarmament Subcommittee. On March 8, the participating Western states (Canada, France, Great Britain, and the United States) introduced a draft resolution that included the prohibition of nuclear weapons and major reductions in all armed forces and conventional armaments.[16] As usual, this resolution placed a heavy emphasis on effective verification and included provisions for an international "control organ." The Western philosophy toward verification was expressed in the explicit statement that no stage of the disarmament process was to begin until "the control organ reports that it is able effectively to enforce it."[17]

The Western resolution was followed by a Soviet draft resolution on March 19, which expressed commitment to all the same goals but followed the traditional Soviet line of calling for substantive acts of disarmament and various pledges, undertaking, and conferences before the creation of a control organ with extensive powers of inspection. Only after significant disarmament had taken place and a "complete prohibition of atomic, hydrogen and other weapons of mass destruction" had been put into effect would a "standing international organ" be created with "powers to exercise supervision, including inspection on a continuing basis."[18]

The Soviet proposal was followed by an Anglo-French memorandum that made a few minor concessions to the Soviet approach. Then, on May 10, the Soviet delegation submitted an extensive new proposal (not just a draft proposal) that made significant concessions to Western demands for effective verification. The Soviet proposal had a number of parts, but the most important for verification was the suggestion that "during the first stage" of the disarmament process, "the international control organ shall establish on the territory of the states concerned, on a basis of reciprocity, control posts at large ports, at railway junctions, on main motor highways and at aerodromes."[19] According to the Soviet proposal, this would provide assurance against any attempt to mobilize forces for a surprise attack and would therefore "create the necessary atmosphere of trust between states, thereby ensuring the appropriate conditions for the extension of the functions of the international control organ."[20]

This wording recalls principle 5 in the previous section, which suggests that some level of trust must exist before effective verification can be achieved. The Soviet suggestion that the control posts be created in the initial stages of the disarmament process can be seen as a serious attempt to confront the dilemma posed by the demand that trust precede the implementation of the verification measures that are needed to built that trust. The seriousness of the Soviet proposal was underlined the following day in a major address by Soviet Premier Bulganin to a Warsaw Treaty Organization conference.[21]

The Soviet concessions were considered highly significant by the Western delegates. The U.S. delegate, James Wadsworth, stated on May 11 that "the Soviet Union has reversed its line and this time seems to be using ideas and language which are similar in many respects to the views put forward for many years by [the Western states]. We welcome this development."[22] The United States still did not feel that the Soviets had come far enough, but there was no mistaking the very positive tone of the U.S. reaction to the Soviet proposal. Unfortunately, for reasons that are outside the scope of this chapter, the United States not only rejected the Soviet proposals but withdrew all of its own previous proposals and broke off the negotiations,[23] substituting later that same year the ill-fated "open skies" proposal.

This incident is the first but certainly not the last in which the Soviet Union has indicated its willingness to relax its insistence that agreements on principle must precede detailed provisions for control. The SALT negotiations have also demonstrated a slow but measurable progress in Soviet flexibility on this issue. For example, at an early stage of the SALT I negotiations, the United States insisted on discussing specific numerical limits on various missile types, but "the Soviets never budged from the principle that numbers would be disclosed and discussed only after agreement on principles."[24] Several years later, however, during the latter stages of the SALT II negotiations, the Soviet Union provided the U.S. delegation with official data on Soviet heavy bomber and launcher numbers, a marked break with traditional Soviet behavior. In fact, when these data were handed over, Vladimir Semyonov, the head of the Soviet delegation, told his U.S. counterpart: [you have] just repealed four hundred years of Russian history. But on reflection, maybe that's not a bad thing."[25] The great significance of this change also impressed the U.S. negotiators, who had persistently argued the virtues of an agreed database to serve as a benchmark for both verification and future negotiations.[26]

As a final comment on this point, it is interesting to note that on at least one important occasion, an American negotiator was attracted by the concept of prior agreement on principle. At one point during the long and frustrating wrangling in the SALT I negotiations, U.S. National Security Advisor Henry Kissinger "said the only way to make progress was to agree in principle on a freeze and then negotiate the ABM agreement and details of the freeze."[27] The ABM Treaty and the Interim Agreement represent the "bearskin" that this concession contributed to obtaining.

Legitimacy

Principles 1 and 3 establish the basis for the Soviet concept of legitimacy in verification. To qualify as an NTM or an acceptable "cooperative measure," any monitoring or inspection scheme must not compromise the national sovereignty of the Soviet Union or go beyond the level of scrutiny demanded by the specific agreement being verified. Measures that violate these criteria do not qualify as NTMs and, in the Soviet view, are therefore not covered by the noninterference provisions that protect NTMs.

It is interesting to note the great similarity between the failure of the "open skies" proposal and the nearly instantaneous rejection by the Soviet Union of the so-called "open invitation" plan offered by Vice-President George Bush at the Geneva negotiations on a chemical weapons treaty in April 1984.[28] Such a proposal clearly falls under the following blanket rejection recently articulated by a Soviet commentator:

> The USSR is categorically opposed to "inspections" like the notorious "Baruch Plan," the "open skies" concept, and others that were put forward by the USA in the past and had the nature of the intelligence-gathering operations. The Soviet Union will not agree to such "verification."[29]

Even more objectionable to the Soviets was the blatant inequality inherent in this proposal, which at first offered only government-owned U.S. facilities for Soviet inspection and then was belatedly amended to include private industrial plants working under government contracts.[30] U.S. officials acknowledged the asymmetry in the plan but argued that it was the best that could be done given U.S. constitutional protections against unreasonable search and seizure of private property.[31] Such concerns were analyzed long ago by U.S. legal experts and were found to be highly dubious;[32] but even if they are granted, this cannot explain how the U.S. government could seriously expect the Soviet government to accept such a proposal, given the deeply held Soviet commitment to the "bedrock principles of international law, fixed in the UN Charter, as sovereign equality and non-interference in the internal affairs of a state. No verification measure is legitimate unless it proceeds from these principles."[33]

Soviet rejection of the Bush proposal does not imply a blanket rejection of on-site inspection. The earliest Soviet proposals for international control of disarmament included provisions for on-site inspection, but only under the conditions of prior disarmament. Their first major concession on this principle, the establishment of control posts, has already been mentioned. This was followed later in 1962, during the nuclear test ban negotiations, by a proposal to monitor a test ban with unmanned seismic stations (so-called "black boxes") installed on the territories of the states that were party to the treaty. These stations would be placed in seismically active areas, where ambiguous events would be most frequent, and they could be visited by international inspectors and technicians for the purposes of maintenance and data collection.[34] Such a system would undoubtedly have greatly reduced, if not eliminated, the need for on-site inspection, thereby reducing the potential for inspectors to gather collateral information. Even so, the Soviets also stated their willingness to accept up to three "challenge" inspections per year, a number quite a few American scientists believed would be ample to deter violations.[35]

Present-day ideas for monitoring a comprehensive test ban put a high value on the use of unmanned regional seismic stations and suggest that with the improvements over the past twenty years in seismic detectors and data-processing techniques, on-site inspection is unnecessary.[36] Nevertheless, the Soviets have not withdrawn their agreement in principle to the use of "challenge" on-site inspections, under which a state challenged by another would be obligated either to accept the inspection or to give a detailed explanation for its refusal.[37] Given the remarkable technical capabilities of modern seismological detectors and data-processing techniques, as well as the rarely discussed but substantial technical problems of on-site inspections,[38] there seems to be no good reason to attempt to push the Soviets toward further compromise on this issue.

There have been other major concessions by the Soviets on the issue of on-site inspection. The Peaceful Nuclear Explosion Treaty (PNET), signed in 1976, contains carefully constructed provisions for the presence of observers at all nonmilitary nuclear explosions. These observers would have considerable freedom to study data, take photographs, make measurements, and observe test procedures to assure themselves that the explosion was fulfilling only its declared peaceful purpose.[39] Unfortunately, the unwillingness of the United States to ratify this treaty has prohibited any test of the efficacy and reliability of these provisions.

Another Soviet acceptance of on-site inspection occurred more recently in the context of the chemical weapons negotiations in Geneva. Here the Soviet side accepted in principle the concept of international observers stationed permanently at facilities declared as destruction sites for chemical weapons stocks.[40] Although it certainly can be argued that it took the Soviets far too long to recognize the obvious necessity of such a verification provision, their ultimate acceptance of it can be seen as an encouraging sign of a continuing willingness to take serious verification proposals seriously.

There are two more issues, one historical and the other current, that illustrate the Soviet approach to legitimacy. The historical case concerns the Soviet acceptance of satellite photoreconnaissance; the current issue involves the encryption of missile test telemetry. It is not necessary here to recall in detail the evolution of Soviet views on satellite photoreconnaissance; it is admirably recounted elsewhere.[41] For our purposes, the essential facts are that the Soviets first bitterly opposed the observation and photographing of their territory by foreign satellites, calling it espionage and a violation of their "air space." This position was consistent with their earlier rejection of "open skies" and was reinforced by the creation of a program to develop antisatellite weapons, presumably to be used to destroy reconnaissance satellites just as they had destroyed the U.S. U-2 and other aircraft that had violated their airspace. However, quite suddenly and unexpectedly in 1963, the Soviet Union reversed itself and accepted satellite photoreconnaissance as legitimate. It did this unilaterally and informally, without negotiation or even great fanfare.

There has never been an official Soviet explanation for the change of heart. From one point of view, it seems quite illogical to oppose over-flights by aircraft and permit them by satellites, when the coverage and resolution of satellite cameras and sensors are in many ways as good or better than those in aircraft. And it remains true that satellites are the most important source of data for U.S. strategic target planning,[42] just as aircraft would have been in the 1950s if "open skies" had been accepted. Yet satellite reconnaissance has become legitimate and accepted, while aerial reconnaissance remains illegitimate and unacceptable—a contrast dramatically and tragically emphasized by the destruction of a South Korean airliner that violated Soviet airspace in 1983.

The most likely explanation for this difference in attitude is the realization by Soviet authorities that the use of reconnaissance satellites is as advantageous to them as it is to the United States, and that the possession of such capabilities by both sides not only contributes to stabilizing the competition between them but also provides accurate targeting data for the Soviet rocket forces as well as the opportunity to observe the activities of many other states. Indeed, Soviet satellites are active in monitoring crisis and conflict situations in all parts of the world, as well as U.S. and NATO military exercises and deployments.[43]

It is important to emphasize the informal nature of the Soviet acceptance of satellite photoreconnaissance. Although this informality has the advantage of obviating the need for lengthy, detailed negotiations, it also means that each side is in principle free to attach whatever limits or reservations it chooses to the use of satellite reconnaissance over its own territory. This is most significant in the case of the Soviet Union's continued assertion that there is a difference in principle between reconnaissance for verification purposes and reconnaissance for the gathering of military intelligence, even though it is almost never feasible in practice to distinguish these activities. For example, a 1979 Soviet article on space law has stated:

> If supervision by means of space equipment goes beyond the purpose of monitoring provided by the treaty and, for example, is carried out for the purpose of getting some intelligence information, this activity must be regarded as unlawful.[44]

A more recent Soviet assessment begins with the clear assertion that "the use of observation satellites is within the norms of existing international law. The space treaty of 1967...does not impose any restrictions on the use of satellites." Yet this same author concludes with a sentence that can only be interpreted as a reservation: "But not a single international legal document directly approves the use of such satellites for monitoring and control."[45] Indeed, photoreconnaissance satellites are never mentioned explicitly in any of the treaties that legitimate the use of national technical means of verification.

Such resevations may be interpreted as keeping open the option of interfering with or attacking functions. The Soviet Union continued to develop, albeit fitfully, an antisatellite (ASAT) capability, even though it was hoped by some that acceptance of the legitimacy of satellite reconnaissance would make such a capability unnecessary.[46] The Soviet testing program has been interrupted several times in the past and is presently observing a unilateral moratorium declared by Secretary Andropov in 1983. Nevertheless, work continues on a large phased-array radar whose most logical primary purpose, according to one analyst, is to contribute to ASAT battle management.[47] It should be added that the United States, which has never questioned the legitimacy of satellite reconnaissance, is also moving forward with an antisatellite weapon whose only plausible functions are to attack Soviet photoreconnaissance, ocean surveillance, or electronic reconnaissance satellites.

Whatever reservations in principle the two sides may have as to the unlimited legitimacy of satellite reconnaissance, there is very little possibility that either side will attempt to enforce its reservations by attacking one of the other's satellites in peacetime. Such an attack would certainly be considered an aggressive act, similar to firing upon a ship in international waters.[48] Such attacks become likely only at times of heightened political tension and would almost certainly contribute to escalating that tension. The act of developing the capability to make such attacks is evidence of a willingness to risk such escalation. But maintaining this option derives much less from questioning the legitimacy of satellites as peacetime monitoring systems than it does from a recognition of their crucial military importance in time of war. On this point, one is unlikely to find major differences of opinion between the Soviet Union and the United States.

The inhibitions against attacking reconnaissance satellites do not extend to the so-called passive measures that can be used to frustrate them. The noninterference clauses prohibit "deliberate concealment measures which impede verification by national technical means,"[49] and even a not-so-strict constructionist interpretation of this phrase leaves ample room for the use of camouflage and deception to conceal activities not specifically covered by treaties. There is every reason to believe that both sides employ such measures to hide sensitive military deployments and activities, and there is no a priori reason to believe that current passive concealment measures constitute violations of existing treaties.

In one particular area, however, allegations of concealment and deception have taken on a special significance. The United States has accused the Soviet Union of violating the SALT II Treaty by encrypting the telemetry from its ICBM tests in such a way as to impede verification of the treaty. The transmission of such telemetry is a routine part of any missile test, and the telemetry from Soviet missile tests has been monitored for many years by U.S. air-, ground-, and space-based antennas. Similarly, the Soviet Union monitors U.S. telemetry with the help of trawlers (equipped with sophisticated antennas) that can approach close to U.S. test sites. The information gained from interception of this telemetry is very useful, if not essential, for the determination of certain properties of ICBMs, such as throw-weight, launch-weight, and number of warheads, features that are limited by the SALT II Treaty. However, it is also very useful in monitoring such things as accuracy and reliability, which are not covered by treaties.

The interception of communications is not generally recognized as a legitimate NTM, and in all other areas of communications much effort is devoted to encrypting or otherwise concealing sensitive messages from the intelligence agencies of other states. The issue of legitimacy is even further complicated by the fact that U.S. air and ground electronic reconnaissance systems are largely based on the territories of third countries, calling into question their legitimacy as *national* technical means. Former Secretary of Defense Harold Brown has testified that "Soviet officials do not accept intelligence gathering systems and stations deployed in third countries as national technical means of verification."[50]

It is in this context that one must consider the single, narrowly defined area in which the interception of telemetry is recognized as legitimate: in the verification of the SALT II Treaty. The treaty contains the following "Common Understanding":

> Each Party is free to use various methods of transmitting telemetric information, including its encryption, except that, in accordance with the provisions of Paragraph 3 of Article XV of the Treaty, neither Party shall engage in deliberate denial of telemetric information, such as through the use of telemetry encryption, whenever such denial impedes verification of compliance with the provisions of the Treaty.[51]

It is important to recognize that this understanding legitimates both the interception of telemetry and its encryption, the only limit on encryption being that it should not "impede" verification. It is this attempt to have it both ways that has led to perhaps the most serious of the current compliance issues between the United States and the USSR.

During the SALT II negotiations, the Soviet Union resisted any attempt by the United States to suggest that there was anything improper about encrypting telemetry, agreeing only in the final stages to acknowledge that there might exist ways in which the encryption of telemetry could impede verification of SALT II.[52] Soviet encryption of missile telemetry began in the mid-1970s after the USSR learned through espionage of the extent and sophistication of U.S. electronic monitoring capabilities, especially the Rhyolite satellite program.[53] Since 1977, when the practice began in earnest, reports of Soviet telemetry encryption have steadily increased in the U.S. media and in congressional speeches and testimony. Finally, in January 1984, President Reagan included charges of Soviet violation of the "Common Understanding" on encryption as one of a long list of alleged Soviet violations that he submitted to Congress.

More recently, there have been unconfirmed reports in the U.S. press that the Soviet Union has gone beyond the passive measure of encrypting its telemetry and has begun the active jamming of U.S. satellites.[54] If these charges are true, this would represent a far less ambiguous challenge to the legitimacy of electronic satellite reconnaissance. One U.S. expert on international law has drawn the interpretation that Soviet acquiescence to photoreconnaissance satellites can be extrapolated to include "any other passive sensor in an overflying satellite."[55] Soviet jamming of U.S. electronic satellites would represent a direct repudiation of this interpretation, suggesting that, to the Soviets, these sensors, however passive, are not operating "in a manner consistent with generally recognized principles of international law."

The charges of satellite jamming may or may not be true, but there seems to be no doubt that extensive encryption is taking place. The Soviets have never denied that they are encrypting telemetry; they deny only that these activities impede verification. According to former Soviet defense minister Ustinov:

> As far as telemetry goes, I don't think there is any sense in discussing this problem. The information essential to verification of the provisions of the Treaty will not be encrypted. Agreement in this has been reached.[56]

Any attempt to analyze Soviet motivations in this case must begin with the realization that such blatant and direct interference with U.S. monitoring efforts cannot be called cheating in the usual sense of trying to hide something to gain military advantage. First, there are often other ways of obtaining the same information as is obtained by telemetry interception. Although these alternative means may not provide the same level of accuracy and reliability, there is no way for the Soviets to be confident that their encryption is successfully concealing treaty violations. Second, the military advantages gained by small changes in throw-weight or other parameters covered by the treaty are so marginal that they could hardly be worth the price that is being paid in terms of increased U.S. hostility and suspicion and the possibility of retaliation.

A more plausible interpretation of these activities would be a Soviet desire, first, to conceal from U.S. intelligence as much data not covered by treaties as possible and, second, to challenge the legitimacy of unrestricted electronic reconnaissance to see how much the United States is willing to concede in other areas to preserve its intelligence assets in this area. Generally, the United States has been reluctant to raise complaints in the Standing Consultative Commission (SCC) about telemetry encryption, because most such complaints would reveal information about the capabilities of United States monitoring and analysis systems. However, when complaints have been raised, the Soviet response has been to ask U.S. representatives to be specific regarding just what information they believe is being encrypted that is necessary for verification—precisely the response one would expect under principle 3.[57] The United States will not comply with this request, partially because to do so would be to reveal the methods by which it analyzes telemetry data, and partially because it is reluctant to acknowledge the very limited amount of telemetry required for verification as compared with that used to monitor such things as reliability, accuracy, and other design parameters uncontrolled by treaty provisions but very useful in military planning.

This kind of dispute can be settled only by negotiation. So long as it is considered legitimate to monitor telemetry for the purposes of verification and at the same time encrypt telemetry for the purposes of concealing militarily sensitive information, there can be no escaping the necessity of coming to an explicit agreement regarding where one practice leaves off and the other begins. The drawing of this line will be very difficult, since there is considerable overlap between the information needed to verify existing treaties and that needed to monitor nontreaty-related capabilities. But unless some line is drawn, the existing ambiguities can be interpreted by each side in its own way, and there can be no guarantee that the interpretations will coincide.

It may be that future treaties should avoid provisions that require telemetry monitoring for their verification. So far, those treaty provisions that do require it have been comparatively unimportant and hardly worth the extra tension and recrimination they have created. However the problem is to be dealt with, it will have to be approached in a cooperative manner. Accusations of cheating do not contribute to creating the appropriate atmosphere for such cooperation.

The Soviet position on telemetry encryption has at least the virtue of logical consistency in the context of the Soviets' overall approach to verification. The U.S. approach, on the other hand, suffers from serious logical inconsistencies. The United States argues that so long as the Soviet Union can encrypt portions of its telemetry, then even if unencrypted information relevation to verification is also provided, the United States will be unable to determine whether there may also be information relevant to verification in the encrypted portion.[58] This is undeniably possible, since many kinds of information can be useful, either directly or indirectly, for determining such parameters as launch- and throw-weight. It is also possible, in principle, to broadcast false data on unencrypted channels while the real data are encrypted. A possible answer to this dilemma is to attempt to convince the Soviet Union to prohibit all encryption. But such a ban would certainly encounter strong Soviet opposition, not to mention the reluctance of the United States to give up its own option to encrypt telemetry under some circumstances.[59] These contradictory elements in the U.S. approach suggest that the United States needs to negotiate a more effective agreement within its own bureaucracy before it can successfully negotiate one with the Soviet Union.

Adequacy

The preceding sections have established what might be called the upper limits of Soviet toleration for verification. It is now appropriate to attempt to infer the existence of *lower* limits to verifiability in the Soviet approach. Such minimal requirements are very difficult to find, of course, mainly because the vast majority of Soviet efforts have gone into fighting off what the Soviets see as unreasonably intrusive and comprehensive U.S. verification proposals. Most of the negotiating time of the two states has been spent at the upper boundary of Soviet tolerance, leaving the lower boundary largely unexplored.

There are some hints in the record of arms control negotiations and compliance diplomacy to suggest a Soviet concern for adequate verifiability in agreements. At one point in the SALT II negotiations, the Soviet side was reportedly willing to offer concessions in the sensitive area of telemetry encryption in exchange for U.S. acceptance of a total ban on cruise missiles.[60] Such an offer can be interpreted in at least two ways: either as an attempt to balance a Soviet concern about verifiability against an American one or as an attempt to take advantage of an American concern about verifiability to extract concessions on actual weapon deployments.[61] It is difficult to separate and rank these possible motivations, but given the obvious difficulty of distinguishing nuclear-armed from conventionally armed cruise missiles and the obvious military importance of the distinction, it seems quite likely that verifiability was a major Soviet concern.

Other evidence for Soviet concerns about verifiability can be inferred from Soviet possession of a sophisticated seismic network for monitoring U.S. underground nuclear tests. Recent Soviet accusations of U.S. treaty violations have pointed to several explosions that have allegedly exceeded the 150 kiloton limit agreed to in the Threshold Test Ban Treaty (TTBT). According to the Soviet charge, "the [U.S.] practice of exceeding the permitted limit of yield for the nuclear devices that are being tested appears to be continuing."[62] As it happens, there is independent evidence that at least two U.S. tests have indeed exceeded the 150 kiloton limit, suggesting that Soviet seismic detection methods are in fact capable of adequately verifying the TTBT.[63]

One further example that suggests a Soviet concern for adequate monitoring capabilities is the Soviet acceptance of satellite photoreconnsaissance. Though surely motivated primarily by military-political intelligence interests, the Soviets' acquiescence to satellite reconnaissance must also have been encouraged by the added sense of confidence it gives them in negotiating agreements with a state whose motives they distrust. The Soviets have relied heavily on satellite evidence to support their complaints in the SCC, and recently in public, about the so-called "environmental shelters" obscuring U.S. ICBM silos undergoing modifications.[64]

Two major features of the Soviet system can account for its very different emphasis on the adequacy of verification from that of the United States. First, there is the ease of Soviet access to the wide variety of information available in open U.S. sources, a major source of reassurance (or alarm) that is unavailable to the U.S. side. Second, decision-making power in the Soviet Union, especially in the area of arms control, is sharply pyramidal. The Soviet form of government requires that only a few people near the top of the hierarchy be reassured by having access to intelligence information and analysis, while in the United States the compliance process must be able to reassure a public and their representatives that all is well, even in an atmosphere clouded by charges of violations based on unsubstantiated leaks of secret intelligence information.

Of these two asymmetries, the second is considerably more important than the first in explaining the relatively lower demands for verification by the Soviet Union. It is undoubtedly true that the absence of open Soviet sources of information makes U.S. intelligence gathering, and therefore verification, more difficult and expensive. However, U.S. intelligence agencies have had many years to adjust to the essentially technical problems posed by Soviet secrecy, and they do not appear to suffer from a serious lack of information on Soviet military activities.[65]

It is in the domestic political role of verification that the Soviet Union enjoys its greatest advantage. The U.S. administration faces the severe task of legitimating arms control agreements (assuming, of course, that it wants to) in the face of the need for a two-thirds ratification vote in the Senate and a public opinion kept in a constant state of alarm by politically inspired intelligence leaks. On the Soviet side, the top decision makers are quite homogeneous politically but can still have disagreements on arms control philosophy and specific proposals. In this situation, the capability to produce hard evidence to demonstrate U.S. compliance with agreements is undoubtedly useful in producing a consensus behind Soviet arms control proposals. But when it comes to public opinion, the Soviet government faces no serious problems, needing only to reassure the public at infrequent intervals:

> In our century of developed electronics and space flights, those who are entrusted with such verification possess all the necessary facilities for immediately finding out any violation of the treaty if it occurs.[66]

The great demands placed on verification to reassure American public opinion lead to a distinction in U.S. thinking between *militarily significant* and *politically significant* violations of treaties.[67] In the ideal Clausewitzian sense, these criteria should be equivalent, since the political significance of a military initiative ought to depend directly on its military significance. Unfortunately, the logic of this position is very difficult to sustain in the U.S. context because of the complexity of and lack of consensus on U.S. military doctrine. The Soviet leaders, on the other hand, are in a far better position to base their demands for verification on the need to detect only militarily significant cheating by the United States.

The Soviet criterion of adequacy does not flow directly from the basic principles, but it is possible to get some idea by combining principles 3, 4, and 7. These suggest that the means of verification must be at least commensurate with specific obligations, that they should derive directly from those obligations, and that they should take into account the cost-benefit relationship between the possible military advantages to be gained by a violation and the risk of detection. This last (perhaps awkwardly translated) principle seems to be saying that even relatively small violations may present unacceptably high risks of detection, but it may also be intended to suggest a more general principle similar to one articulated by former Secretary of Defense Harold Brown in testimony on the SALT II Treaty:

> In short, there is a double bind which serves to deter Soviet cheating. To go undetected, any Soviet cheating would have to be on so small a scale that it would not be militarily significant. Cheating on such a level would hardly be worth the political risks involved. On the other hand, any cheating serious enough to affect the military balance would be detectable in sufficient time to take whatever action the situation required.[68]

Soviet belief in this double-bind principle would be consistent with a focus on militarily significant violations and could explain the Soviets' demands for reassurance that are consistently lower than Americans, faced by a far more volatile domestic political situation, are willing or able to settle for.

This raises the question of how far Soviet negotiators are willing to go to accommodate the seemingly insatiable demands of the U.S. Congress and public for reassurance. Some concessions have already been made, such as the willingness to tolerate with only mild protest the Carter administration's decision to release summaries of the confidential deliberations of the SCC to support its assertion that the Soviet record of compliance was satisfactory. It can also be argued that many, if not most, of the detailed verification concessions made by the Soviet side in previous negotiations have been motivated by a recognition that without them, there would be no ratification of the treaty by the U.S. Senate.

Unfortunately, it now appears that even the many concessions that have been made are inadequate. There has been no ratification of a U.S.–Soviet arms control treaty by the Senate since 1972, including three treaties whose verification provisions broke new ground and were considered adequate by the administrations that negotiated them. What appeared to be a slowly growing convergence on verification during the 1960s and 1970s has again become a wide and deep chasm. It is far too much to expect that the Soviet Union will see it as entirely its responsibility to reclose this gap.

Trust

Of all the principles listed by Ambassador Israelyan, principle 5 is the one on which the Soviet and U.S. approaches to verification differ most dramatically.

Virtually all discussions of verification in the United States, whether by liberals or conservatives, begin with the basic premise that the Soviet Union cannot be trusted to abide by its commitments. A few examples:

> The Chairman of the Senate Foreign Relations Committee, who in his report on the verifiability of the SALT II Treaty begins with the statement: "It is agreed that the United States cannot rely upon or trust the Russians to comply with [the Treaty's] terms."[69]

> Former CIA Director William Colby, who is a strong advocate of a mutual nuclear freeze but for whom "the first and most obvious fundamental is, of course, that we should not 'trust' the Russians."[70]

> Democratic presidential candidate Walter Mondale, who stated emphatically in his second debate with President Reagan: "I don't trust the Russians."[71]

Such statements have become de rigueur in the United States—a kind of incantation to demonstrate that the speaker is not a sentimental disarmer or unwitting dupe of Soviet trickery. They are part of a credibility ritual that Americans have come to expect of anyone with pretensions to expertise in arms control verification. Yet the practical consequences of such an attitude are never honestly explored. This is no problem for those Americans who oppose arms control agreements with the Soviet Union; such a lack of trust is, in fact, one of the foundation stones of their position. For advocates of arms control, however, the lack of trust must somehow be neutralized if arms control agreements are to be negotiated. It is here that the traditional American faith in technology is called to the rescue—verification will be the substitute for trust and will even contribute to building trust:

> Verification systems which are now essential because of lack of trust, can, by the assurance of compliance they can provide, become one of the most powerful tools for building the sought-for mutual trust.... In sum we have the following equation: the more absolute the verification—born in mistrust—the greater the progress toward absolute trust.[72]

This quotation may overstate the case a bit, but it typifies the Western notion that verification can serve as a substitute for trust and can lead to the growth of trust.

Needless to say, the Soviets are skeptical of this belief. Principle 5 states that verification "should not be built upon the principle of total distrust by States of one another," and former Soviet President Brezhnev has been quoted as telling a U.S. Senator:

> The danger today is not that the current methods of verification are inadquate, but that this issue might be used to fuel a propaganda campaign that would

only trigger distrust between our countries and poison the political atmosphere.[73]

Whereas American expressions of distrust of the Soviet Union are frequent and direct, Soviet statements implying or suggesting distrust of the United States, *with respect to its intention of complying with arms control agreements,* are really quite rare. Gerard Smith, the chief U.S. negotiator in SALT I, has remarked that during the entire two years of difficult and occasionally acrimonious negotiations, "The closest the Soviets ever came to suggesting that the United States might violate an agreement was a statement that a party to an agreement might evade its terms by helping to build up allied strategic forces."[74] Yet there are limits to such restraint, and occasionally a Soviet spokesman will remind the world that "we have no reason for trusting others any more than others trust us."[75]

It is worthwhile to examine in greater depth the reasoning of the author of this remark, because it helps clarify the Soviet perspective on where verification must leave off and trust begin. He is addressing the "concept of distrust," which carries the following conditions:

> Every party to a convention is regarded as a potential violator of its provisions, as one who will do everything possible to ensure that his neighbors ban and destroy their weapons while he himself keeps his so that he can use them either for deterrence or for a direct attack. . . . In these conditions. . . no matter how much we expand and complicate the verification system. . . we shall never reach the point at which we can be sure that no uncertainties have been left.[76]

Ambassador Israelyan goes on to examine the practical consequences of adopting such a principle in the context of a chemical weapons ban. In particular, the principle of total distrust implies that it would be insufficient to accept declarations by states of their stocks of chemical weapons and production facilities and then confine monitoring to the destruction of these declared stocks and facilities. In that case, he asks:

> Do we now have to place under control the entire production of these [common] substances? Or do we have to fill enterprises with hundreds and thousands of foreign inspectors? . . . Can we be sure that a suspect State is not using these chemicals for prohibited purposes? Would we really have to place under control all metalworking enterprises [which might produce metal casings for chemical munitions]?[77]

There is undeniable validity in Israelyan's contention that there must be limits to distrust if arms control or disarmament is to succeed, as there is in Brezhnev's contention that too much verification can actually stimulate distrust. There is insufficient space here to make this argument in detail; this is done elsewhere.[78] It can be noted, however, that the same understanding has appeared from time to time in Western analyses of verification. For example:

> If we assume something approaching 100 percent willingness to cheat, then verification by technical means becomes politically ineffective. In an atmosphere of intense distrust the verification system will be asked to verify things that resist verification and to provide unreasonable reassurances.[79]

In addition:

> Transparency has revealed defense establishments of great technical complexity, in the process of constant change. Where the meaning of certain activities is inherently obscure, greater amounts of information are bound to lead to conflicts of interpretation and thus of policy choice. Transparency has a confidence-eroding as well as a confidence-building dimension.[80]

This is most likely what the Soviets have in mind when they emphasize the distinction between monitoring disarmament and monitoring armaments.

In short, although it is obvious that one can have too little verification, it is also necessary to understand that one can demand too much. This is not to say that the United States must accept the Soviet view of where this boundary lies, but it does mean that U.S. advocates of arms control must take a more sophisticated and realistic approach than they have thus far to the problems of trust and confidence building if they are to educate the American people to the true functions and limitations of verification. Nothing can be gained and much can be lost by holding out unreasonable promises regarding what verification would be able to accomplish if only the Soviets would allow it to happen.

It is a basic fact of psychology that if evidence of compliance with agreements is to build confidence and trust, it must have some preexisting trust to build on.[81] This might be called a willingness to be convinced or a "disposition to be reassured."[82] It may well be that the growth of trust will depend on greater openness, but it is no less true that greater openness will depend on the growth of trust.

Just how this process can start is unclear, and the present political climate gives little cause for optimism. Some kind of political leap of faith is required— perhaps something like that envisioned by Secretary of War Henry Stimson in 1946. Stimson, at first an advocate of U.S. monopoly on all information relating to the atomic bomb, became disillusioned with this policy and advocated a direct approach to the Soviet Union to explore the possibilities of collaborating on the control of atomic energy. In his argument to President Truman he wrote:

> The chief lesson I have learned in a long life is that the only way you can make a man trustworthy is to trust him; and the surest way to make him untrustworthy is to distrust him and to show your distrust.[83]

Despite the great advances in monitoring and analysis techniques that have taken place since Stimson wrote these words, their essential truth is unchanged. Arms control advocates in the United States would do well to place at least as much emphasis on the need for some level of trust as on their self-defeating litany of distrust.

Conclusion

The fact that arms control negotiations take place at all is evidence of a mutual concern for the prevention of war and the reduction of armaments. If such negotiations are to succeed, each side must be willing to take some risks, based on the confidence that the other side shares these fundamental concerns. Each side must also respect to the greatest extent possible the particular political, historical, and technological constraints operating to restrict the freedom of maneuver of the other side.

The progress of SALT, nuclear nonproliferation, test ban, and chemical weapons negotiations of the 1960s and 1970s, though slow and often frustrating, showed a clear tendency for convergence between the positions on verification taken by the United States and the USSR. This convergence met increasing opposition in the United States during the 1970s, and many of the people and interests that constituted this opposition are now in positions of authority in the U.S. arms control bureaucracy. It is important to understand, however, that this opposition was really less concerned with problems of verification than it was, and still is, with the entire arms control philosophy of previous administrations.

In this situation, verification has often served as a surrogate issue that is somehow easier to argue about than the more fundamental conflicts over military-strategic doctrine that are the real sources of disagreement. As a result, verification has been asked to bear too great a burden, and in the inevitable distortions of political debate, the Soviet positions on verification have not been given an honest and objective hearing in the United States.

It is important to emphasize in concluding this analysis that to take the Soviet approach to verification seriously does not require that one agree with it in detail, or even in principle. It requires only the recognition that the Soviets themselves take it seriously as their best attempt to reconcile the contradictory demands of pursuing arms control and an arms race simultaneously within the constraints posed by their own security needs and domestic political situation. This, in turn, requires a willingness to refrain from gratuitous expressions of distrust and premature accusations of violations based on ambiguous evidence.

An open-minded examination of the Soviets' approach to verification reveals a substantial degree of validity, particularly in their recognition of the advantages of agreeing in principle before haggling over details, in their understanding of the need for some a priori assumption of trust, and in their skepticism about the practical and political usefulness of comprehensive plans for on-site inspection. On the other hand, they can be criticized for an overly formal and unrealistic attempt to separate verification activities from the much larger spectrum of intelligence gathering, which in fact makes verification possible in the first place. One would also like to ask the Soviet Union to show more sensitivity than they have in the past to the demands of domestic U.S. politics, but one would feel more comfortable in making this request if the United States were also displaying a greater sensitivity to legitimate concerns of the Soviet Union.

Notes

1. W. Slocombe, "Verification and Negotiation," in *The Nuclear Weapons Freeze and Arms Control,* Proceedings of a symposium held at the American Academy of Arts and Sciences, Center for Science and International Affairs, Harvard University, January 13–15, 1983, p. 87.

2. S.B. Payne, Jr., *The Soviet Union and SALT,* (Cambridge, Mass.: MIT Press, 1980), p. 81.

3. T.N. Dupuy and G.M. Hammerman, *A Documentary History of Arms Control and Disarmament* (New York: Bowker; and Dunn Loring, Va.: T.N. Dupuy Associates, 1973), pp. 345–348.

4. A. Chayes, "An Inquiry into the Workings of Arms Control Agreements," *Harvard Law Review* 85(March 1972): 937.

5. V. Israelyan, CD/PV.119, Committee on Disarmament, Final Record of the 119th Meeting, 31 March 1981, Geneva, pp. 16–17.

6. R. Parkinson, *Clausewitz: A Biography* (London: Wayland, 1970), p. 314.

7. J. Goldblat, *Agreements for Arms Control: A Critical Survey,* (London: SIPRI, Taylor & Francis, 1982), p. 155 (emphasis added).

8. V. Israelyan, "Soviet Initiatives on Disarmament," *International Affairs* (Moscow), July 1977, p. 55.

9. *Documents on Disarmament 1945–1959,* U.S. Department of State Publication 7008 (Washington, D.C.: U.S. Government Printing Office, August 1960), Vol. I, pp. 486–488.

10. Ibid., p. 487.

11. D.A. Rosenberg, "The Origins of Overkill: Nuclear Weapons and American Strategy, 1945-1960," *International Security* 7(Spring 1983): 38.

12. Ibid., p. 50.

13. G.M. Steinberg, *Satellite Reconnaissance: The Role of Informal Bargaining* (New York: Praeger, 1983), p. 96.

14. C. Jönsson, *Soviet Bargaining Behavior: The Nuclear Test Ban Case* (New York: Columbia University Press, 1979), p. 72.

15. A.S. Krass, *The Technology and Politics of Verification* (London: SIPRI, Taylor & Francis, 1985), chapter 3, section II.

16. *Documents on Disarmament,* pp. 448–450.

17. Ibid., p. 449.

18. Ibid., pp. 450–452.

19. Ibid., pp. 456–467.

20. Ibid., p. 466.

21. Ibid., pp. 467–471.

22. Ibid., p. 473

23. P. Noel-Baker, *The Arms Race* (London: John Calder, 1958), pp. 12–30; R.J. Barnet, *Who Wants Disarmament*, (Boston: Beacon Press, 1960), pp. 27–45.

24. G. Smith, *Doubletalk: The Story of SALT I* (New York: Doubleday, 1980), p. 170.

25. S. Talbot, *End Game: The Inside Story of SALT II* (New York: Harper & Row, 1979), p. 98.

26. R. Earle II, private communication, 16 October 1984.

27. Smith, *Doubletalk,* p. 230.

28. G. Bush, Address before the Committee on Disarmament on banning of chemical weapons, Geneva, 18 April 1984, U.S. Department of State, Bureau of Public Affairs, Washington, D.C.

29. Major General Lebedev, "Washington's Speculations Around Verification Issues," *Pravda,* May 3, 1984.

30. W. Pincus, "US Clarifies Stand on Chemical Pact," *Washington Post,* May 1, 1984, p. 12.

31. R.J. Smith, "A Novel Proposal on Chemical Weapons," *Science,* May 4, 1984, p. 474.

32. L. Henkin, *Arms Control and Inspection in American Law* (Westport, Conn.: Greenwood Press, 1958), pp. 64–75.

33. R. Zheleznov, "Monitoring Arms Limitation Measures," *International Affairs* (Moscow), July 1982, p. 77.

34. G.T. Seaborg, *Kennedy, Khrushchev, and the Test Ban* (Berkeley: University of California Press, 1981), p. 177.

35. Ibid., p. 191.

36. L.R. Sykes and J.F. Evernden, "Verification of a Comprehensive Nuclear Test Ban," *Scientific American* 247(October 1982): 47–55.

37. "Tripartite Report to the Committee on Disarmament," in *World Armaments and Disarmament: SIPRI Yearbook 1981* (London: Taylor & Francis, 1981), pp. 383–387.

38. Krass, *Technology and Politics of Verification,* chapter 4.

39. Goldblat, *Agreements for Arms Control,* pp. 221–222.

40. "Moscow Yields on Point of Chemical War Ban," *New York Times,* February 22, 1984, p. 4.

41. S.A. Cohen, "The Evolution of Soviet Views on Verification," in W.C. Potter, ed., *Verification and SALT: The Challenge of Strategic Deception* (Boulder, Colo.: Westview Press, 1980); Steinburg, *Satellite Reconnaissance.*

42. D. Ball, "Targeting for Strategic Deterrence," Adelphi Paper No. 185, (London: IISS, 1983), p. 26.

43. *World Armaments and Disarmament: SIPRI Yearbook 1984* (London: Taylor & Francis, 1984), pp. 352–356.

44. Cohen, "The Evolution of Soviet Views," p. 54.

45. Zheleznov, "Monitoring Arms Limitation Measures," p. 79.

46. Steinberg, *Satellite Reconnaissance,* p. 4.

47. J. Pike, "FAS Public Interest Bulletin" (Washington, D.C.: Federation of American Scientists, March 1984), pp. 3–9.

48. G. Bunn, "Legal Context of Arms Control Verification," Paper presented to the MIT Conference on Technical Aspects of Verification, February 1-3, 1984, p. 5.

49. SALT II Treaty, Article XV.3; see Goldblat, *Agreements for Arms Control,* p. 280.

50. *Military Implications of the Treaty on the Limitation of Strategic Offensive Arms and Protocol Thereto (SALT II Treaty),* Committee on Armed Services, U.S. Senate, 96th Cong. 1st sess., 30 July–2 August 1979 (Washington, D.C.: U.S. Government Printing Office, 1979), vol. 1, p. 228.

51. SALT II Treaty, Second Common Understanding to Paragraph 3 of Article XV; see Goldblat, *Agreements for Arms Control,* p. 280.

52. Talbot, *End Game,* p. 238.

53. D. Ball, "The Rhyolite Program," Reference Paper No. 86, Strategic and Defense Studies Centre, Research School of Pacific Studies, Australian National University, Canberra, November 1981, p. 15.

54. W. Andrews, "Soviets Reportedly Are Jamming US Satellites Used as Monitors," *Washington Times,* June 4, 1984, p. 3.

55. Bunn, "Legal Context," p. 5.

56. Cohen, "The Evolution of Soviet Views," pp. 50–51.

57. E. Ulsamer, "The Soviets Test a New ICBM," *Air Force Magazine* 67(January 1984): 17.

58. Ibid.

59. *The SALT II Treaty,* Hearings before the Committee on Foreign Relations, U.S. Senate, 96th Cong. 1st sess. (Washington, D.C.: U.S. Government Printing Office, 1979), vol. 1, p. 267.

60. Talbot, *End Game,* p. 223.

61. Slocombe, "Verification and Negotiation," p. 87.

62. "The United States Violates Its International Commitments," *News and Views from the USSR,* Soviet Embassy Information Department, Washington, D.C., January 30, 1984, p. 5.

63. R.J. Smith, "Scientists Challenge Claims of Soviet Treaty Violations," *Science,* June 17, 1983, p. 1254.

64. "Compliance with SALT I Agreements," Special Report No. 55, U.S. Department of State, Bureau of Public Affairs, Washington, D.C., July 1979, p. 4.

65. W. Colby, "Verification of a Nuclear Freeze," in *The Nuclear Weapons Freeze and Arms Control,* Proceedings of a symposium held at the American Academy of Arts and Sciences, Center for Science and International Affairs, Harvard University, January 13–15, 1983, p. 73.

66. Cohen, "The Evolution of Soviet Views," p. 68.

67. S.M. Meyer, "Verification and the ICBM Shell Game," *International Security* 4(February 1979): 48.

68. *Report of the Senate Committee on Foreign Relations on the SALT II Treaty,* 19 November 1979 (Washington, D.C.: U.S. Government Printing Office, 1979), p. 221.

69. Ibid., p. 189.

70. W.E. Colby in *Military Implications,* vol. 3, p. 1025.

71. Transcript of the Reagan–Mondale debate on foreign policy, *New York Times,* October 22, 1984, p. B6.

72. R.E. Roberts, "Verification Problems—Monitoring of Conversion and Destruction of Chemical-Warfare Agent Plant," in SIPRI, *Chemical Weapons: Destruction and Conversion* (London: Taylor & Francis, 1980), pp. 129–130.

73. *The SALT II Treaty,* vol. 5, p. 261.

74. Smith, *Doubletalk,* p. 323.

75. Israelyan, DC/PV. 119, p. 16.

76. Ibid., p. 14.

77. Ibid., p. 15.

78. Krass, *Technology and Politics of Verification,* chapter 3, section VI.

79. R.J. Barnet, "Why Trust the Russians?" *World Policy Journal* 1(Spring 1984): 467.

80. J.A. Schear, "Verifying Arms Agreements: Premises, Practices and Future Problems," *Arms Control* 3(December 1982): 91.

81. J.H. de Rivera, *The Psychological Dimension of Foreign Policy* (Columbus, Ohio: Charles E. Merrill, 1968), chapters 2 and 9.

82. L. Freedman, "Assured Detection: Needs and Dysfunctions of Verification," in U. Nerlich, ed., *The Western Panacea: Constraining Soviet Power through Negotiation,* vol. II, (Cambridge, Mass.: Ballinger, 1983), p. 254.

83. H.L. Stimson and McG. Bundy, *On Active Service in Peace and War* (New York: Harper Brothers, 1948), p. 644.

4
Verification of Test Ban Treaties

Warren Heckrotte

T he issues surrounding a ban on nuclear weapons tests fall into two general categories: (1) the consequences of the ban and (2) the verification of such a ban. The first category has two parts: the perceived political gains that would derive from a test ban and the perceived costs of a test ban. It is the trade-off between these two parts that generates the pressures for and the opposition to a ban. The decision to negotiate a test ban represents a governmental decision that the gains outweigh the costs. The negotiations themselves are not directly concerned with these issues but dwell almost entirely upon the element of verification. The importance of verification from the point of view of the United States—an importance clearly established by the historical record—is directly related to the matter of the technical-military costs. Verification is required by the United States to ensure as much as possible that the Soviets will also incur the costs—that they will not, by cheating, be able to avoid the technical-military penalties of a ban—and that the United States will have confidence in their compliance. The partisans on the test ban issue put different weights and assessments on these various elements. It is not the purpose of this chapter to provide a comparative analysis of these elements and thus of the merits or demerits of a nuclear test ban, nor to review technical analyses of verification methods. Rather, the purpose is to review the elements of verification with a focus on the attempts to negotiate with the Soviet Union verification provisions that the United States has required as the basis for a nuclear test ban.

The Eisenhower administration made the first attempt to achieve a nuclear weapons test ban. The motivation was to meet the national and international pressure for such a ban that had been spurred in substantial part by the concern over fallout and also by the hope that a ban would be a first step toward more substantial measures of arms limitations. The beginning of negotiations was made contingent by the Eisenhower administration upon the development of a control or verification system. In the relatively short period of seven weeks in 1958, Western and Eastern scientists drafted an agreed report—the so-called Experts Report—which concluded that it was technically feasible to set up a workable and effective control system and described the elements of such a system.

The basic technical elements of monitoring possible nuclear explosions in the atmosphere, underground, and underwater were laid out in this report, including a recognition of the role of on-site inspections (OSIs) for the identification of ambiguous seismic events. A later agreed-upon report described the technical elements for monitoring outer space for possible nuclear explosions. The administrative framework for verification was to be an international control authority that would be in charge of the monitoring function. It was left to the political negotiations to translate this work into a treaty. After three years of effort, the negotiations failed.

Of the variety of issues that confronted the negotiators, those that centered on the installation of a seismic monitoring system and the role of on-site inspections of seismic events suspected of being possible underground nuclear explosions dominated the proceedings. These two issues continue to this day to dominate the discussions of verification of a test ban, and it is on these two matters that the judgment of the adequacy or effectiveness of verification for a test ban has been largely made.[1] For seismic monitoring, the problem is to establish a sufficient number of seismic stations within the borders of the parties, with appropriate administrative arrangements; for on-site inspections, the problem is establishing procedures to initiate and to carry out the inspections. The implementation of these measures into treaty text invokes substantial difficulties vis-à-vis the Soviet Union because of the intrusive nature of these measures.

During the first test ban negotiation, the public perception of these difficulties was centered on the differences between the sides over the appropriate yearly quota of on-site inspections. A close reading of the record, however, shows that the difference was more profound than such a simple numerical difference. The Soviets sought arrangements that would have permitted them to limit or control monitoring and verification procedures within their borders. The United States, in contrast, sought arrangements and procedures that could not be legitimately controlled or interfered with by a party within its borders.[2] The Soviets were frank in expressing their concern that the monitoring and verification arrangements the United States sought could serve as a vehicle for espionage. This concern over espionage was in turn related to a perceived inferiority relative to the West. Soviet unwillingness to accept verification procedures sought by the United States reinforced the belief that the Soviets were unwilling to accept reasonable control restraints—a view that persists to this day.

Following the breakdown of these negotiations, the two sides continued in international forums to espouse their interest in a ban on nuclear weapons tests, but the substance of the debate was a sterile reiteration of the respective views regarding whether or not on-site inspections were necessary for adequate verification. The Limited Test Ban Treaty of 1963 avoided these verification difficulties by putting aside the matter of underground testing and thus the matter of seismic monitoring and on-site inspection. The treaty does not mention verification, which is by national technical means (NTM).[3]

A break in this stalemate over verification came with the Threshold Test Ban Treaty (TTBT) of 1974 and its corollary treaty, the Peaceful Nuclear Explosion Treaty (PNET) of 1976. The TTBT established a 150 kiloton yield limit for underground nuclear weapons tests. The treaty provided for verification by national technical means, which in this instance meant seismic monitoring. Each party, using its own seismic network, can determine the seismic magnitude of a weapons test explosion carried out by the other and then, by use of a suitable relation between magnitude and yield, estimate the yield. To limit in some measure the uncertainties associated with this method of yield estimation, the treaty imposes a number of stipulations, including an exchange of scientific and technical data. No means were provided, however, for the parties to confirm independently the accuracy of the data supplied by each to the other.

The TTBT was negotiated in a short span of five weeks in June–July 1974, in time for signature at the Nixon-Brezhnev summit conference. This schedule was met only by postponing consideration of the issue of nuclear explosions for peaceful purposes (engineering and scientific projects). By 1974, economic and political considerations had caused the United States PNE program (Plowshare) to wither away. Accordingly, the United States was prepared to ban PNEs. By this time, however, the Soviets had developed an extensive PNE program of their own,[4] and they insisted on the right to continue it under the TTBT, including high-yield, multiple-explosion projects. It was recognized by both sides that it would take more time than was then available to develop verification procedures ensuring that PNEs did not provide opportunities for weapons testing that were denied under the TTBT's 150 kiloton yield limit. The two sides agreed to take up PNEs in a separate negotiation. Thus, the United States was prepared to accept PNEs to get the TTBT if suitable verification arrangements for PNEs could be developed. The Soviets were prepared to accept some elements of verification to get the TTBT and preserve in some measure their PNE program. At the time, the Soviets said that they would allow U.S. observers at PNE events. It appeared that the long-held Soviet opposition to on-site inspection was about to change.

The PNE negotiations began in October 1975 and were completed in April 1976. There were six rounds, or sessions,[5] all of which took place in Moscow. The negotiations did not begin with the two sides plunging into a consideration of detailed treaty text. First there was the task of setting the framework of the problem. What, for example, was the scope of the PNE projects that the Soviets intended to carry out? Different projects could present different verification problems. What did the Soviets have in mind in saying that observers could be present at PNE projects? This first stage of general discussions occupied the first three rounds of the talks; not until the fourth round were the problems sufficiently thought out and mutual understandings achieved to begin consideration of the treaty text.

Attempts by the U.S. side to ferret out the intent of the Soviet position that observers would be permitted at PNE projects did not meet with prompt success. The United States argued that observers should be present at most PNE events, a view to which the Soviets were unreceptive. The initial Soviet approach was "verification by cooperation." Participation of U.S. personnel in Soviet PNE programs, it was claimed, would enable them to see that the program was peaceful. It was not an approach that stood up under even a cursory analysis, and it did not satisfy the United States with regard to the role of observers. It did, however, establish a persistent theme: the role of cooperation in verification. Not until the middle of the second round did the two sides begin to define the role of observers or inspectors.

The Soviets sought to permit so-called group explosions. A group explosion is the simultaneous firing of a number of neighboring explosions, which in some PNE applications is an engineering and economic necessity. In keeping with the previous accord on the TTBT, no single explosion should exceed 150 kilotons, although the total yield might exceed that limit. The United States took the position that it saw no practical way to determine individual yields of group explosions by verification arrangements and argued that group explosions with a total yield over 150 kilotons should be banned. There was a sharp collision over this matter that lasted for some time. Finally, the head of the Soviet delegation put the question: Would the United States agree "in principle" to permit group explosions with a total yield over 150 kilotons if there were a satisfactory means to verify that individual yields did not exceed 150 kilotons? The U.S. response was positive.

With that response in hand, and not until then, the Soviets proceeded to describe a technique by which, they claimed, the individual yields could be measured. This involved placing instruments to measure ground motion at appropriate locations in the vicinity of the explosions. The United States questioned them on how it could have any confidence in such measurements. They responded that U.S. personnel would be there to make the measurements. The Soviets had finally agreed "in principle" that U.S. observers or inspectors could be present at some PNE events. Much work remained, however, to translate this agreement in principle into explicit provisions that established the rights and functions of the personnel.

When it came to writing the text, the Soviets objected to the term *inspectors,* which they felt carried an insidious implication. (The Soviets' objection reflected their general sensitivity to terminology, although the basis for their concern was not always evident.) In response, the U.S. delegation invented the phrase "designated personnel" as a neutral name for members of the inspection team.

The activities of the designated personnel were a primary consideration. The Soviets stated that these activities should not interfere with the conduct of the project and that they should be able to ensure the safety of the designated personnel. Thus, they claimed, they should know where the designated personnel were and what they were doing. This was not unreasonable. Nonetheless, there was clearly a pressing Soviet concern that the designated personnel might obtain "information not needed for the purpose of verification." This phrase, often used, was invented by the Soviets, harkening back to the early days of test ban negotiations, when they expressed the view that verification activities were simply a disguise for espionage. There were many times, as the debate over a particular verification issue grew heated, when they would again suggest that the United States was seeking such extraneous information.

The Soviets sought to limit the number of designated personnel, the time they could spend at the site, their area of access, and their freedom of access. These issues were not, however, dealt with in an arbitrary or polemical manner by either side. Each side brought substantive arguments and detailed analysis to support its position. The Soviets sought to minimize; the United States sought to maximize. The issues were finally settled by a compromise. One principle governing the Soviets' position, which they made explicit more than once, was that the requirements had to be justified for the purpose of verification. They would not agree to more extensive procedures or to a greater degree of precision than was required for technical adequacy. Verification, they said, is not a research program. On several occasions, the United States had to fall back because its proposals could not be justified on the grounds of verification, although they would have been nice to have had for scientific or technical reasons.

The Soviets continued to interject cooperation as an element in the verification procedures. This would have entailed Soviet personnel working alongside U.S. personnel carrying out verification procedures. From the Soviet point of view, such an arrangement would provide the means of controlling any perceived abuse of verification activities. From the U.S. perspective, though, such an arrangement could be used to thwart the purpose of verification. This the United States could not accept; verification that was not solely the responsibility of the verifying side would amount to self-inspection. Nevertheless, the United States recognized that to be carried out successfully, such verification activities would require some form of cooperation. For example, the designated personnel would be dependent on the other side for living arrangements, food, transportation, and possibly placement of verification equipment. Considerable discussion and time were devoted to developing a text that acknowledged the role of cooperation without compromising the integrity of the verification procedures.

The nature of some of the negotiating difficulties deriving from characteristics of the two societies can be illustrated by an example. The subject in this case was a dispute over the acquisition of photographs. One might expect this to be a simple matter. Both sides agreed that photographs should be used to record the activities of the designated personnel. The difference arose over the

U.S. position, based on self-evident merit, that designated personnel should take the photographs they require. The Soviets objected, stating that designated personnel could not take photographs. This was not a matter of logic. They provided no explanation and gave no elaboration of the grounds for their concern. They made it clear that this was an issue on which they would not compromise.

It should be noted that in the Soviet Union, taking photographs is an activity regarded far more seriously by the authorities than it is in the United States, as some American tourists have learned to their dismay. It was finally agreed that a member of the host party would take photographs as requested, using equipment supplied by the designated personnel, under procedures that were carefully spelled out after laborious negotiations.

The activities of the designated personnel formed one set of primary issues. Another major set of issues concerned the equipment and procedures for measuring the individual yields in a group explosion. As previously noted, the Soviets had suggested one method for measuring the individual yields in a group explosion. A U.S. analysis found the method inadequate. The Soviet side appeared neither dismayed nor surprised; it is possible that the Soviets had proposed it simply as a starter. The United States proposed another method, whereby an electrical cable is introduced into the emplacement hole for the explosive. The lower end of the cable is located near the explosive and the other end is attached to electronic equipment at the surface. When the explosive is fired, the lower end of the cable is systematically crushed by the expanding shockwave from the explosion. The crushing can be measured electronically as a function of time, enabling the yield to be deduced.

After further lengthy discussion, the Soviet side accepted this approach in principle. Its actual implementation, though, raised a number of difficult and highly technical issues that were resolved only by tough negotiations. Most of these negotiations were peculiar to this verification technique, but one stands out because it applies to on-site verification equipment in general, and its resolution will no doubt be applied to other treaties involving on-site inspections.

The issue, once again, was the Soviet concern that "information not needed for the purpose of verification" would be sought or obtained. Accordingly, the Soviets wanted assurances that the equipment did not have the covert capability to obtain such information. There is some irony in this situation: The United States seeks verifications that the Soviets don't cheat on the treaty, and the Soviets seek assurances that the United States doesn't cheat with respect to the purpose of the tools of verification. The concerns on both sides are strongly felt.

The first step in the solution was to provide the Soviets the opportunity to examine the equipment before it was used and to retain the equipment for further examination after the data were obtained. However, the United States had two concerns—that the Soviets might damage the equipment during the inspection or that they might modify it so that it would provide erroneous data. Accordingly, the U.S. side proposed that its designated personnel be present while the Soviets examined the equipment before it was used. The Soviets would not accept this, however. Although they did not say so, it was understood that they would not want the United States to know their methods for checking out the equipment, for such information could be of value to the United States.

The issue led to a deep and serious standoff. The next step was taken by the Soviets. They proposed that the United States furnish two identical sets of equipment, one to be selected by them for inspection in private and the other, which would be used for recording the data, to be inspected by them in the presence of our designated personnel. After being used, the equipment would be retained by the Soviets for further examination before it was returned. The Soviets had accepted, in effect, the U.S. position. Then, in a fundamental turnabout, the United States withdrew its position and rejected the Soviet acceptance. This was a serious step, for one does not lightly withdraw a position, particularly after it has been accepted. Predictably, it brought forth a harsh response from the Soviet side, which questioned the good faith of the United States.

The reason for this turnabout was that the United States had reevaluated the procedures for inspecting the equipment and had concluded that it should neither be examined before use nor retained after use by the other side. It had concluded that should the other side have access to the equipment, its integrity could not be ensured, even if it were inspected in the presence of designated personnel. Furthermore, if questions later arose regarding the quality of the data, it would be necessary to examine the recording equipment. The U.S. side thus argued that it should retain the equipment after the explosion.

In spite of the sharp difference, the issue reflected a correlation of concerns: both sides wanted assurances that the equipment was what it was supposed to be, no more and no less, and each side clearly understood the concerns of the other. There was no way to give both parties absolute assurance that their concerns were met. The United States took the approach that the two sides, having similar concerns, should equally share the risk. It therefore proposed that two sets of equipment be brought to the site. The Soviets would select the set to be used by the designated personnel and would retain the other for examination. They would have no access to the equipment to be used by the designated personnel. It was unlikely, it was argued, that the United States would "doctor" one set, given a 50 percent chance that the Soviets would select it. Next, each set of equipment would contain two recorders, both of which would record data. After the explosion, copies of the data would be provided to each party. Then, by a process of chance (a flip of a coin), one side would get one recorder and the other side the other. Again, it was argued, neither side would be likely to doctor the equipment on-site, given at least a 50 percent chance of being caught. This approach was a simple and concrete example of verification by deterrence. After some time, the Soviets accepted this approach.

There were many other issues, of course, but this example illustrates the character of the issues and the respective approaches of the two sides toward their resolution. The treaty is a lengthy document, spelling out in complex technical detail the spectrum of provisions needed to provide for verification.[6] No other arms control treaty approaches it in substantive scientific technical provisions. Its lengthy thoroughness followed from a basic premise of the United States that verification provisions should be spelled out in full detail as precisely as possible in the treaty text. Only in this way could the United States ensure that it would obtain the verification capability it sought. It was recognized by both sides, though, that not all problems could be anticipated and dealt with in the treaty text. Accordingly, the PNET provides for a joint consultative commission made up of U.S. and Soviet representatives to deal with the problems that would inevitably arise in the implementation of the treaty provisions.

The TTBT states that the treaty would go into effect on March 31, 1976, but the PNET was not completed until early April 1976, and it was understood that the TTBT would not be ratified until its companion treaty was ready. Following the custom of international law, however, the two sides agreed to observe the 150 kiloton limit as of March 31, 1976. The PNET was signed by both parties May 28, 1976. However, the United States has not ratified the TTBT and PNET and, apart from the 150 kiloton yield limit on testing, none of their provisions is now in effect.

Verification of the 150 kiloton yield limit is now carried out solely by national technical means, without the assistance of the cooperative arrangements provided for in the TTBT or the assistance that would follow from the yield and other information that is to be provided for every PNE event. Over the years, the *seismically* estimated yield of a number of Soviet weapon tests have been significantly in excess of 150 kilotons. This has given the United States concern regarding whether the Soviets are adhering to the 150 kiloton yield limit.

The Reagan administration's assessment of this matter was put forward on January 23, 1984, in the document, "The President's Report to the Congress on Soviet Noncompliance with Arms Control Agreements." In the part dealing with the TTBT, the report finds:

> While the available evidence is ambiguous, in view of ambiguities in the pattern of Soviet testing and in view of verification uncertainties, and while we have been unable to reach a definitive conclusion, this evidence indicates that Soviet nuclear testing activities for a number of tests constitute a likely violation of legal obligations under the TTBT.

The Reagan administration has sought to engage the Soviets in discussions to improve the verification of the TTBT, but the Soviets have rejected the approach and have said that they are observing the 150 kiloton threshold.[7]

There are uncertainties in the determination of yield by seismic means—both inherent uncertainties of a random character and systematic uncertainties that, in principle, can be reduced.[8] The existence of these uncertainties was recognized at the time the TTBT was negotiated. These uncertainties do, indeed, lead to some ambiguity, which inevitably provides a basis for differences of opinion. Some division exists within the scientific community involved with these matters, but the majority view appears to be that there is not a basis for asserting that the Soviets have violated the agreement.[9]

In the summer of 1977, sixteen years after the first comprehensive test ban negotiations had ended in failure, the United States, the United Kingdom, and the Soviet Union again began full, serious negotiations for a Comprehensive Test Ban Treaty (CTBT). The intent of such a treaty is to prohibit all nuclear weapons testing, including underground nuclear tests. After twelve rounds, the talks recessed in November 1980 with substantive issues still unresolved, awaiting the decision of the newly elected Reagan administration on the future of the negotiations. It was not until July 20, 1982, that the administration stated that negotiations would not be resumed, citing inadequacies of verification for the basis of this decision. (The status of the CTBT negotiations is summarized in a report prepared by the three negotiating partners and submitted to the Geneva Committee on Disarmament in July 1980.[10] As in other cases, the agreement among the three negotiating partners provided that details of the negotiations beyond those contained in the report would be kept private.)

The issue that dominated the early stages of the CTBT talks was the status of PNEs. Just as they had for the TTBT, the Soviets sought to have PNEs accommodated. In negotiating the PNET the verification task was to ensure that no weapons benefits could be obtained through PNEs above and beyond what could be obtained under the TTBT. Under a CTBT, it would be necessary to ensure that no weapons benefits whatsoever could be obtained from PNEs.

The United States took the view that even if it were possible to devise verification procedures that could identify an attempt to carry out a nuclear weapons test under the guise of a PNE event (which is doubtful), the production, fielding, and firing of explosive devices for peaceful purposes could lead to weapons benefits. In the absence of a U.S. PNE program, a CTBT permitting PNEs would provide a clear advantage to the Soviets. For these reasons, the United States strongly opposed a PNE accommodation. On November 2, 1977, Secretary Leonid Brezhnev announced that the Soviets would accept a moratorium on PNEs for the duration of a CTBT. This outcome of an issue that many perceived as a major obstacle to a CTBT seemed to indicate a serious commitment on the Soviet side to achieve a CTBT.

With the PNE issue put aside, full attention was turned to the issue of verification. The idea of an international authority that formed the administrative base for verification during the first test ban negotiations had been given up years ago. Now each party to the treaty would be responsible for carrying out monitoring and verification procedures. International procedures were recognized only to the extent of providing for an international exchange of seismic data. A party could submit its seismic records to an international data center and could receive from the center the data submitted by other participating countries. Thus, this system would enable smaller countries without significant NTM to make their own assessment of whether the treaty was being complied with. The draft text also recognized the right of a party to request of another party an on-site inspection to seek clarification of an ambiguous event—a request that could be accepted or rejected by the requested party.

In addition, the treaty being negotiated recognized that parties could develop additional measures to facilitate verification of compliance. These additional verification measures, upon which the bulk of the negotiations concentrated (and which would apply to the three negotiating partners only), were provisions relating to on-site inspections and to seismic stations internal to the borders of each of the three parties. This reflects the assessment of the United States that NTM are not sufficient and that verification provisions should be spelled out in full detail as precisely as possible.

For years, the symbolic difference between the United States and the USSR over verification of a CTBT was reflected in the issue of on-site inspections (OSIs), the United States requiring them and the Soviets denying their necessity. The United States had sought OSIs as a potential means of resolving the character of an ambiguous seismic event—an event that could not be identified by seismic means as either an earthquake or an explosion.

The U.S. side had held the position that there would be a guaranteed right to some agreed number of inspections each year. This right to an OSI would by no means be unconditional; it would be circumscribed by various technical criteria that would establish whether an inspection of a particular seismic event could be carried out.

This approach to OSIs was challenged by Sweden in the 1960s with the suggestion of "challenge" or "voluntary" inspections. A voluntary OSI works in the following way: If the character of an event detected in the territory of one party appears ambiguous to another party (and thus might be a nuclear explosion), the latter party can request permission to inspect the region around the event. The requested party can either reject or accept. If permission is rejected, the requesting party may withdraw from the treaty. Neither the United States nor the USSR accepted the idea, and the United States sharply criticized it, claiming that voluntary OSIs would not provide the assurance needed for adequate verification.[11]

In 1976, the Soviets broke with the past by proposing a draft CTBT at the United Nations that provided for voluntary OSIs. In the CTBT negotiations that began in 1977, they reaffirmed their willingness to accept voluntary OSIs. In response, the United States reassessed its position in the early stages of negotiations, switched from its long-held position of insisting on guaranteed OSIs, and concluded that voluntary OSIs could serve as an equal deterrent to cheating if the rejection of a request could be established as a serious matter that, in effect, differed little from thwarting a guaranteed OSI. It was also necessary that effective procedures for the conduct of an OSI be established in the agreement.

The distinction between guaranteed and voluntary inspections is not so great as it might seem if there were not an acceptable international authority to apply the criteria that form an integral part of guaranteed inspections. Any imaginable bilateral arrangements that provided for guaranteed inspections would likely require the parties to agree that the criteria were met for a particular seismic event so as to justify an inspection. Under this circumstance, the distinction between guaranteed and voluntary inspections in the test ban context is largely lost. At the base of this view is the assumption that no state would give another state carte blanche to cross its borders to investigate possible or alleged improprieties.

The United States and the Soviet Union had developed mutually acceptable provisions for the OSIs in the PNET. Furthermore, the provisions for OSIs under a CTBT should be simpler, since the technically detailed provisions in the PNET for data exchange and yield-measuring equipment are not needed in a CTBT. There are major differences, however, between an OSI under a PNET and an OSI under a CTBT. For a PNE event, the time and location of the OSI are determined by the party carrying out the event, and the verification procedures are invoked automatically to monitor ongoing activity. Under a CTBT, the location of the OSI is determined by the requesting party on the basis of the location of an ambiguous event in the territory of the requested party. The OSI is initiated by the requesting party to resolve, if possible, the ambiguous character of the event. Such a request could be interpreted by the requested party as a suspicion (if not an accusation) of violation and thus could become a sensitive political matter.

These differences in the character of an OSI under a CTBT and an OSI under a PNET inevitably produced new or enhanced concerns over the issues that otherwise were often quite similar. These issues centered on procedures for the initiation of an OSI, rights and functions of designated personnel, and procedures for the use of equipment brought by the designated personnel. For an OSI under a CTBT, such equipment includes radiation-monitoring devices to survey the inspection area for any radioactivity characteristic of a nuclear explosion, seismic recorders to detect local seismic signals characteristic of a past nuclear explosion, and instruments to search for possible artifacts of a nuclear test. (All of these items were considered in the 1958–1961 CTBT negotiations.) Each type of equipment entails procedures for its use, as well as a methodology and set of standards for analyzing the acquired data. The results of the data analysis would play an important role in the conclusions reached by the verifying side regarding the character of the ambiguous event that had led to the on-site inspection.

Significant progress was made in developing provisions for OSIs, although some substantial problems remained at the time the negotiations recessed in November 1980. Another major verification issue during the CTBT talks concerned the installation of seismic stations in the territories of the Soviet Union, the United States, and the United Kingdom. Each station would send seismic data to the other two parties for the purpose of verification. This data, in conjunction with those obtained by NTM, would be used to detect, locate, and identify seismic events. The data would contribute to the justification for a request for an OSI of an ambiguous seismic event. In the U.S. view, the stations should contain automatic, tamper-detecting, high-quality instruments with agreed-upon characteristics. Such stations eliminate the need for a permanent foreign staff to assist in the operation of the stations (by way of providing assurances that the stations were being operated properly) and thus would remove what had been an element of intrusiveness connected with internal seismic stations. The provisions for such stations raised substantial technical issues, such as numbers, locations, technical characteristics, and procedures for installation, operation, maintenance, and so forth. The negotiations, however, were dominated by a political dispute that left substantive issues unresolved. As the situation was later summarized by President Jimmy Carter, the British and the Soviets "could not agree on how many of the sensing devices should be in Great Britain, with the Soviet leaders insisting that all three of our nations must have exactly the same number, and the British equally adamant that in their much smaller country a smaller number of these expensive instruments would be adequate.[12]

The CTBT negotiations recessed in November 1980, but political matters external to those negotiations had not been propitious for the resolution of the outstanding issues.[13] Whether these issues could have been resolved under other circumstances is, at best, a matter of conjecture. Nevertheless, there has been a radical change in the Soviet approach to verification for a comprehensive test ban. The experience of the PNET and CTBT talks has shown that the Soviets will accept some measure of intrusive verification as necessary for reaching agreement on test ban treaties. Political problems of test ban verification provisions that were unsolvable twenty-five years ago may be capable of resolution now.[14]

Even though substantial agreement was reached on some matters—and full agreement possibly could have been reached—would the verification arrangements being considered have been accepted by the United States as "adequate" or "effective"? During congressional testimony in 1978, a Department of Energy spokesman stated in the context of measures being negotiated that there was "no guarantee that the Soviet tests at the level we find necessary for maintaining long-term confidence in our nuclear weapons stockpile can be detected and identified with confidence."[15] More recently, the Reagan administration has said, in rejecting a resumption of CTBT negotiations, that the Soviet Union would not accept measures that would provide for effective verification, thus implicitly criticizing the arrangements considered in the CTBT negotiations.[16]

What is "adequate" or "effective" verification? A definition provided officially in 1972 was "that which would reduce to an acceptable level of risk that clandestine test programs of military significance could be conducted under a CTB."[17] This definition recognizes that, in practice, no verification system can guarantee that no nuclear explosions take place. In application, the definition is surely subjective; disagreements will be found over "acceptable level of risk" and "military significance." There will be those who seek a verification system that provides a high probability that an attempted clandestine explosion above some threshold of concern would be detected and identified. In contrast, there will be those who would be satisfied with a much lower probability of detection and identification above some threshold of concern and who see the efficacy of the verification system as a deterrent. The former view will require greater technical proficiency and probably more intrusiveness; the latter view will require less technical proficiency and less intrusiveness. Behind these judgments lie varied perceptions of the Soviet Union, its behavior, and the utility of arms control. These differences cannot be solved by technical considerations, for they rest on political perceptions of the gains and costs of the agreement with the Soviet Union.

Putting aside these issues, one can nevertheless foresee, at this time, that seismic verification of a comprehensive test ban could be beset by the presence of uncertainty—the circumstance when the tools of verification can neither prove violation nor demonstrate compliance with regard to events of potential significance. As has been noted, this is a problem that exists now with the TTBT.

It is reasonable to assume that if a party sought to violate a comprehensive test ban by clandestine testing, it would require sophisticated precautions to minimize the seismic signal or explosion-like characteristics of the tests. The most direct way would be to use decoupling—firing the explosive in a very large cavity.[18] The seismic signal from a decoupled explosion is substantially reduced, so that it is equivalent to a yield about fifty to a hundred times smaller than the actual yield. There are large areas in the Soviet Union with geologic media suitable for the construction of large cavities.

Suppose that it is decided that the seismic monitoring system should be capable of detecting a one kiloton test. Because of the possibility of decoupling, this means that the system must detect a decoupled shot of one kiloton or, in effect, a yield of about one one-hundredth of a kiloton. Seismologists agree that it is possible to design a system of seismic stations within the Soviet Union that would provide that capability, although they differ as to the number and character of the seismic stations required.[19]

However, at the low seismic magnitude associated with low-yield decoupled explosions, there will be many hundreds of unidentified events—seismic events that, though detected, cannot be definitely classified as either an explosion or an earthquake—that will be ambiguous. Some number could no doubt be ruled out because they occurred in locations that precluded a clandestine test, but a substantial number would remain as ambiguous events.

On-site inspections were introduced as a verification tool because of the recognition that there would be ambiguous events. However, even a single on-site inspection is a substantial endeavor, and one cannot realistically expect—either technically or politically—to carry out inspections of even a small fraction of the ambiguous events that would exist at these low magnitudes.[20]

With a large number of ambiguous seismic events, one would be left with uncertainty. One would not have a demonstration of compliance, nor would one be likely to obtain proof of a violation, even if the Soviets were to carry out a decoupled clandestine test. Two things can be said in amelioration of this observation. First, it is possible that research into the physics of decoupling will find that the signal reduction is not as great for the high-frequency content of the seismic signal and that identification procedures exist for this frequency range of signals (that is, to distinguish between a decoupled explosion and an earthquake).[21] Second, the analysis rests on seismic verification, and it largely ignores the role of nonseismic NTM, which might reveal the presence of an evasion attempt. It is probably difficult to assess the capabilities of such tools to detect an evasion attempt so as to say in what measure these means could fill the gap in the seismic monitoring capabilities. On the other hand, any consideration of such an attempt by a potential evader would have to recognize the existence of such means. Inevitably, they contribute to the deterrence of evasion.

In conclusion, very real, substantial progress has been made in solving the classical political problems attendant to the verification provisions for a CTBT. However, technical problems of seismic verification remain, even though significant technical and scientific progress has been made over the years. The technical problems turn largely on the possibility of decoupling. This possibility leads to the conclusion there could be many low-magnitude seismic events each year in the Soviet Union that could not be identified as either a decoupled explosion or an earthquake. Thus, there would be uncertainty regarding compliance or noncompliance with a CTBT. In amelioration of this assessment, it is possible that further research could conclude that decoupling is less effective than now thought. Also, it is possible that nonseismic NTM may be assessed to fill, in some measure, the gap in seismic monitoring capability.

Notes

1. The capability to verify compliance in other environments—for example, outer space—would inevitably arise as an issue if a Comprehensive Test Ban Treaty (CTBT) were ever negotiated. Verification for these environments would rest on national technical means and thus would probably not be a subject of negotiations.

2. A review of these negotiations can be found in Glen T. Seaborg, *Kennedy, Khruschev and the Test Ban,* (Berkeley: University of California Press, 1981). A detailed exposition of the U.S.-Soviet differences, together with relevant documents, can be found in *Geneva Conference on the Discontinuance of Nuclear Weapon Tests, History and Analysis of Negotiations,* Department of State Publication 7258, October 1961.

3. National technical means (NTM) of verification is a euphemism for verification equipment and methods operated by one party outside the recognized boundaries of the party whose activities are being monitored. For a nuclear test ban, such means include seismic stations and satellites.

4. A description of the Soviet PNE program is given in Iris Borg, "Nuclear Explosives—The Peaceful Side," *New Scientist,* March 8, 1984, pp. 10–13.

5. In the later CTBT negotiations, the head of the Soviet delegation questioned the term *rounds.* He said it made the proceedings sound like a boxing match.

6. The text can be found in *Arms Control and Disarmament Agreement, Texts and Histories of Negotiations,* United States Arms Control and Disarmament Agency, Washington, D.C., 1982.

7. *Tass,* 13 April 1983.

8. Systematic uncertainties could be reduced by the use of calibration explosions at the test sites under procedures by which the yield could be ascertained by the other party. The TTBT provides for the exchange of the yields of two explosions from each geophysically distinct testing area for the purpose of calibration. However, there is no provision by which the correctness of these yield values could be ascertained.

9. *Science,* June 17, 1983, p. 1254.

10. "Tripartite Report to the Committee on Disarmament," CD/130 (July 30, 1980), p. 5.

11. Statement by ACDA Deputy Director Fisher to the Eighteen Nation Disarmament Conference: Cessation of Nuclear Tests, April 4, 1966. *Documents on Disarmament 1966,* U.S. Arms Control and Disarmament Agency, 1967, pp. 190–199.

12. Jimmy Carter, *Keeping Faith* (New York: Bantam Books, 1982), p. 229.

13. One of these matters was the delay in concluding SALT II. See ibid., p. 231. The subsequent failure to ratify SALT II ended any expectation of moving on with the CTBT.

14. One may ask why this change has come about. A possible answer is provided by a Soviet author, R. Zheleznov, in his article, "Disarmament Is the Realistic Road to Peace: The Problem of Monitoring Arms Limitations Measures," *Mezhdunarodnaya Zhizn* 6 (May 1982): 77–87. Addressing the period of the late 1960s and 1970s, he writes: "the problem of monitoring began to make headway when, under the conditions of the further change in the correlation of forces in the world arena and the establishment of approximate East–West strategic military parity, favorable preconditions emerged... for a number of agreements, along with relevant monitoring provisions." To this one can add that the Soviets do not require the verification measures one finds in the CTBT

for themselves—they have said more than once that they are really not necessary. They accept them as the price to pay to get agreement with the United States.

15. House Committee on Armed Services, Intelligence and Military Applications of Nuclear Energy Subcommittee, *Effects of a Comprehensive Test Ban Treaty on the U.S. National Security Interests,* 95th Cong., 2d sess., 1978, p. 57. In the subcommittee's report on these hearings, it recommended that any treaty permit testing up to 10 kilotons (p. 11).

16. The White House, Office of the Press Secretary, "Background Briefing on Test Ban Treaty," July 20, 1982, p. 3.

17. Statement by the U.S. Representative Martin to the Conference of the Committee on Disarmament: Comprehensive Test Ban, August 24, 1972. In *Documents on Disarmament,* U.S. Arms Control and Disarmament Agency, 1972, p. 589.

18. The idea of decoupling was introduced into the first test ban negotiations in 1959. See Seaborg, *Kennedy, Khruschev and the Test Ban,* pp. 18–19. In 1966, the United States conducted a low-yield (0.38 kiloton) nuclear explosive decoupling experiment using a cavity that had been formed by a 5.3 kiloton nuclear explosion in a salt formation. The decoupling factor was about 70.

19. L. Sykes and J. Everndon, "The Verification of a Comprehensive Test Ban," *Scientific American* 247(1982): 47–55; W.J. Hannon, "Seismic Verification of a Comprehensive Test Ban," *Energy and Technology Review,* Lawrence Livermore National Laboratory, May 1983, pp. 50–65. Sykes and Everndon call for fifteen single stations. Hannon calls for thirty array stations. This difference can be ascribed to several factors. Hannon argues that there are many more low-magnitude events than Sykes and Everndon assumed. The author has adopted Hannon's view on these factors. Obtaining agreement with the Soviets for a large number of internal seismic stations could prove to be a problem.

20. If the number of ambiguous events were small, then the issue of the technical effectiveness of an OSI would arise. This note sketches a few considerations.

If the ambiguous event were actually an earthquake, and a request for an OSI of this event were granted, the outcome of the OSI would probably be that no evidence of a nuclear explosion was found. One could not expect to *prove* that the event was an earthquake. Some would not find this outcome reassuring. If the request were not granted, and the reasons given were not persuasive, one would have a political problem (see later discussion).

If the ambiguous event were actually a clandestine nuclear explosion, the challenge for an effective OSI would be to locate with good accuracy (within a few kilometers) the source of the event. The on-site measurements that might detect evidence of a nuclear explosion can have a chance of succeeding only in the immediate vicinity of the explosion. The seismic signals from a low-magnitude event will not serve to locate the event to this accuracy. The area of uncertainty in the location will be many hundreds of square kilometers or even larger. The location to the accuracy necessary for the tools of an OSI to come into play will require other means. These could be NTM or, possibly, an aerial survey. In the abstract, it is probably not possible to quantify the possibility of a correct selection.

If an incorrect location were sought for the OSI, permission for the inspection could be safety granted. The conclusion would be as for the earthquake case.

If the correct location were selected for the OSI, it is doubtful that the perpetrator would agree to it, in spite of the precautions that would have been taken: radioactivity may leak in very small but detectable amounts to the surface; weak seismic signals are emitted from the immediate region of the explosion for many months after the event; and artifacts (including the presence of a cavity) may be found. With rejection of the request, and if the reasons were not persuasive, one would have a political problem, as in the previous example.

Is rejection tantamount to an admission of guilt? Probably yes to some, but not necessarily to others. The assessment and actions taken would depend on the circumstances at the time.

The deterrent capability of OSIs would depend on the assessments by a potential evader of the likelihood that a clandestine test would be detected, that a request for an OSI would be made, and that a correct determination of the location would be made, and on a consideration of the political consequences of the rejection of an OSI if a request were made.

21. W. J. Hannon, "Seismic Verification."

5

Verification of Limitations on Antisatellite Weapons

William J. Durch

Introduction

Space weapons became part of the public agenda with President Reagan's March 23, 1983, "Star Wars" speech. Space arms control became prominent soon thereafter, but the political and technical history of these subjects is extensive. By reviewing that history, this brief introduction sets the stage for a discussion of verification issues relevant to antisatellite (ASAT) arms control measures. Such issues have figured prominently in the Reagan administration's declaratory policy for ASAT arms control and should not, in any case, be addressed in technical isolation.

Developments in ASAT Technology

Superpower interest in space weapons dates to the earliest years of the space age, and H-bombs in orbit topped the list of space arms control concerns in the late 1950s and early 1960s.[1] The Soviet Union seems to have had an orbital bombardment system under development in the early 1960s and tested a fractional orbit bombardment system in 1967–1971. But earth orbit proved inferior to ballistic delivery of nuclear weapons—particularly in accuracy, reliability, and peacetime weapon security. The United States contemplated but did not flight-test both a satellite inspector system (SAINT) and an orbital bomber/reconnaissance vehicle (the X-20 Dyna Soar).[2] The United States did deploy nuclear-armed interceptors on Kwajalein Atoll (1963) and Johnston Island (1964), along the path that a U.S.-bound orbital bomb would be expected to take. The Kwajalein ABM test site was apparently relieved of its ASAT mission in 1964, when the Johnston Island system became operational. The latter was tested (without warheads) some thirteen times from 1964 through 1968. It was deactivated in 1975.[3]

In 1968, the Soviet Union began testing a nonnuclear ASAT, a radar-guided interceptor designed to home on its target after one or two orbits and explode. The highest intercept to date with this system has been at 1,700 kilometers. All tests with a new infrared sensor have been failures. The last three tests of the radar homing version (two in 1977 and one in 1981) have apparently been successful.[4]

The United States began its current "miniature vehicle" (MV) ASAT development program in early 1978. The MV is a nonnuclear, hit-to-kill system launched from an airborne F-15 fighter; it does not enter orbit but climbs directly toward targets in low earth orbit.[5]

No Soviet ASAT tests occurred from 1972 through 1975, June 1978 through March 1980, or July 1982 through the end of 1984. It is not unreasonable to characterize each suspension as a negotiating pause: the first for SALT I (and, while negotiations were progressing under Nixon and Ford, SALT II), the second for the Carter negotiations, and the third to encourage a Reagan round. There may also be some technical explanation for this pattern, and some analysts have suggested—based on the timing of the tests and their orbital characteristics—that the Soviet ASAT program is aimed more at Chinese than U.S. satellites.[6] Regardless of the explanation for the unhurried pace, it is distinctly lacking in urgency, unlike typical Soviet weapons development test patterns.[7] U.S. Defense Department publications suggest that the USSR may place higher priority on development of directed-energy ASATs, particularly large, ground-based lasers.[8] Such systems have both advantages and drawbacks, which will be discussed shortly.

Arms Control Proposals, Negotiations, and Agreements

A number of arms control agreements currently in force prohibit certain military uses of space. The Limited Test Ban Treaty of 1963 forbids nuclear tests in outer space; the Outer Space Treaty of 1967 bans the stationing of weapons of mass destruction in space; the Antiballistic Missile (ABM) Treaty of 1972 bans the development, testing, and deployment of space-based ABM systems and components; and the strictures of the Environmental Modification Convention of 1977 apply to space as well as to earth.[9] No agreement to date, however, restricts the development, testing, or deployment of antisatellite weapons, with the foregoing exceptions; that is, nuclear warheads for such weapons may not be based or tested in space, nor may ASATs be "capable of substituting" for ABMs. (ABM–ASAT interactions will be discussed later at some length.) Soviet compliance with all of the foregoing agreements is monitored via national technical means (NTM).

In March 1977, during the Vance mission to Moscow, the United States proposed the establishment of a number of bilateral U.S.–Soviet arms control working groups, one of which addressed ASATs. U.S. and Soviet delegations held three rounds of talks, one in 1978 and two in 1979, before the cooling climate of U.S.–Soviet relations and other political traumas put this and other Carter administration arms control initiatives on ice.[10]

In August 1981, the Soviet Union tabled a draft treaty on space weapons in the United Nations, a document generally thought to have been tabled mostly for its propaganda value. In April 1983, following the "Star Wars" speech, Soviet President Yuri Andropov called for comprehensive limitations on space weapons. Four months later, the Soviet Union tabled a revised (and more serious) draft space weapons treaty. The Reagan administration routinely rebuffed these Soviet overtures, maintaining as late as spring 1984, in a legislatively mandated report to the Congress, that verification difficulties posed nearly insurmountable obstacles to ASAT limitations.[11]

In June 1984, the Kremlin proposed bilateral talks on this subject with the United States, and the Reagan administration appeared to take up Moscow's offer.[12] The apparent turnabout could be accounted for without ascribing to the administration any fundamental change of heart. Congressional pressure to seek ASAT limits had been building. An amendment to the Fiscal Year 1984 Defense Authorization Act forbade the testing of ASAT "warheads" against objects in space unless the president certified that the United States was "endeavoring in good faith to negotiate" an ASAT ban with the Soviets and that "pending agreement on such a ban," testing was necessary "to avert clear and irrevocable harm to the national security." In May 1984, the House of Representatives added language to the 1985 Defense Authorization Act that prohibited U.S. ASAT testing so long as the USSR also refrained from testing. (A moratorium on such tests was offered by Andropov in August 1983.[13]) Language finally approved in October was less restrictive, allowing three tests against objects in space after March 1, 1985, and not limiting tests without targets ("point-in-space" tests).[14] A positive response to the Soviet negotiating offer thus would have been one way to encourage Congress ultimately to adopt less restrictive language and clear the way for the point-in-space MV test of November 1984.

Second, with the talks on strategic and theater nuclear missiles in abeyance following deployment of Pershing 2 and cruise missiles in Western Europe, ASAT was the only live prospect for arms control talks during the fall presidential campaign. If talks did get under way in the two months prior to the election, there was little risk of either breakdown or agreement.

Ultimately, the summer initiative collapsed. The United States insisted that the agenda be open to discussion of issues related to START and INF, which was unacceptable to the Soviet Union. The USSR, on the other hand, insisted that the United States agree to a moratorium on ASAT tests during the negotiations, an approach supported by many U.S. advocates of ASAT arms control but not by the administration.[15] In the Shultz-Gromyko talks the following January, however, the Soviet Union appeared to relent on both the moratorium issue and the issue of a broader negotiating agenda, agreeing to a tripartite structure of strategic, intermediate, and space weapons talks.

Arms Control Measures for Antisatellite Weapons

Issues of Definition and Coverage

Before launching into a discussion of verification issues for specific types of ASAT arms control agreements, we must define what is to be controlled—a task that analysts and negotiators have found difficult. Much of the difficulty has to do with the fact that systems not normally thought of as ASATs possess residual antisatellite capabilities. (These systems will be discussed individually.) Some of the difficulty has to do with the lack of an internationally agreed boundary between national airspace and outer space. (We will return to this issue in discussing ASAT test bans.) Some of the difficulty, finally, also has to do with differing national objectives. During the Carter round of ASAT talks, for example, the United States sought limits on weapon systems designed to damage or destroy space objects. The USSR sought to ban the *acts* of damaging, destroying, *or displacing* space objects.[16] One approach to this problem may be to define rather narrowly the capabilities constrained by agreement but to define rather broadly the actions so constrained. Thus, for example, an agreement might ban only "weapons" whose primary mission is the damage or destruction of space objects, where *weapon* is defined as a means of rendering a target permanently inoperative or permanently degraded in operational capability. But actions to damage or destroy space objects might be banned whatever the means used to take such actions.

Such an agreement (to be discussed further) would leave unconstrained certain systems that are technically capable of doing some damage to at least some space objects. Three kinds of systems with residual ASAT capability receive the most attention: maneuverable spacecraft, nuclear-armed ballistic missiles, and ABMs.

Maneuverable Spacecraft. In this category are found both human-piloted and automated systems. Piloted craft include the American shuttle, the Soviet Salyut/Soyuz system, and the expected Soviet shuttles. The automated systems include the Soviet Progress supply vehicle, U.S. and Soviet reconnaissance and surveillance satellites, and, potentially, every satellite carrying fuel and thrusters for station-keeping purposes.

The March 1984 Reagan administration ASAT report emphasized the dilemmas of definition and verification that the existence of these spacecraft could pose for an ASAT agreement.[17] But the report failed to keep the problem in perspective, in effect equating the risk posed by systems neither intended nor tested for antisatellite missions with the threat posed by dedicated ASATs, present and prospective. (We will return to the question of risk later.) The report also noted the potential difficulty of distinguishing surreptitious tests of constrained systems from orbital rendezvous of benign intent.

Experience gained from routine rendezvous may indeed hone a capability to intercept cooperative low-altitude targets, but it may be less applicable to intercepting targets that prefer not to be hit. Moreover, the only Soviet spacecraft routinely engaged in orbital rendezvous are the Soyuz and Progress. Soviet reconnaissance satellites, also maneuverable, appear to use the basic Soyuz/Progress satellite body. All are launched by large A-class boosters, which burn kerosene and liquid oxygen (LOX).[18] Such boosters must be fueled up just before launch, because LOX cannot be stored in booster fuel tanks for any great length of time. Moreover, the Soyuz/Progress craft have severely fuel-constrained maneuvering capacity. This is not the sort of system of which a quick-reaction ASAT capability is made.

A new generation of Soviet launch vehicles nearing operational capability may herald a new generation of maneuvering spacecraft as well. But the new boosters are very large (7–18 meters across at the base, 60–70 meters in length) and cryogenically fueled. They would appear to be, if anything, less well suited to ASAT missions than their predecessors.[19]

On the U.S. side, the space shuttle has a demonstrated satellite retrieval capability, having brought two errant communications satellites back to earth. But the shuttle would be a poor vehicle with which to harass satellites, both because it is limited in altitude and maneuver capability and because it is expensive, manned, and vulnerable to a target satellite's possible self-destruct capability. (Similar arguments would apply to use of a Soviet shuttle for ASAT purposes.) Unmanned orbital transfer vehicles deployed from a shuttle's cargo bay might be used in an ASAT mode, but such expensive vehicles would necessarily be few in number and more difficult to replace than the Soviet satellites against which they might be sent. On the other hand, any weapon payload that a shuttle might carry *would* be constrained by the kinds of limits on ASAT means to be discussed here.

The cost to legitimate uses of space of constraining maneuverable spacecraft would seem to be far greater than the arms control benefits to be derived from such constraints. Such systems' residual antisatellite capabilities would not seem to pose great threats to the integrity of a regime limiting dedicated ASATs.

Strategic Nuclear Systems. Nuclear weapons carried by ballistic missiles and midcourse ABM interceptors could be used to destroy an opponent's satellites. They are exceedingly blunt instruments, however, and an attacker using them would have to anticipate destroying a number of "friendly" satellites in the process. A deliberate nuclear attack on space systems outside the context of a wider nuclear war is also highly improbable. Any country that is prepared to unleash a nuclear barrage in space is unlikely to shrink from simultaneously resorting to such weapons on earth. Thus, any country that is irresponsible enough to fire nuclear "warning shots" into space is likely to see its warnings taken even more seriously than it intended. Little attention need be paid to potential reprogramming of intercontinental ballistic missiles (ICBMs) and submarine-launched ballistic missiles (SLBMs) for antisatellite missions. If such weapons are ever used as ASATs, there will be much bigger things to worry about.

ABM Capabilities. Certain kinds of ballistic missile defense (BMD) systems give their owners antisatellite capabilities and create problems for antisatellite limitation agreements. Certain ASAT technologies can, on the other hand, provide a means of circumventing development restrictions written into the ABM Treaty. This section discusses ground-based and then space-based ABM systems.

Ground-Based ABM Capabilities. There is a strong technical relationship between direct-ascent ASAT and ground-based, midcourse BMD technologies. The apogee of a minimum-energy ICBM trajectory is more than 1,000 km, and midcourse velocities are nearly orbital. Thus, much of the technology applicable to nonnuclear, midcourse missile intercept is also applicable to ASAT. The U.S. Air Force ASAT program, for example, inherited its "miniature vehicle" from the Army's BMD program.

Because a midcourse ABM interceptor can reach altitudes of several hundred kilometers, and because the ABM Treaty permits deployment of 100 ABM interceptors, zero direct-attack ASAT capability is not achievable in an ASAT agreement. The ASAT capability of treaty-permitted BMD should not be exaggerated; neither side could intercept satellites in Molniya (highly elliptical) orbits with southern perigees, nor satellites with orbits inclined at less than about 45 to 50 degrees (current ABM deployment areas are Grand Forks at 48 degrees north and Moscow at 56 degrees), nor satellites orbiting above the interceptors' operational ceilings. If the ABM interceptors are nuclear-armed, as the Soviet Galosh is reported to be, they are not a plausible threat to space assets except in a nuclear war, when a variety of other nuclear hardware could be brought to bear as well. But nonnuclear, high-altitude ABM interceptors could readily target satellites entering their range envelopes if their guidance and tracking systems were fed data from a space track network. In June 1984, the U.S. Army conducted the first successful midcourse intercept of a Minuteman reentry vehicle, using a nonnuclear, direct-impact interceptor.[20] Its target could just as well have been a low-orbit satellite whose ground track passed near the Kwajalein launch site.

Ground-based lasers at ABM test sites could also pose a threat to satellites in low earth orbit. Two such lasers at the USSR's Sary Shagan test site in Soviet Central Asia reportedly have some capability to damage satellites in orbits of a few hundred and a few thousand kilometers altitude, respectively.[21] Such weapons cannot penetrate cloud cover, however, and must wait for prospective satellite targets to pass overhead. An ASAT agreement would not necessarily affect the development and testing of such ABM lasers at designated test sites, but it could serve to prevent the proliferation of lasers with ABM potential under the guise of a ground-based laser ASAT program.

An ASAT agreement that limited testing of *any* weapon, whatever its primary mission, against space objects would serve to reduce decision makers' confidence that a dual-capable system could successfully engage satellite targets on short notice. But testing of nonnuclear, midcourse ABM hardware and software would continue to provide experience with engagement of objects in space. This connection between midcourse BMD and ASAT could only be broken by prohibiting the testing and deployment of nonnuclear, exo-atmospheric BMD interceptors, which would require modification of the ABM Treaty. Such modification, in conjunction with an ASAT agreement, would clearly limit BMD research and development to endo-atmospheric systems suited basically to defense of hardened point targets. (The feasibility and potential impact of such modifications are the subject of a different study, currently under way.)

Space-Based ABM Capabilities. Ground-based, midcourse ABM may serve to undermine ASAT limits, but space-based, boost-phase BMD provides extensive ASAT capabilities automatically. If the ABM Treaty were terminated to permit investment in boost-phase missile defenses, it would not be technically possible to restrict their ASAT capabilities, because ASAT requirements would never exceed those of BMD.

ASAT is generally a less demanding task than ballistic missile defense, because an ASAT's presumptive targets follow paths that are known and fairly predictable. The number of targets is small compared to the number involved in a full-scale strategic missile launch. Moreover, the number of *time-critical* satellite targets would be some relatively small fraction of the total, whereas all targets would be time-critical for boost-phase BMD, the mission of space-based missile defenses. A laser operating as an ASAT could thus afford much longer per-target dwell times than in the case of BMD—damaging targets by warming them slowly rather than by burning or breaking them up (via impulse loading). A beam with a delivered intensity only ten times that of unfiltered sunlight could, over a period of minutes, heat a nominal satellite target by several hundred degrees Celsius, well beyond the ability of its thermal control system to compensate and thus well past the point of electronic component failure. A laser in low earth orbit capable of destroying missile boosters at a range of 3,000 km could overheat a satellite in geosynchronous orbit at a range of 40,000 km.[22]

Even if it were technically possible to separate the ASAT and BMD missions, it would most likely not be politically feasible. The vulnerability of orbiting "Star Wars" stations to laser or kinetic ASATs, not to mention nuclear weapons, is essentially unavoidable. Missile defense stations would present very attractive, high-value strategic targets. A serious "Star Wars" development and deployment program thus would stimulate ASAT programs designed to counter it, and DSAT (satellite defense) programs designed to protect its products once they reached orbit.[23]

Monitoring Technologies

To date, the verification process has relied primarily on national means (technical and otherwise) to monitor treaty partners' compliance with arms control agreements. Technical means used to monitor strategic arms agreements have been ably detailed elsewhere.[24] Of these means, photographic and electronic intelligence satellites would be of high value for monitoring ground-based, ASAT-related activities. (Their limitations with respect to specific types of ASAT agreements will be discussed later.) Any agreement limiting space-based or space-directed weapons would require additional means of monitoring activities in space itself.

The United States maintains an extensive ground-based spacetrack system employing both radars and high-powered imaging systems. Its components are listed in Table 5-1. Phased-array radars such as EPARCS, PAVE PAWS, and COBRA DANE can track several hundred objects at once and are thus invaluable for monitoring the movement of objects in orbit. But their range is limited to about 5,000 km, and their resolution is relatively low.[25] Optical systems, by contrast, can have much greater range and resolution but trade those features for a much narrower field of view and restriction to nighttime operation (like other astronomical observatories). The main telescopes of the Ground-based Electro-Optical Deep Space Surveillance (GEODSS) system, for example, are said to be able to detect a sunlit "soccer ball" at geosynchronous range, roughly 36,000 kilometers.[26] At lower altitudes, resolution may be assumed to be greater and to be limited largely by atmospheric distortion. Technologies such as adaptive optics, which combine sophisticated light wave sensors and deformable mirrors, can eliminate much of that distortion and increase resolving power to the limit defined by a system's focal length, aperture diameter, and focal plane resolution.[27]

The initial mission of the space shuttle *Columbia* demonstrated the power of U.S. ground-based (and, perhaps, space-based) optical surveillance systems. Shuttle cargo-bay cameras spotted damage to thermal tiles on *Columbia's* tail section, prompting concern about the integrity of other tiles critical for safe reentry. NASA sought Air Force assistance in photographing the shuttle's underside. Two Air Force telescopes, Teal Amber (sited at Malabar, Florida) and Teal Blue (sited on Mt. Haleakala, Maui), were brought into play, reportedly without success because of cloud cover or bad look angles.[28] Nonetheless, that these facilities were called upon to image shuttle tiles averaging 20 centimeters on a side suggests that they are capable of extremely high-resolution coverage of objects in low earth orbit.

Table 5-1
U.S. Ground-Based Space-Tracking Capabilities

The Space Detection and Tracking System (SPADATS) receives data from a wide variety of systems, both radar and optical, located around the world:

1. Ballistic Missile Early Warning System (BMEWS) — Twelve large radars located at Clear, Alaska; Thule, Greenland; and Flyingdales, England, provide ground-based ICBM early warning and secondary spacetrack capability in the north polar region, with a range of about 4,000 km.

2. Enhanced Perimeter Acquisition Radar Attack Characterization System (EPARCS) — Phased-array Safeguard ABM detection and tracking radar located at Concrete, North Dakota. Range about 4,000 km.

3. PAVE PAWS — Submarine-launched ballistic missile detection and tracking radars at Otis AFB, Massachusetts, and Beale AFB, California (two more are under construction in Georgia and Texas). Range, about 5,500 km.

4. COBRA DANE — Large phased-array radar on Shemya Island, western tip of the Aleutians. A primary national technical means for monitoring Soviet ICBM reentry vehicles targeted on the Kamchatka impact area.

5. Pacific Barrier (PACBAR) — Series of three radars located at San Miguel, Philippines (GPS-10); Kwajalein Atoll; and the Western Space and Missile Center, Vandenberg AFB, Calif. The latter radar is capable of tracking satellites in up to 800 km orbits.

6. Spacetrack and other radars — At Pirinclik, Turkey (FPS-17/79); Ascension Island, So. Atlantic (FPQ-15); Antigua, in the Caribbean; Florida (FPS-85); Kaena Point, Hawaii; Westford, Mass. (Haystack, 120-foot dish).

7. Optical systems — Baker-Nunn cameras located in New Mexico, California, Hawaii, New Brunswick, Pulmosan (S. Korea), Mount John (New Zealand), and San Vito (Italy); Teal Blue/MOTIF (Maui Optical Tracking and Identification Facility on Mt. Haleakala, Hawaii, a laser radar with adaptive optics); Teal Amber (Malabar, Florida, telescope with mosaic, charge-coupled device focal plane sensor and adaptive optics); and GEODSS (Ground-based Electro-Optical Deep Surveillance) system, with operational sites at Mt. Haleakala, Taegu (S. Korea), and White Sands (New Mexico) and two other sites on Diego Garcia and in Portugal slated for initial operational capability in 1985 and 1986, respectively.

8. Naval Space Surveillance (NAVSPASUR) system — Three transmitting and six receiving sites in the southeastern United States.

Sources: Aviation Week and Space Technology, June 16, 1980, pp. 240–242; Feburary 22, 1982, p. 65; September 3, 1984, p. 313. Thomas Karas, *The New High Ground* (New York: Simon & Schuster, 1983), pp. 34–36, 154–156. *The Military Balance, 1983–84* (London: IISS, 1983), pp. 4–5. C.D. Miller and J.D. Sigler, "Pacific Barrier Radar III," Paper No. 83–2782, American Institute of Aeronautics and Astronautics. *New York Times*, May 31, 1983. Joel W. Powell, "Photography or Orbiting Satellites," *Spaceflight* 25 (February 1983): 82–83.

Other reports claim that U.S. photoreconnaissance satellites—Big Bird or KH-11—were used to make the damage assessment.[29] It appears, however, that the only Big Bird aloft in spring 1981 reentered just before *Columbia* was launched.[30] Of two KH-11s in orbit, only one appeared to come sufficiently close to image *Columbia's* tiles. The closest daylight approaches (280 and 83 kilometers) occurred over the United States, with the reconnaissance satellite, on its closest approach, passing above and behind a receding *Columbia* at high relative velocity. The opportunity to photograph *Columbia's* tiles at closest approach probably lasted no more than 10 to 30 seconds, depending on the resolving power of the KH-11 optics. (Most open sources do not credit the KH-11 with very high-resolution capabilities.) A higher-resolution "close look" reconnaissance satellite apparently was in orbit during this period, but such vehicles appear not to have a real-time data transmission capability.[31]

It may be desirable to track space objects *from* space. In principle, space-based radars could be deployed to extend active tracking of space objects to much higher altitudes. The U.S. Air Force has an interest in such radars for purposes of tracking aircraft and cruise missiles.[32] But radar requires more electric power than solar arrays can deliver. Nuclear reactors are more suitable. Since 1967, the Soviet Union has used short-lived nuclear reactors to generate about 10 kilowatts of power for its radar ocean reconnaissance satellites (ROR-SATs).[33] In early 1983, NASA joined the U.S. Departments of Energy and Defense in an effort to develop jointly a 100–kilowatt space power reactor, with an orbiting prototype scheduled for 1995.[34] Until the latter 1990s, then, any American space-based surveillance system is likely to use passive infrared sensors, which require much less power. Such a sensor, designed to track satellites against the cold background of space, was to be test-flown in the Air Force Space Infrared Experiment. The program was canceled, however, because of its high cost overruns. Another effort, DARPA's Advanced Sensor Demonstration Program, will place a staring infrared array designed to detect and track targets against a space background in geosynchronous orbit in fiscal 1987.[35]

Verification: Standards and Risks

As most treatments of this subject point out, monitoring and verification are two distinct functions.[36] Monitoring is an intelligence activity that takes place whether or not there are arms control agreements in force. Verification is the often political, always judgmental process that makes use of monitoring data in deciding whether observed Soviet behavior is in compliance with the negotiated constraints imposed by an arms control agreement.

Standards of verification—the criteria against which Soviet behavior is judged—should vary according to the risks and uncertainties associated with specific agreements, where *risk* means "probable threat," not just "bounded uncertainty."[37] The risk posed by monitoring uncertainties will depend on the military value of feasible undetected treaty violations, the military value of legal activities that could nonetheless undermine the intent of an agreement, the overall security benefits of the agreement, and the options available to offset the consequences of another party's cheating or abrogation of the agreement.[38]

One may conceive of agreements in which monitoring uncertainty may be high but the associated risks may be relatively low. An example might be an agreement involving dismantling of the current Soviet ASAT. There, the risk of covert stockpiling must be weighed against the risk of near-certain Soviet deployment of more capable space-directed weapons in the absence of agreed constraints. The level of risk can be further reduced by making American satellites less susceptible to destruction or less critically important to U.S. wartime operations. Such measures would be no more costly under a regime constraining ASAT than in the unconstrained case; and to the unconstrained case must be added the cost of ASAT development, deployment, operations, and maintenance.

In other agreements, uncertainty may be low but the risks may be high. An example might be a stand-alone ASAT nonuse agreement. Such an agreement might be relatively straightforward to monitor via the ground-based space track network, supplemented by attack sensors (including laser light detectors) deployed aboard satellites. Certainty that ASATs were not being used against one's satellites in peacetime would not, however, reduce the risk of wartime ASAT use against those same satellites, because a nonuse agreement alone would not constrain ASAT development, testing, or deployment.

The level of risk considered tolerable will also clearly depend on levels of offsetting benefits realized through arms control. In the case of ASAT, the cost-benefit calculus is complex and time-dependent, and it will not be delved into at length here. Briefly, American costs in giving up a direct-attack ASAT capability must be measured against its expected military utility in specific scenarios. U.S. national space policy gives ASAT a joint mission of deterrence (of Soviet ASAT use) and defense (against certain Soviet spacecraft, particularly ocean reconnaissance satellites).[39] It is not clear that both missions could be carried out at once; the USSR is unlikely to refrain from ASAT use if the United States is destroying Soviet satellites—even less so if, as in many potential conflict scenarios, U.S. forces rely more on space support than Soviet forces do. Moreover, it is not clear that a principal defensive mission could be carried out at all; effective use of ASAT to protect U.S. forces against Soviet ROR-SATs and their companion electronic intelligence (ELINT) ocean reconnaissance satellites (EORSATs) would in all likelihood require its use before any other shots were fired. In a crisis, the mission of those satellites would be to provide advance data on the positions and movements of American forces, thereby vectoring Soviet forces to their targets. The satellites would have made their contribution to the "battle of the first salvo" before a crisis escalated into war. Unless the United States wished to precipitate conflict, U.S. forces would have to rely on electronic countermeasures (jamming, spoofing, emissions control) for protection against the periodic overflights of these spacecraft.

The benefits to the United States of limits on ASAT weapons are long term rather than short term. ASAT limits would work to enhance the future security of other uses of space, both civilian and military; to limit a potential threat to crisis stability; and to limit opportunities to circumvent the ABM Treaty. The benefits to the Soviet Union of such limits are similarly future-oriented and appear to derive from an ambitious manned space program and from concerns that American technology would outpace Soviet technology in an unconstrained arms race in space. As the following discussion will suggest, agreements intended to reap the greatest benefits of arms control ten and twenty years hence may pose the greatest verification uncertainties at present. Whether those uncertainties could also pose great security risks is an issue best taken up for each type of agreement in turn.

Verification of Specific Agreements

This section examines a "zero-zero" agreement, which requires dismantling of all existing direct-attack ASAT systems; a "zero development and testing" regime, which uses the passage of time to create de facto zero-zero conditions through progressive atrophy of existing systems; and a "one each" agreement, which allows either party one type of direct-attack ASAT, capping the development of new means. The discussion of these three approaches to ASAT arms control will be followed by a discussion of an ASAT nonuse agreement and cooperative measures, such as on-site inspection, that might supplement monitoring by national technical means.[40]

Banning Weapons for Damaging or Destroying Space Objects. This approach would require dismantling of existing weapon systems, and it implies a ban on testing (treated separately). Banning ASAT capabilities eases some monitoring problems, since monitors need not tally numbers of operational units or measure their performance against prescribed limits. On the other hand, it may be very difficult to assure the dismantlement of any existing capabilities via national technical means.

The current Soviet interceptor is launched from two pads at Tyuratam by the same booster (the F-1-m, derived from the SS-9 ICBM) that launches RORSAT and EORSAT missions.[41] Since the inclinations of all these missions are all essentially 65 degrees, and congressional reports suggest that Soviet launch practices specialize launch pads for particular inclinations, it is not unreasonable to assume that these missions share launch facilities as well. The ASAT orbiter is roughly four meters long and two across.[42] It could easily be stored in structures also used for RORSAT/EORSAT payloads. Thus, effectively dismantling the current Soviet ASAT capability would probably entail dismantling its launch facilities and the RORSAT/EORSAT program. The latter capability is not one that the Soviets are likely to give up; nor would the United States be likely to offer commensurate capabilities in exchange if Moscow were to offer such a deal.

On the other hand, given the limited capabilities of the current Soviet ASAT and the residual ASAT capability potentially available to both sides in the form of electronic countermeasures and treaty-limited BMD, verification of a dismantling pledge could afford to be somewhat less stringent than might otherwise be the case. Moreover, the military utility of covertly retained co-orbital vehicles would very likely decline over time for lack of testing. Tests using an F-1 booster and an interceptor of known characteristics weighing several tons would be difficult to conceal (see later discussion).

Dismantling the U.S. F-15/MV ASAT capability would seem even more problematic than dismantling the Soviet system, once the MV has been thoroughly tested. The two-stage ASAT booster and its payload are about 5 meters long. The missile is fitted to an F-15 fighter that has undergone minimum modifications. A covert ASAT capability thus might be maintained anywhere F-15s are deployed. This is not to suggest that the United States would cheat on an ASAT ban, but rather that cheating would be hard for another country's verification process to rule out. The relatively greater openness of the U.S. defense budget process might make covert production difficult, though classified programs have been secretly undertaken before (the U-2, a number of satellites, and "stealth" technology are examples).[43] But covertly produced ASAT interceptors would have to remain hidden indefinitely, as would any related training and exercises. Any inadvertent revelations would disclose not only U.S. capabilities but deliberate and militarily significant cheating on an arms control agreement—an enormous propaganda windfall for Moscow and a blow to U.S. government credibility. So the political risk to the United States of covert interceptor stockpiling probably would not be worth it. Moreover, possible U.S. stockpiling of miniature vehicles need not be a great source of concern to Soviet military planners if the USSR does not expect to rely heavily on satellites in an East–West war. Together, these factors may make Soviet leaders less concerned about the fine points of verifying U.S. compliance with a dismantlement agreement even after testing of the F-15/MV has been completed.

Banning Tests of ASATs in Space or Against Space Objects. A test ban would not necessarily prohibit retention of existing ASAT weapons nor testing in the lab or, in this case, in the atmostphere. It would be designed to erode confidence in existing ASAT capabilities over time by increasing uncertainty about hardware reliability, adequacy of software, and proficiency of controllers. It would therefore establish a "balance" in effective ASAT capabilities over time without specifically requiring dismantlement of any current system. If the ban were established after a U.S. space-test program with the MV system, the effect would be equivalent to a "one current-type" limit (see later discussion), with an added testing constraint. Both sides' systems would sit on the shelf until and unless they were used in conflict, without benefit of recent test launches into space or against space targets.

In its latest series of ASAT tests, the USSR has had mixed success. Soviet confidence in the ability of even the original active radar homing version to operate successfully against an uncooperative satellite at an untried inclination, after a long period without testing, is likely to be low. The poor performance of the infrared version would not encourage Soviet planners to expect secret system upgrades to perform as designed upon first launch in a crisis.

Quantity can make up for qualitative shortcomings, to some extent, but the Soviets have never attempted to control more than one ASAT at a time. Until the large midsummer 1982 strategic exercise, which incorporated an ASAT launch, the USSR had never conducted any other space launches while an ASAT mission was in progress.[44] A system configured like the F-15/MV, on the other hand, would be more capable of multiple-launch and shoot-look-shoot strategies (fire an interceptor, see if you hit the target, fire again if you didn't), given adequate space track support and proper spacing of aircraft. That potential capability would be offset by the limited amount of testing the system would have had should an ASAT test moratorium go into effect in, say, 1985.

If a test ban governed only tests "in space or against space objects," a negotiated definition of *space* might seem in order. The concept of national airspace evolved to permit states to prohibit unauthorized flights over their territories and to take defensive actions against violators.[45] Up to the present, no boundary between sovereign national airspace and outer space has been incorporated into international law, but spacecraft have been tacitly exempted from challenge (though Soviet declaratory policy on this subject has changed a good deal over time). A number of states, the USSR among them, have suggested a boundary in UN debates. The Soviet Union has supported a limit of 100–110 km.[46] The orbital perigees of "close-look" reconnaissance satellites approach that altitude. A cooperative U.S.–Italian space shuttle experiment will winch a tethered subsatellite down there as well. Future orbital transfer vehicles may breach that altitude while using atmospheric braking upon return from high orbit. Air defenses capable of intercepting targets at nearly 100 km altitude could be difficult to distinguish from missile defenses proscribed by the ABM Treaty, yet they would be difficult to prohibit if they were tested only against "boost-glide" targets that reentered the atmosphere from orbit on non-ballistic trajectories. A transatmospheric vehicle (TAV), a lineal descendant of the Dyna Soar and Aerospaceplane concepts of the early 1960s, is on U.S. Air Force drawing boards, and the USSR may be developing its own spaceplane.[47] Thus, projecting a threat against which boost-glide air defenses might be necessary is not difficult.

Leaving *space* undefined may pose verification problems, however. ASAT tests might be conducted at a very high altitude short of some unilaterally defined threshold of space, undermining an ASAT ban but remaining within its letter. But it is not clear that fixing an airspace boundary would resolve potential problems posed by direct-ascent interceptors and ground-based beam weapons. It would seem possible, for example, to test a direct-ascent missile or a ground-based laser at altitudes below 100 km (against hypersonic high-altitude drones, for example), whether or not that was the official airspace boundary. (It would be difficult to test the current Soviet ASAT in such a manner. In a normal test, the booster would climb well above 100 km before third-stage burnout and payload separation. A test that kept the interceptor below 100 km would allow scant opportunity for intercept before atmospheric friction caused orbital decay and reentry.)

The U.S. ability to monitor Soviet ASAT tests appears adequate to support a test ban. For the co-orbital interceptor, launch and intercept locations and times, modes of intercept, and assessments of success or failure are reported routinely.[48]

Regarding directed-energy weapons, the 1984 edition of the Defense Department publication *Soviet Military Power* indicates that the USSR has "two ground-based test lasers that could be used against satellites" and depicts a laser based at Sary Shagan. It does not indicate whether these lasers have been tested against satellites.[49] Because such tests could occur only when target satellites passed over the test range, the optical and thermal signatures of satellites recently having done so could be measured and compared with baseline figures to detect changes suggesting laser damage—a big job but not intrinsically undoable. Satellites carrying laser light detectors in geosynchronous or Molniya orbits over the Soviet Union might also be useful means of monitoring such tests.

Detecting tests of space-based ASAT lasers would be less difficult. The spacecraft in question would be very large (a high-energy laser is extremely power-hungry[50]) and thus likely to be placed in low orbit. A low orbit not only minimizes the size of the booster required but permits the weapon to be serviced by Soviet cosmonauts whose Soyuz spacecraft are severely altitude-limited.[51] Judging by the frequency of repairs to the manned Salyut station, a Soviet space laser would require constant maintenance. Moving in low orbit, the laser would routinely come within view of the Air Force telescopes described earlier. Its configuration—large fuel supply, pointing and tracking telescope, and large fighting mirror—would be uniquely identifiable. Its use would change its thermal signature and, if it was a chemical laser, would possibly envelope it in a cloud of discharged gases. (Chemical lasers are thought likely to be the first deployed in space because they do not require large amounts of electrical power. Their chemicals lase at fairly high efficiencies, and the resulting beam in the infrared range can be focused by optical mirrors, though the mirrors would need to be 4 to 10 meters in diameter. For good technical discussions of high-energy lasers, see Carter, Hecht, and Wilkening.[52])

Permitting One Current-Type or One Generic-Type ASAT.[53] This approach acknowledges the existence of an "ASAT floor" and seeks to constrain direct-attack ASAT capabilities to roughly that level. It concedes low earth orbit but seeks to confine ASAT capabilities to that region. Thus, its potential impact on crisis stability would not be as great as an outright ban on

ASAT weapons. Ocean surveillance and photoreconnaissance satellites, for example, would be within "current-type" ASAT range. On the other hand, most early warning and communications satellites would be out of range.

A "one current-type" approach might ban further modernization of current ASAT interceptors, where "current" would include the U.S. F-15/MV system and the Soviet co-orbital vehicle, but not directed-energy systems. Monitoring problems associated with this approach would be akin to those encountered in the SALT II "new types" provisions. How great a difference in performance would constitute a prohibited change from the current type? Would a 10 percent increase in booster acceleration for the MV or a 10 percent increase in the Soviet ASAT's observed rate of closing on its target be important to constrain? Would it be detectable? Do we know whether the Soviet system has ever been tested at the edge of its performance envelope? Clearly, estimates can be made on the basis of the presumed load of fuel carried by an interceptor and the characteristics of its engine, guidance, homing sensor, and warhead. But the definition of "current-type" would have to admit of a performance band.

It is not clear that this uncertainty would pose a significant risk to U.S. security. The Soviet ASAT would have to more than quadruple its current altitude capability to threaten the next tier of American satellites, the NAVSTAR constellation in semisynchronous orbit (20,000 km). But the "current-type" approach would present clear opportunities for incremental performance changes that push against the limits of the agreement and thus would allow considerable opportunity for friction in its implementation.

A "one generic-type" approach would be more explicitly performance-oriented, setting standards that treaty-permitted ASAT weapons could not exceed. Within those standards, which could specify attack modes, technologies (for example, types of sensors), or altitude capability, the sides could modernize or replace systems.

This approach gives the two sides more freedom of maneuver in developing their ASAT technology, but the same monitoring problems remain. It would always be possible, for example, to test a new system at less than its full potential (though, again, rough estimates of that potential might be made). It could also be difficult to tell whether older ASAT systems were being swapped for newer ones or kept in the inventory (the dismantlement problem discussed earlier). Finally, the type of ASAT permitted would have to be kinetic if the agreement imposed an altitude limit. Because of its ready access to power, the lethal range of a ground-based laser ASAT could extend well beyond low earth orbit, and a laser in low orbit could probably reach geosynchronous altitude. It might be possible to devise strict limits on laser brightness or intensity, but not without infringing on developmental ABM lasers allowed under the ABM Treaty. (Such an impediment to laser ABM development can, of course, be viewed as desirable.)

If it did ban directed-energy weapons, including developmental ABM weapons, a "one...type" approach would create a safe zone for satellites beyond low earth orbit, and new military satellites would tend to be placed within that zone.

Neither the current nor the generic approach would admit of quantitative limits on retained interceptors. Numbers on hand could no more be counted reliably by national technical means than could interceptors covertly stored under a dismantling regime. In this case, however, the stability of the agreement might actually be served by a lack of quantitative limits. Both sides could maintain a comfortable inventory of weapons. Since current ASATs aren't really intended to fight each other, the relative sizes of the ASAT inventories would not matter as much as their size relative to respective target sets.

Banning the Use of ASATs in a Rules-of-the-Road Agreement. Without a limit on means, this approach would offer, at best, tenuous protection to satellites in periods of tension or conflict, but it could work to reduce the probability of provocative actions during peacetime, and it could reduce misunderstandings or miscalculations about the other side's actions in space. It could also be a useful adjunct to any of the constraints on capabilities discussed earlier.

A rules-of-the-road agreement could be modeled on the U.S.-Soviet Incidents at Sea Agreement of May 1972[54] and could be applied not only to dedicated ASAT systems, but to capabilities whose development, testing, and deployment would not be directly constrained by an ASAT testing or possession ban—high-power microwave antennas, nonnuclear electromagnetic pulse generators, general-purpose spacecraft, and ABM interceptors, for example. In addition to banning actions intended to damage, destroy, or displace space objects without the consent of their state of registry, such an agreement could specify types of behavior in space, or with respect to space objects, that are to be prohibited. Launch constraints, speed-of-approach limits, minimum separation between spacecraft (keep-out zones), on-site or space inspection, and consultative mechanisms might contribute to verifying compliance with a rules-of-the-road agreement. They would set markers the transgressing of which would give cause for protest, establish official avenues for protest, and add to the verification database. Some of these measures would also provide a means of coping with the potential verification problem posed by "space mines." Space mines would share their target's orbit, or a nearly intersecting one, but would maintain a discreet distance until commanded to alter course, approach, and explode.[55] They could be openly deployed or masquerade as silent replacements for active satellites (so-called dark spares), or they might be satellites with other primary functions but with explosive secondary missions (self-destruct charges are not uncommon aboard sensitive military satellites).

Launch Constraints, Approach Limits, and Keep-Out Zones. Certain procedures for launching spacecraft could make their use as orbital ASATs more difficult and would clearly signal a violation of the agreement if they were contravened. An example would be a requirement not to launch a satellite within two degrees of the orbital inclination and right ascension of another state's satellite.[56] Such requirements might place a heavy burden on space track and might reduce satellite launch windows. On the other hand, access to and use of space is bound to become more constrained as space becomes more heavily used; just as there are sealanes in busy international straits, there are already minimum separation distances for communication satellites using geosynchronous orbit.

Speed-of-approach limits could increase attack warning time or clearly single out attacking vehicles by their closing speed alone. Such limits would work best in conjunction with keep-out zones, which foreign spacecraft could legally infringe on only with the consent of the satellite's owners.

Keep-out zones might be useful, but they could be difficult to monitor and enforce. Zones large enough to buffer their satellites against energetic mines could prove quite unwieldy—moving bubbles of sovereignty that could make technical violations hard to avoid. A high number of such routine encounters would dilute the intended effect of the zone. Moreover, the space track system cannot watch all space objects all of the time (each GEODSS main telescope, for example, can search roughly 20 percent of its slice of sky every night).[57] If it were to discover a dark companion to an important satellite where no companion ought to be, the owner of the shadowed satellite might not have much immediate recourse. Without space inspection (see next subsection), it would be difficult to verify the threat; even with inpection, it could be difficult to specify the object's country of origin (especially as more countries develop launch capability).

On-Site and Space Inspection Regimes. On-site inspection (OSI) was at one time a standard feature of U.S. proposals in arms control and disarmament. With the advent of NTMs, particularly space-based reconnaissance, the requirement for OSI became less significant for many treaties, though in some cases it is still considered necessary. The USSR historically has been resistant to the idea, though in 1976 it agreed to elaborate inspection measures in support of the Peaceful Nuclear Explosions Treaty (PNET), and in 1980 it showed willingness to include certain OSI provisions in a Comprehensive Test Ban Treaty (CTBT).[58] In the case of ASAT, launch site and/or payload inpection may be thought to have particular utility, but there are clear problems.

Ad hoc inspections limited to launch sites and their immediate vicinity (whether or not such inspections are subject to veto by the inspected party) would be unlikely to uncover treaty violations, because activities in violation of treaty provisions (for example, production and storage of boosters or prohibited payloads) could be undertaken off-site. On the other hand, launch site OSI probably would deter the stockpiling of ASATs at the launch site or the advance mating of ASATs and boosters for rapid launch.

Neither side would want to allow the other the option of engaging in intelligence "fishing expeditions," and this would necessitate prior agreement on the nature of permissible inspection equipment and on procedures to be used by designated inspection personnel. There is precedent for agreement on such difficult matters in the elaborate inspection procedures negotiated for the PNET. But there remains the problem of targetting OSIs. In the Soviet case, this would involve one or two F-booster launch sites. In the U.S. case, however, it could involve every airfield at which F-15s are based or from which they operate. And since any launch vehicle could be given a space mine as a payload, any space launch could theoretically be subject to challenge.

If inspection rights were not confined to launch sites, the potential for harassment would be greater. An inspection quota could reduce the proportion of nuisance inspections, but resistance to inspection requests could raise suspicions, create grounds for charges of cheating, or encourage creation of "Potemkin violations" to run down the other side's inspection quota. On the other hand, if inspections were not confined to launch sites, the utility of off-site cheating would tend to decline. The issue is whether potential compliance gains would make sufficient military difference to adequately offset the political stress they might cause.

In monitoring regimes in which proximity is crucial to picking up a signal (for example, in International Atomic Energy Agency safeguards for nuclear fuel cycles or in seismic detection of nuclear tests), automated systems may be more reliable and less intrusive than on-site inspections involving human inspectors. Black boxes stay in one place, and their monitoring is continuous. If the system has been carefully designed, the party on whose soil or in whose facilities the boxes rest need not be concerned about extraneous intelligence collection. (See the Heckrotte chapter in this volume.)

Automated monitoring of ASAT constraints may have some limited utility. If the object were to ascertain, for example, that a certain facility had indeed been shut down (a launch pad or a ground-based laser facility), then heat, motion, and light sensors might accomplish that task. If the task were to ascertain which, if any, of several similarly sized and similarly shrouded payloads in a ready facility were prohibited items, then automated sensors would not help.

A space inspection regime would follow the example of the Outer Space and Antarctic Treaties, which provide for in situ inspection of installations, facilities, and equipment. In the former case, all such installations on the moon or other celestial bodies (but not those in space) are to be open to representatives of other states-parties, on a basis of reciprocity, upon "reasonable notice." In the latter case, inspections are specifically provided for, and all installations, and so forth, are to be "open at all times" to designated inspectors who are to have "complete freedom of access at any time to any and all parts of Antarctica."[59]

Such an inspection regime might be appropriate to space if the environment were to be demilitarized. However, the sorts of limited measures contemplated in this chapter would be designed in part to safeguard, not eliminate, other military uses of space; and there is little point to negotiating a procedure that could readily be undertaken unilaterally as an NTM function. Moreover, unilateral space inspection could raise concerns that such inspections could mask attacks or espionage. Keep-out zones might reduce the former risk, and a two-key inspection system might address the latter.

Under a two-key system, a dark satellite detected within another satellite's keep-out zone could be subject to close inspection if it were not identified and its orbit shifted by its owner. Close inspection could be accomplished using a teleoperated maneuvering system (TMS), similar to the orbital transfer vehicles contemplated for NASA's space station complex. Inspections would be requested by the infringed party. The TMS could be operated by a technically competent third party not allied militarily to either superpower or, perhaps, by a joint U.S.–Soviet team. This system would help assure that inspections were neither used as a pretext to examine sensitive satellites at close range nor conducted by the owners of the infringing spacecraft. If rogue mines become a future problem, the TMS could be equipped as a mine sweeper, with carefully negotiated and closely controlled capabilities to disable such rogue spacecraft.

This approach would not eliminate all risk of infringement on sensitive intelligence assets; however, as the international use of space continues to grow and as technology marches on, it is not clear that the missions of such satellites can remain as closely guarded as they have been heretofore. Neither is it clear that acknowledging the general nature of a satellite's missions necessarily affects the execution of that mission in detail. If the superpowers are unwilling to risk the disclosures that a space inspection system might entail, then spacecraft hardening and maneuverability, comprehensive tracking capabilities, and terrestrial backup systems might mitigate the potential threat posed by space mines.

Consultative Mechanisms. Any ASAT agreement would be helped by the existence of a mechanism to which either side could repair to hammer out details of implementation or to challenge suspected treaty violations. The Standing Consultative Commission (SCC) serves this function for U.S.–Soviet strategic arms control agreements. Embassy channels and an annual compliance conference serve a similar purpose for the U.S.–Soviet Incidents at Sea Agreement.[60]

The value of such channels for raising questions about practices uncovered by monitoring means cannot be lightly dismissed. A formal agreement legitimates questioning that would be brushed aside by the USSR under other circumstances. Because such consultative mechanisms provide routine channels for grievances, problems can be addressed out of the political limelight;

thus, they are more likely to be resolved than if they were first breached in public, necessitating public reply. The USSR seems to prefer such confidential government-to-government arrangements, and they appear to work reasonably well.[61]

Conclusions

Monitoring of Soviet military programs and activities can afford to be no less rigorous in the absence of arms control than in its enforcement. Missing relevant and militarily significant activities under either circumstance can mean the future emergence of an unanticipated threat to U.S. security. Because the same means are used in both cases, what isn't noticed in the one case probably won't be noticed in the other. Yet different standards are often applied to the two cases. In general, monitoring is called upon to indicate threat. Arms control monitoring, especially under the Reagan administration, has been called upon to prove the absence of threat, and proving a negative is a logical impossibility. The verification process that monitoring supports will always proceed on the basis of incomplete data, as do most intelligence assessments. Its core concerns should be whether an agreement halts the development of threats that it is supposed to halt and that would have materialized in its absence, and whether significant threats to U.S. security or to the integrity of the agreement, for which timely countermeasures cannot be taken, can arise undetected.

This chapter has attempted to address such concerns with respect to potential antisatellite arms control agreements. Some potential agreements do pose uncertainties for monitoring and verification, but the uncertainties must be evaluated in terms of the security risks they might pose, and those risks must be weighed against the risks posed by unconstrained ASAT, development and deployment.

Some of the potential risk in an ASAT accord could be reduced by satellite survivability programs and related measures that would be prudent and useful to undertake whether or not ASAT limits were in force. Survivability programs now under way aim at improving the ability of satellites to detect and report interference or disabling attacks, their ability to maneuver, and their autonomy (ability to maintain attitude, orbital position, thermal equilibrium, and the like, for long periods without direction from the ground).[62] Other desirable measures would include prepositioning spare satellites and dispersing capabilities across a number of spacecraft, so that attacks would produce gradual degradation of capabilities rather than their catastrophic loss. Current examples of dispersed systems are AFSATCOM communication transponders, which ride on a variety of satellites, and the NAVSTAR Global Positioning System, whose eighteen satellites will each contribute independently to a global navigation net. A reconstitution capability using protected launch vehicles or substitute systems that are not space-based would be another useful hedge.

The ASAT arms control measures discussed in this chapter are limited in scope—even the one intended to eliminate all dedicated, direct-attack ASAT capabilities. Such an agreement would leave intact nondestructive means of meddling with satellites and such destructive means as ABM interceptors. Because of the interaction between ASAT and ABM, no ASAT agreement could be effective without the continuing existence of the ABM Treaty. Any ASAT agreement would be bolstered by measures to strengthen that treaty, and the treaty, in turn, would be bolstered by an ASAT accord.

Of the types of agreements surveyed, the combination with the best uncertainty-risk trade-off would seem to be an indefinite test ban on both kinetic and beam weapons, accompanied by a rules-of-the-road agreement. The risks posed by such an agreement seem manageable in context. The risks posed to future uses of space in the absence of agreement may not be so manageable. Not every aspect of Soviet behavior relevant to such an agreement could be monitored, but the risks posed by such unmonitored behavior seem acceptable when balanced against the unconstrained case, the prospective benefits of arms control, and the hedges available to the prudent policymaker.

Notes

1. Works published in this period addressed orbital nuclear bombs and space-based missile defense, but not ASAT. See, for example, Lincoln Bloomfield, ed., *Outer Space: Prospects for Man and Society* (Englewood Cliffs, N.J.: Prentice-Hall, 1962); and Joseph M. Goldsden, ed., *Outer Space in World Politics* (New York: Praeger, 1963).

2. See Stephen M. Meyer, "Space and Soviet Military Planning," in William J. Durch, ed., *National Interests and the Military Use of Space* (Cambridge, Mass.: Ballinger, 1984), pp. 77–78; and Bhupendra Jasani, "Space: Battlefield of the Future?" in Michiel Schwartz and Paul Stares, eds., *Space: Past, Present and Future,* a special issue of *Futures,* October 1982, p. 437.

3. U.S. Congress, House Committee on Science and Technology, *U.S. Civilian Space Programs, 1958–78, Vol I.* Committee Print, serial D, January 1981, App. G.

4. Nicholas Johnson, *The Soviet Year in Space* (Annual) (Colorado Springs, Colo.: Teledyne-Brown Engineering, 1981–1983).

5. Richard L. Garwin, Kurt Gottfried, and Donald L. Hafner, "Antisatellite Weapons," *Scientific American,* June 1984, pp. 49 ff.

6. See, for example, Marcia S. Smith, "Antisatellites (Killer Satellites)," Issue Brief No. IB81123, Science Policy Research Division, Congressional Research Service, Library of Congress, August 1981. Cited, with further discussion, in Donald L. Hafner, "Approaches to the Control of Antisatellite Weapons," in Durch, *National Interests,* p. 268n.

7. Meyer, "Space and Soviet Military Planning," p. 79.

8. U.S. Department of Defense, *Soviet Military Power, 1984* (Washington, D.C.: U.S. Government Printing Office, 1984), pp. 35–36.

9. U.S. Arms Control and Disarmament Agency (ACDA), *Arms Control and Disarmament Agreements, 1980 Edition* (Washington, D.C.: Government Printing Office, 1980) pp. 34–42; 48–55; 137–47; 161–63; 190–98.

10. D. Goedhuis, "Some Observations on the Efforts to Prevent a Military Escalation in Outer Space," *Journal of Space Law* 10(1982): 13–30.

11. For an assessment of the two Soviet drafts, see Malcolm Russell, "Soviet Legal Views on Military Space Activities," in Durch, *National Interests*, pp. 218–222. See also the interview given by Andropov to *Der Spiegel*, April 19, 1983; Soviet text broadcast by Moscow TASS (in English), 1515 GMT, April 24, 1983, and reprinted in *Foreign Broadcast Information Service (FBIS)*, Vol. III (USSR), April 25, 1983 (ASAT offer, p. AA5).

12. "Report to the Congress: U.S. Policy on ASAT Arms Control," March 31, 1984, pp. 3–4; Leslie Gelb, "U.S. Agreed to Talk About Space Arms Without Clear Plan," *New York Times*, July 3, 1984, pp. A1, A6.

13. Anthony Barbieri, "Andropov Proposes Ban on Outer Space Weapons," *Boston Globe*, August 19, 1983, p. 3; John Burns, "Andropov Issues a Promise on Antisatellite Weapons," *New York Times*, August 19, 1983, p. A1.

14. U.S. Congress, Senate, Statement of Hon. Paul Tsongas, *Congressional Record*, July 18, 1983, p. S10261. The Tsongas amendment is Sec. 1235 of PL.98-94. For the 1985 authorization, see *Congressional Record*, May 23, 1984, pp. H4717–4738, and June 12, 1984, pp. S6945–6975, and *Congressional Quarterly*, October 20, 1984, p. 2733.

15. *Time*, July 16, 1984, p. 30; Bernard Gwertzman, "U.S. Makes New Offer on Space Weapons Talks," *New York Times*, July 25, 1984, p. 15; "TASS Statement," *Pravda*, July 29, 1984, p. 2, cited in FBIS/USSR, July 30, 1984, p. AA2; and TASS, "Weinberger Reiterates Unacceptable Position," July 29, 1984, cited in ibid, p. AA7.

16. Don Oberdorfer, "U.S. and Soviets Will Discuss Ban of Killer Satellites," *Washington Post*, April 10, 1979, p. A4; Richard Burt, "Soviet Said to Ask Space Shuttle Halt," *New York Times*, June 1, 1979, p. A6.

17. "Report to the Congress," pp. 5–7.

18. P.S. Clark, "Aspects of the Soviet Photoreconnaissance Satellite Programme," *Journal of the British Interplanetary Society* 36(February 1983): 169; U.S. Congress, Senate Committee on Commerce, Science and Transportation, *Soviet Space Programs, 1976–80, Part 1*, 97th Cong., 2d sess., Committee Print, December 1982, pp. 72–73 and App. III.

19. "Soviets Ready New Boosters at Tyuratam," *Aviation Week and Space Technology*, August 27, 1984, pp. 18–21.

20. Clarence A. Robinson, Jr., "BMD Homing Interceptor Destroys Reentry Vehicle," *Aviation Week and Space Technology*, June 18, 1984, pp. 19–20.

21. U.S. Department of Defense, *Soviet Military Power, 1984*, p. 35; *Aerospace Daily*, July 19, 1984, p. 35.

22. Dean A. Wilkening, "Space Based Weapons," in Durch, *National Interests*, pp. 147–149.

23. Ashton B. Carter, "Directed Energy Missile Defense in Space," Background paper for the Congressional Office of Technology Assessment, April 1984, pp. 46–48; Wilkening, "Space Based Weapons," pp. 157–160.

24. See, for example, Bruce Blair and Gary Brewer, "Verifying SALT Agreements," in William C. Potter, ed., *Verification and SALT: the Challenge of Strategic Deception* (Boulder, Colo.: Westview Press, 1980); Ted Greenwood, "Reconnaissance and Arms Control," *Scientific American*, February 1973, pp. 15–25; and "Reconnaissance, Surveillance and Arms Control," Adelphi Paper No. 88 (London: International Institute for Strategic Studies, 1972). See also the Richelson chapter in this volume (chapter 10).

25. Blair and Brewer, "Verifying SALT Agreements," pp. 35–37; *The Military Balance, 1983–84* (London: International Institute for Strategic Studies, 1983), p. 5; and "U.S. Upgrading Ground-Based Sensors," *Aviation Week and Space Technology*, June 16, 1980, pp. 240–242.

26. "U.S. Upgrading Ground-Based Sensors," *Aviation Week and Space Technology*, June 16, 1980, pp. 240–242. See also "The GEODSS Difference," *Sky and Telescope*, May 1982, pp. 469–473.

27. Blair and Brewer, "Verifying SALT Agreements," p. 37; Carter, "Directed Energy Missile Defense in Space," pp. 23–24.

28. Joel W. Powell, "Photography of Orbiting Satellites," *Spaceflight* 25(February 1983): 82–83.

29. Ibid., citing *Science Digest* 89(July 1981): 32; and Anthony Kenden, "Was 'Columbia' Photographed by a KH-11?" *Journal of the British Interplanetary Society*, 36(February 1983): 73–77.

30. *SIPRI World Arms and Disarmament Yearbook, 1982* (Cambridge, Mass.: Oelgeschlager, Gunn & Hain, 1982), p. 295.

31. Kenden, "Was 'Columbia' Photographed," presents an exhaustive analysis based on *Two Line Orbital Elements*, published by NASA's Goddard Space Flight Center. See also *SIPRI Yearbook, 1982*, p.306.

32. Edgar Ulsamer, "Approach Set on Space Radars," *Air Force*, February 1984, p. 17.

33. See *Aviation Week and Space Technology*, January 31, 1983, p. 20; and William J. Broad, "Nuclear Power for Militarization of Space," *Science*, December 17, 1982, p. 1201.

34. Philip J. Klass, "Agencies Agree on Space Power Effort," *Aviation Week and Space Technology*, February 21, 1983, pp. 22–23.

35. U.S. Congress, House of Representatives, *Conference Report on the Fiscal Year 1985 Department of Defense Authorization*, 97th Cong., 2d sess., H.Rpt. 97–749, August 16, 1982; and Gowri Sundaram, "U.S. Military Space Programs," *International Defense Review* 8(1984): 1030.

36. See, for example, the earlier companion volume to this one: William C. Potter, ed., *Verification and SALT: The Challenge of Strategic Deception* (Boulder, Colo.: Westview Press, 1980).

37. For a more thorough discussion, see Stephen M. Meyer, "Verification and Risk in Arms Control," *International Security* 8(Spring 1984): 111–126.

38. This section and the ones that follow are adapted, except as noted, from the author's July 1984 report, "Antisatellite Weapons, Arms Control Options, and the Military Use of Space," written under contract No. AC3PC103 for the U.S. Arms Control and Disarmament Agency (ACDA). Views expressed in that report and summarized here are those of the author. Their publication does not in any way imply their approval or endorsement by ACDA.

39. White House, "Fact Sheet on Military Space Policy," *Weekly Compilation of Presidential Documents* 18(July 4, 1984): 872–876.

40. Other regimes for controlling space weapons are of course conceivable. Those chosen for discussion here seem to meet a basic criterion for domestic acceptance of arms control treaties—namely, the appearance of fairness. In SALT, the criterion is met by equal quantitative ceilings on delivery systems. It makes little operational difference that the agreement does not allocate equal capabilities to the two sides; the destructive power of nuclear weapons washes out the details of the balance. With respect to ASAT, it is the limited nature of current capabilities that permits a similar political balance to be crafted at zero systems, at zero recently tested systems, or at one system each, with or without continued testing and development.

41. U.S. Department of Defense, *Soviet Military Power, 1984*, p. 34.

42. U.S. Congress, *Soviet Space Programs, 1976–80*, p. 46.

43. See, for example, James Bamford, *The Puzzle Palace* (Boston: Houghton Mifflin, 1982), pp. 187, 195 ff.

44. Johnson, *Soviet Year in Space, 1982*, p. 25.

45. D.H.N. Johnson, *Rights in Air Space* (Dobbs Ferry, N.Y.: Oceana, 1965), pp. 12, 21.

46. For a discussion of the boundary question, see Philip D. O'Neill, Jr., "The development of International Law Governing the Military Use of Outer Space," in Durch, *National Interests*, pp. 182–183. For discussion of Soviet policy, see Russell, "Soviet Legal Views," pp. 210–213.

47. "ASD [Aeronautical Systems Division] Research on Lifting Bodies and Related Vehicles," an Air Force summary published in *Aerospace Daily*, July 23, 1984, pp. 118–120; and "Soviets Ready New Boosters," p. 19.

48. See, for example, Johnson, *Soviet Year in Space, and SIPRI Arms and Disarmament Yearbook*, annual lists of satellite launchings; and the regular "Satellite Notes" section in *Journal of the British Interplanetary Society.*

49. U.S. Department of Defense, *Soviet Military Power, 1984*, pp. 34, 36.

50. See Wilkening, "Space Based Weapons," p. 148.

51. Johnson, *Soviet Year in Space, 1983*, p. 42.

52. On manning and maintenance, see ibid.; Meyer, "Space and Soviet Military Planning," pp. 81–82; also the regular "Salyut Mission Report" in *Journal of the British Interplanetary Society.*

53. This section draws on work done by Donald L. Hafner in "Approaches" and in "Outer Space Arms Control: Unverified Practices, Unnatural Acts?" *Survival*, November/December 1983, pp. 244–247.

54. For the text of the agreement, see *New York Times*, May 26, 1972, p. A4.

55. The space mine question cuts two ways; the kind of threat posed to workaday military satellites could also be posed to space-based "battle stations." See "Space-Based Missile Defense," a report of the Union of Concerned Scientists, April 1984, pp. 49–50.

56. Suggested by Hafner, "Approaches," p. 264.

57. "The GEODSS Difference," *Sky and Telescope*, May 1982, p. 471.

58. For PNET provisions, especially the detailed protocol on inspections, see ACDA, *Arms Control and Disarmament Agreements, 1980*, pp. 171–189; see also Warren Heckrotte's chapter in this volume (chapter 4). On the CTBT negotiations, see "Tripartite Report to the Committee on Disarmament," by the United States, the USSR and the United Kingdom, July 31, 1980.

59. ACDA, *Arms Control and Disarmament Agreements,* pp. 22–24, 54.

60. See U.S. Congress, Senate Committee on Foreign Relations, *Briefing on SALT I Compliance,* 96th Cong., 1st sess., especially "A Concise History of the Standing Consultative Commission," an appendix including the Memorandum of Understanding that established the SCC. On compliance with the Incidents at Sea Agreement, see the transcript of a press briefing by Navy Secretary John Lehman at the Pentagon, June 10, 1983.

61. *Briefing on SALT I Compliance,* testimony of SCC Commissioners Robert Buchheim and Sidney Graybeal. See also Robert Buchheim and Dan Caldwell, "The U.S.–USSR Standing Consultative Commission: Description and Appraisal," Working Paper No. 2, Center for Foreign Policy Development, Brown University, May 1983; and the Caldwell chapter in this volume (chapter 11).

62. See Sundaram, "U.S. Military Space Programs," passim.

6
Monitoring Bombers and Cruise Missiles

Dean A. Wilkening

To date, arms control agreements have dealt with only a fraction of the air-breathing systems threat—namely, "heavy" bombers. The SALT II Treaty defined heavy bombers either by aircraft type—currently B-52s and B-1s for the United States and Tupolev-95 (Bear) and Myasishchev (Bison) types for the Soviet Union—or by their ability to carry cruise missiles with a range in excess of 600 kilometers. Future bomber types are included if they can carry out the mission of a heavy bomber. Cruise missile carriers (CMCs) were counted separately under the 1,320 MIRVed missile/CMC sub-ceiling, whereas other heavy bombers counted against the 2,400 (or 2,250) total launcher limit. Until December 31, 1981, the protocol to the SALT II Treaty banned the deployment of ground-launched or sea-launched cruise missiles.[1] However, such deployments are now a moot issue, since the United States has deployed ground-launched cruise missiles in Europe and is reported to have deployed Tomahawk cruise missiles aboard U.S. attack submarines.[2] Except for SALT II, qualitative and quantitative limits do not exist for bombers and cruise missiles. In particular, intermediate-range aircraft (for example, FB-111s and Backfires) and dual-capable, theater-based aircraft are not limited under any existing arms control agreement.

This chapter discusses the extent to which bomber/cruise missile characteristics and activities can be monitored by national technical means (NTM). Particular attention is paid to those characteristics and activities that are relevant to arms control. National technical means—which refers to various technical means by which monitoring data can be gathered, usually involving satellite reconnaissance—are not the sole means for monitoring, though they may be the most dependable.

Monitoring involves collecting and evaluating intelligence data in an effort to identify and count different aircraft types and to determine their characteristics. Monitoring an opponent's forces should be distinguished from the process of verifying whether the opponent's actions violate particular treaty provisions.

The author wishes to acknowledge helpful discussions with Frank Fukuyama, along with helpful comments from the participants of the Conference on Verification and Arms Control, Los Angeles, January 25–26, 1984.

The former is essentially a technical process, the latter a legal judgment. Verification relies on data provided by one's monitoring capabilities; however, since these data often lead to equivocal assessments, careful judgment is required before one can verify treaty compliance. In particular, one must take into account an opponent's ability to evade detection should it choose to deliberately violate a treaty. In other words, monitoring has more to do with detecting, identifying, and measuring, whereas verification involves judging treaty compliance.[3]

Whether a treaty is "adequately" verifiable involves still broader political and military judgments. To assess whether compliance can be adequately verified, we must understand the risks that potential violations pose to our national security, as well as our ability to counter any noncompliance. These risks must be weighed against the political and military advantages derived from the treaty. Judgments concerning adequate verification are influenced by past experience with the other party, the present political climate, and by one's view of the other party's intentions. Furthermore, adequate verification should not be viewed as an absolute condition, since the overall benefits derived from a treaty may compensate for any weakness in our ability to verify compliance. This is particularly true if those provisions that are difficult to verify involve low risk.[4]

It is beyond the scope of the present discussion to determine whether arms control treaties involving bombers and cruise missiles can be adequately verified. What will be discussed, however, is the confidence one might have in monitoring bombers and cruise missiles. The following arguments are based on elementary technical considerations as well as a familiarity with past arms control agreements.

Monitoring confidence is judged as either high, medium, or low, depending on how difficult it is to obtain the requisite information via national technical means. High confidence reflects an optimistic assessment of monitoring capability, while low confidence implies that NTM alone probably cannot provide sufficient data to assess treaty compliance reliably. In some cases, this difficulty reflects physical limits to one's ability to make observations. More often, however, it reflects the ease with which an opponent (that is, the Soviet Union) could deliberately conceal that which one is trying to observe. Concluding that deliberate concealment is relatively easy does not imply that concealment would, in fact, take place. However, given the Soviets' penchant for secrecy, claims that they have deliberately concealed activities in the past, and a cautious estimate of one's monitoring capabilities, it is reasonable to assume that if certain activities can be concealed, they will be difficult to observe. In assessing monitoring confidence, human intelligence sources are not taken into account. Furthermore, no credit is given for fortuitous events, such as information obtained from a defector. National technical means are assumed to be the sole source of intelligence data.

Monitoring data can be observed directly, derived, or inferred. Counting aircraft inventories is an example of direct observation. Derived quantities are calculated using certain assumptions; for instance, a bomber's payload can be derived from a knowledge of the aircraft's range along with assumptions about its structural design. Inferred data arises when observed activity can be plausibly linked to the characteristic one wishes to determine; for example, the capability to carry nuclear weapons can be inferred from the aircraft's alert status. Typically, U.S. aircraft designated for nuclear missions are placed on quick-reaction alert to enhance their survivability. Whether this corresponds to Soviet practice is another matter, which points to the weakness of inferred characteristics.

Characteristics that can be observed directly are more desirable from the standpoint of verification, since they are more reliable. Consequently, it behooves the United States to construct arms control agreements using direct observables as much as possible so that verification ambiguities become less likely. Furthermore, direct observables are more important if one chooses to respond to a treaty violation, since evidence based on them has more influence on public and international opinion.

In general, bans are easier to monitor than treaties involving numerical limits, since one reliable counterexample suffices to verify noncompliance. The confidence with which numerical limits can be monitored depends on the counting accuracy. Quantitative limits (for example, aircraft numbers, dimensions, and the like) are easier to monitor than qualitative limits (for example, guidance accuracies or a bomber's electronic countermeasure capability), since quantitative limits usually involve direct observables. Deployment is usually easier to monitor than production, since the former involves direct observation. For the same reason, testing and deployment are easier to monitor than research and development. Large, fixed objects are easier to monitor than small, mobile ones for the simple reason that the latter are easier to conceal. Similarly, platforms that perform a single function (for example, strategic nuclear bombers) are easier to monitor than dual-capable platforms (for example, radars capable of operating in an air defense mode and an ABM mode or fighter-bombers capable of delivering either nuclear or conventional ordnance), provided that one wishes to distinguish between different types of dual-capable platforms. Few direct observables seem to exist that distinguish between dual-capable platforms. "Concealment," whether intentional or not, occurs by virtue of their identical appearance.[5]

Bombers

This section gives examples of bomber characteristics relevant for arms control, along with the confidence with which they can be monitored. In particular, it discusses counting specific aircraft types and determining aircraft range, payload, and the capability for delivering nuclear weapons. Monitoring bombers presents problems because aircraft are versatile platforms. Basically, it is hard to distinguish between the nuclear missions one wishes to constrain and missions left unconstrained (antisubmarine warfare, reconnaissance, in-flight refueling by tankers, transport, and so on). The ability to carry weapons, either internally or externally, is the only fundamental characteristic that distinguishes bombers (including cruise missile carriers) from other types of aircraft.

Identifying and Counting Aircraft

The SALT II Agreement used functionally related observable differences (FRODs) to determine which aircraft types were counted as heavy bombers. FRODs were defined as those observable differences that indicate whether the airplane in question "can perform the mission of a heavy bomber." Examples of FRODs were never given, since those details were left to the Standing Consultative Commission (SCC). Bomb bay doors might be one example.

The drawback with FRODs is that they are few in number and not necessarily reliable. For example, the lack of bomb bay doors does not preclude external weapon carriage, nor is it clear how long it would take to install bomb bay doors. This is especially true for Soviet nonstrike aircraft, since they use the same airframe as Soviet bombers. (The Soviet Union has about 75 Tu-142 reconnaissance and antisubmarine warfare aircraft—Bear versions D, E, and F—and approximately 113 Tu-95 bombers—Bear versions A, B, and C.[6]) Furthermore, bomb bay doors are difficult to observe in the first place, since satellite photoreconnaissance occurs from an overhead perspective. Identifying bomb bay doors might require intercepting the bombers as they leave Soviet airspace, which implies that we would observe only those planes the Soviets wanted us to see. Thus, whereas, in principle, FRODs allow one to distinguish aircraft types with high confidence, in practice they are of more modest utility.

Monitoring the ability to carry weapons externally might be equally difficult, since pylons are hard to observe from an overhead perspective. Moreover, pylons can carry a variety of objects (for example, short-range air-to-surface missiles, external fuel tanks, or electronic countermeasure pods) that are not necessarily related to weapon carriage. Hence, the ability to carry weapons externally can only be inferred if pylons are observed. Even if pylons are not observed, this does not prove that a plane cannot carry weapons externally. External hard points are the critical feature for this capability. Hard points are specific locations on the fuselage or wings that are structurally reinforced to handle heavy weights. It is at these points that pylons are attached. Consequently, for monitoring purposes, the absence of pylons should not be relied upon to disprove the capability to carry weapons externally. Hard points may prove to be difficult to observe.

If reliable FRODs do not exist, externally observable differences (EODs) often allow one to distinguish between aircraft types. Though EODs can be detected with high confidence, they do not unequivocally indicate whether an aircraft can perform bombing missions. Examples of EODs are differences in aircraft dimensions, landing gear housings, external radomes and miscellaneous "blisters" (bulges in the fuselage), and "strakelets" (small, aerodynamic fins).

Though the United States apparently could distinguish Bison tankers from Bison bombers using EODs, the Soviets were required to give their thirty-one Bison tankers FRODs within six months after the SALT II Agreement was signed to confirm that these aircraft could not perform bombing missions. Apparently, the United States was not convinced that these tankers could not easily be converted into bombers.[7] Depending on how extensive the modifications must be before an aircraft can perform bombing missions, EODs can be used to identify bombers with moderate to low confidence.

Once a given aircraft type has been identified, the total inventory can be counted with reasonably high confidence. Witness the fact that thirty-one Bison aircraft were singled out as tankers in SALT II. (The total Bison force was about seventy-four planes in 1979.[8]) One can surmise that aircraft counts are accurate to within several planes, at least for aircraft no longer in production. The uncertainty arises because the planes cannot all be observed simultaneously. For aircraft still in production, greater uncertainties arise because the inventory is increasing at an uncertain rate.

Identifying and counting cruise missile carriers (CMCs) will no doubt be important for arms control. The SALT II Treaty set a precedent in this regard by separating CMCs from heavy bombers and counting them as MIRVed launch platforms under the 1,320 MIRVed missile/CMC subceiling. In the treaty, only EODs (in this case, strakelets) were required to distinguish B-52G air-launched cruise missile (ALCM) carriers from non-ALCM carriers.[9] FRODs were required for CMCs other than existing heavy bomber types.[10]

CMCs can be distinguished from other bombers or transport aircraft with, at best, modest confidence. Cruise missiles carried internally are hard to detect. Special doors for dispensing ALCMs from transport aircraft would provide a FROD for monitoring purposes. However, without such a FROD, the confidence with which one could identify these CMCs would probably be low.[11] Cruise missiles carried under the wings can be monitored with high confidence, provided that the aircraft is observed fully loaded. If they are carried under the fuselage, observation becomes more difficult. If the CMC is not fully loaded, the capability for external carriage must be inferred by observing pylons or hard points.

In summary, total aircraft inventories can probably be counted with high confidence. The real problem for monitoring lies in determining which aircraft types can perform bombing missions. This problem is exacerbated by the Soviet tendency to use bomber airframes for their nonstrike aircraft. The confidence with which one can identify designated bombers is high. Determining that nonstrike aircraft cannot perform bombing missions can be accomplished with moderate to low confidence, depending on how extensively the aircraft must be modified. However, high monitoring confidence might not be required for adequate verification, since nonstrike aircraft presumably are required for other vital military missions.

Aircraft Range

Knowing an aircraft's range helps distinguish between heavy bombers, medium bombers, and fighter-bombers. Aircraft that can deliver payloads over intercontinental distances are categorized as heavy bombers, since they constitute a strategic threat. A plane's takeoff gross weight roughly correlates with aircraft range, which explains why strategic bombers are called "heavy"; however, relying on takeoff gross weight alone can be misleading. Typically, the range that defines "intercontinental" falls between 8,000 kilometers and 10,000 kilometers. (In SALT II, intercontinental ballistic missiles were defined as those land-based missiles with a range greater than 5,500 kilometers.) The variation results from differences in the launch points and the proximity of recovery bases. One might also consider one-way missions.

A plane's actual range depends on numerous mission-related details—for example, the payload weight, whether the plane refuels in flight, whether the route is direct (for example, a circuitous route might be required to avoid local air defenses), the range of standoff weapons, and requirements for low-altitude flight and supersonic dash. Because mission ranges vary so widely, this measure should not be used to distinguish heavy bombers. For the purposes of arms control, the unrefueled cruising range (or ferry range) provides a better measure, since its value is intrinsic to the plane.

The unrefueled cruising range is the distance a plane can fly at optimal altitude (high altitudes) without refueling. It can be derived from the Breguet range equation with the following four inputs: (1) the plane's optimal cruising velocity, (2) the lift-to-drag ratio (a measure of the plane's aerodynamic efficiency), (3) the specific fuel consumption (a measure of the engine efficiency), and (4) the fraction of the takeoff gross weight devoted to fuel.[12] The unrefueled cruising range can be determined, at best, with moderate confidence, since most of these inputs are derived or inferred from direct observations. To give just one example of the first input: a plane's optimal cruising speed can be roughly determined from the sweep angle on swept-wing aircraft.

The problem for arms control is to decide which bombers can fly intercontinental distances. Since the cruising range is extended by 30 to 40 percent with one in-flight refueling, one must account for refueling capability. This was the essence of the Backfire debate during SALT II. According to the International Institute for Strategic Studies (IISS) publication *The Military Balance, 1983–84,* the unrefueled cruising range of the Backfire is 8,000 kilometers.[13] If this is correct, the plane has marginal intercontinental capability. However, since early versions of the Backfire were observed with a refueling probe, the plane potentially had an intercontinental capability, regardless of whether intercontinental missions were intended. Verifying that this refueling capability was removed, as required by the SALT II Treaty, became central to the debate. Although one can probably observe that refueling probes have been removed, they are the least important indicator of refueling capability. The internal plumbing and controls are more crucial, since they take longer to install. However, the presence of this equipment cannot be detected with much confidence.

Lest one jump to the conclusion that in-flight refueling cannot be adequately verified, one should bear in mind that almost any aircraft can be converted for refueling within several weeks. During the Falklands War, the British gave Nimrod early-warning aircraft an in-flight refueling capability within seventeen days.[14] Including designated tankers in arms control agreements would help account for an opponent's ability to conduct intercontinental strikes; however, the British again demonstrated that other aircraft can be quickly converted into tankers. During the Falklands War, C-130 transports and Vulcan bombers were converted into tankers within six to seven weeks.[15]

Thus, NTM can probably measure a bomber's unrefueled cruising range with moderate confidence and identify the capability for in-flight refueling with high confidence, provided that external refueling probes are visible. If the Soviets deployed a refueling capability covertly, it would be hard to detect. Whether one can verify in-flight refueling adequately depends on the likelihood that such covert deployments will occur. One should remember that, in any event, aircraft can be converted within several weeks.

Bomber Payload

The best measure of a bomber's offensive potential is the payload that can be delivered over a given distance. This is analogous to ballistic missile throw-weight. Payload is hard to derive from NTM because it is a sensitive function of aircraft range. For example, reducing a bomber's range by 10 percent by offloading fuel increases the payload that can be delivered over this distance by approximately 50 percent. Alternatively, if one holds the range constant, but the plane refuels once in flight, the payload could increase, in principle, by around 300 percent. Thus, it is misleading to specify the mission payload without specifying the mission range and whether the plane is refueled in flight.

Nevertheless, nominal range-payload values can probably be derived with moderate confidence if one estimates the plane's structural and aerodynamic characteristics. This monitoring capability may not provide adequate verification, since people will invariably disagree on the assumed mission characteristics. This occurred during the Backfire debate in SALT II. Different range-payload estimates for the Backfire were derived by assuming recovery bases in Cuba, one-way missions, and/or high-altitude (maximum range) flight profiles (one assumes that low-altitude penetration is less critical against U.S. air defense).

Nuclear Capability

Including dual-capable fighter-bombers in the arms control process, especially those based in the European theater, remains a thorny issue. Neither the Soviet Union nor the United States is eager to have arms control agreements aimed at nuclear forces constraining their conventional forces. Consequently, one must distinguish which dual-capable aircraft are, in fact, nuclear-capable. This is difficult (some say impossible) essentially because nuclear warheads weigh about the same as conventional munitions. (Nuclear warheads typically weigh between 200 kilograms and 1000 kilograms, depending on the type and yield.) Consequently, any fighter-bomber that can deliver conventional munitions most likely can deliver nuclear weapons as well. This problem does not arise with heavy or medium bombers, despite their conventional roles, because there are fewer aircraft and the majority are designated specifically for nuclear missions.

To identify those fighter-bombers that are nuclear-capable, one might attempt to detect special communication, command, and control (C^3) links associated with nuclear release and to determine whether the planes are hardened for operation in a nuclear environment or whether they have the enduring alert capability usually associated with designated U.S. nuclear strike aircraft. Since nuclear capability can only be inferred from such indicators—and evidence for these characteristics or activities is likely to be equivocal—I conclude that one can identify nuclear capable fighter-bombers with low confidence.

Conclusions

This section has illustrated the confidence with which one can monitor bomber characteristics by examining four examples: (1) identifying and counting aircraft types, (2) determining bomber range, (3) determining bomber payload, and (4) determining whether a bomber is nuclear-capable. In principle, aircraft types (bombers, cruise missile carriers, nonstrike aircraft, and so forth) can be identified by functionally related observable differences (FRODs). In practice, however, unambiguous FRODs are rare. As a result, aircraft types are typically identified on the basis of externally observable differences (EODs). Since EODs are not necessarily functionally related to the mission, aircraft that can perform bombing missions can be identified with, at best, moderate confidence. Once identified, aircraft types can be counted with reasonably high confidence. Range-payload characteristics can be determined with moderate confidence, since they can be derived from externally observable features. The capability for in-flight refueling can be identified with high confidence, provided that external refueling probes are observed, Without this FROD, monitoring confidence drops to a low level. Finally, one can probably identify nuclear-capable bombers with moderate confidence, except for nuclear-capable fighter-bombers, which can only be identified with low confidence.

Whether this monitoring ability is sufficient to adequately verify arms control treaties depends on numerous political and military factors. Several military considerations that might be important are discussed briefly in the last section of this chapter.

Cruise Missiles

Cruise missiles present greater difficulty for arms control monitoring. Their small size (at least for modern long-range cruise missiles like the Tomahawk and the current U.S. Air Force ALCM) makes them difficult to count whether or not deliberate concealment is practiced. If one thinks of a cruise missile as an additional warhead, then counting cruise missile inventories should be compared to counting total warhead inventories—a task that I assume cannot be accomplished with NTM alone. Counting CMCs as MIRVed launchers in SALT II is consistent with this perspective, since cruise missiles become analogous to ballistic missile reentry vehicles. However, cruise missiles are more often thought of as launchers, since they fly substantial distances under their own power. This perspective leads to a greater desire for monitoring capability, since arms control agreements (such as SALT II) frequently use launchers as a metric.

Cruise Missile Numbers, Type, and Range

Cruise missile inventories can be inferred by multiplying the number of launchers by the number of cruise missiles each launcher can carry. Summing over all launcher types provides an estimate of the total stockpile. Actually, these estimates measure the carrying capacity of the force, rather than the number of weapons deployed. Alternatively, one could estimate cruise missile inventories by monitoring production rates. This approach suffers from difficulties in monitoring the production of small items, as well as from opportunities for concealment (discussed later). Consequently, the confidence with which one can measure cruise missile inventories is probably low.

As with dual-capable fighter-bombers, nuclear cruise missiles are virtually impossible to separate from their conventionally armed counterparts. Schemes that detect the radioactive decay from a nuclear warhead (as the Swedes did with the Soviet submarine that ran aground on October 27, 1981) might detect nuclear cruise missiles; however, the short detection range for radioactivity and obvious countermeasures, such as shielding the warheads, limit the utility of this approach.

Range is more difficult to monitor for cruise missiles than for bombers. The factors in the Breguet range equation are harder to measure, since cruise missiles are small and easy to conceal. A rough estimate might be derived from the missile's volume. (It has been suggested that tactical cruise missiles be defined as missiles with volume less than one-half cubic meter.[16]) One can estimate cruise missile volume with high confidence if one can see the missile. However, this approach suffers from the ease with which cruise missiles can be concealed. Also, there is a problem with older cruise missile types, since they tend to be large for their range. Observing flight tests would be a third way to verify cruise missile range. Observing cruise missile test flights is not a trivial proposition (as will be discussed later), since they have low "observables"— that is, optical, infrared, and radar signatures. Furthermore, the point is often made that cruise missiles need not be tested to full range to ensure their reliability and accuracy. In short, if deliberate concealment does not take place, cruise missile range can probably be estimated with moderate confidence. With concealment, monitoring confidence becomes rather low. One can at least be thankful that questions relating to in-flight refueling don't arise.

Thus, monitoring cruise missile numbers, type (conventional or nuclear), and range with high confidence is hard to accomplish using NTM. Deliberate concealment would reduce the level of confidence considerably.

Other Monitoring Schemes

Table 6–1 summarizes the confidence levels associated with other monitoring approaches. Two arms control regimes are considered—bans and aggregate limits. Each observable is examined for its applicability to cruise missiles in general and to those armed with nuclear warheads. In most cases in which moderate to low confidence occurs, the moderate level pertains to situations in which no concealment occurs; otherwise, low confidence is more appropriate. The following sections provide a more detailed discussion of each observable. As mentioned earlier, monitoring bans is easier than monitoring limits, since it only requires the detection of one counterexample, whereas accurate counting is necessary for monitoring limits.

Flight Tests. Cruise missile flight tests are probably difficult to detect. Unlike ballistic missiles, cruise missiles fly close to the earth, where detection (especially by radar) is difficult. Moreover, they don't need to be tested to their full range as ballistic missiles do—though, given the difficulty detecting the test, it hardly matters what the range is. Telemetry, another signature that makes ballistic missile tests observable, could be difficult to detect, since the transmitter would need only enough power to reach a nearby aircraft that follows the cruise missile during its flight. On the other hand, ballistic missile

Table 6–1
Confidence Associated with Monitoring Schemes for Long-Range Cruise Missiles

Observable	*Bans*		*Limits*	
	All	*Nuclear Only*	*All*	*Nuclear Only*
NTM Monitoring				
Flight test	Moderate-low	Low	Low	Low
Radar mapping	Low	Low	Low	Low
Production	Moderate-low	Low	Low	Low
Launchers				
Bombers (ALCM)	Moderate-low	Low	Moderate-low	Low
Submarines (SLCM)	Moderate-low	Low	Moderate-low	Low
Surface ships (SLCM)	Low	Low	Low	Low
GLCM	Moderate-low	Low	Moderate-low	Low
Associated equipment or operational procedures	Low	Low	Low	Low
Cooperative Monitoring				
External	Moderate	Moderate	Moderate	Moderate
Internal	High	High	High	High

telemetry must be sent back from 1,000 kilometers above the earth. Thus, a ban on testing cruise missiles with ranges in excess of 600 kilometers could probably not be monitored with high confidence.

Bans on flight tests only for nuclear cruise missiles cannot be monitored with confidence. The payload has little to do with flight testing, except that conventional cruise missiles would need to be tested with greater terminal accuracies. Cruise missile limits cannot be monitored using flight tests, since testing is tenuously related to the number of systems deployed.

In any event, since the United States has tested cruise missiles beyond 600 kilometers, this approach will probably not attract much enthusiasm from the Soviets.

Radar Mapping. Modern cruise missiles usually require accurate maps to provide precision guidance. Monitoring the development of these maps might be another approach to cruise missile arms control. For example, terrain contour matching (TERCOM) guidance requires accurate radar maps of selected portions of an opponent's territory. If TERCOM maps required active radar sounding, one could monitor this activity with high confidence. This is not the case, however, since terrain altitude data obtained from surveys or stereophotography can be transformed into synthetic TERCOM maps.[17] Moreover, other guidance technologies exist that do not require active mapping techniques.

In general, guidance technologies are difficult to monitor, since their development is primarily a research activity. Evidence from flight tests often gives the first indication of new or improved guidance systems. It is impossible to ban mapping techniques that apply only to nuclear cruise missiles, since they use the same guidance system as conventional cruise missiles (except for the terminal fix, which must be more accurate for conventional cruise missiles). Numerical limits cannot be monitored via the guidance technology, since no relationship exists between the two.

Production.   Bans on cruise missile production would probably be difficult to monitor, simply because the weapons are so small. Manufacturing could take place separately, with final weapon assembly done covertly. The separate parts would be hard to distinguish from parts for drones and other small aircraft. Certainly, the nuclear warheads would be produced separately, making a ban solely on the production of nuclear cruise missiles impossible to monitor. Production limits would be even more difficult to monitor than bans on production, simply because it is harder to determine absolute production levels than to detect production activity when there is supposed to be none.

Launchers.   Monitoring cruise missile deployments by observing their launch platforms poses fewer problems for NTM. However, since many launch platforms serve dual purposes, it may be hard to distinguish cruise missile launchers according to a unique functionally related observable difference. Nevertheless, verifying a ban by monitoring cruise missile launchers might be moderately reliable.

As discussed earlier, bombers carrying ALCMs can usually be distinguished using externally observable differences. Since the Tomahawk submarine-launched cruise missile SLCM can be launched from torpedo tubes, monitoring a SLCM ban by observing launch tubes, aboard either submarines or surface ships, would be difficult. However, if launch tubes designed specifically for SLCMs (for example, vertical tubes) were deployed, a ban might be effectively monitored. This is less true for surface ships, since it is too easy to conceal SLCM launchers below deck. A ban on ground-launched cruise missile GLCM launchers might be successfully monitored, since current GLCM launchers look sufficiently different from other military vehicles. However, a concerted effort to deploy GLCMs deceptively, on otherwise innocuous-looking trucks, would be very difficult to detect.

Monitoring a ban on nuclear cruise missiles via their launchers would be difficult to accomplish, since there would probably be few observable differences between conventional and nuclear launchers. Certain activities might arouse suspicion if they were observed at cruise missile sites—for example, special handling and storage procedures associated with radioactive warheads—but one could only infer the existence of nuclear cruise missiles from such activities. Consequently, one could not monitor a ban with much confidence. For the same reason, limits on nuclear cruise missiles only would be difficult to monitor.

Thus, one can probably monitor limits on total cruise missile deployments with moderate confidence, provided that one can distinguish the launch vehicles. However, deliberate efforts to conceal cruise missile launchers would lead to low monitoring confidence.

Associated Equipment and Procedures. If special equipment or operating procedures are essential to cruise missile storage, handling, or launching, one might detect the presence of related activities or vehicles instead of the cruise missiles themselves. One obvious example is the cruise missile launcher, which has been discussed separately because of its monitoring importance. Another example is detection of special handling procedures associated with nuclear warheads, though radiation safety and special security precautions are associated with other nuclear missions as well. It is difficult to invent other examples, because the equipment associated with cruise missiles is relatively small and probably indistinguishable from countless other pieces of military equipment. Since one can only infer cruise missile activity by identifying associated equipment, this monitoring technique is probably of low reliability.

Cooperative Arrangements. Stepping beyond the realm of NTM, it is useful to ask how confident one could be of cooperative monitoring arrangements, such as on-site, on-demand inspections. Without spelling out the detailed procedures for such inspections, one can distinguish two cases: external inspection which means that one is allowed to inspect questionable locations or launch platforms but is not allowed to board any aircraft, submarine, or surface ship or to enter any sensitive facility; and internal inspection, which describes a situation in which one can enter any suspected cruise missile site.

External inspection does not necessarily help much since cruise missiles can easily be stored out-of-sight. Radioactive detectors might help locate nuclear warheads at certain sites, however it would probably be difficult to distinguish cruise missile warheads from other nuclear warheads stored at the same site. External inspection might give one a better view of possible production facilities, launchers, or associated equipment; though it is not clear that one could gain decisive information about cruise missile activity (nuclear or otherwise).

Obviously, internal inspection allows one to monitor a great deal. Cruise missile bans could easily be monitored; however, cruise missile limits could not be monitored with high confidence unless each party was allowed a large number of on-site inspections. It should be equally obvious that internal inspection is a complete nonstarter politically. Covert operations are the only source of internal inspections, and they can hardly be called cooperative.

Conclusions

The picture that evolves is rather gloomy. At best, NTM can monitor cruise missile characteristics and activities with moderate levels of confidence. Any effort to deliberately conceal cruise missiles reduces this confidence to a low level. In general, bans can be monitored with greater confidence than limits, though the summary in table 6–1 is hardly reassuring.

Adequate Verification

Despite the fact that monitoring air-breathing systems with high confidence appears to be very difficult, this does not necessarily imply that arms control agreements cannot be adequately verified. Certainly, as one's monitoring confidence diminishes, the prospects for adequate verification dwindle. However, broader political and military considerations must be included before judgment can be passed. This section briefly addresses several military factors that might influence judgments on adequate verification—namely, the effect of air-breathing systems on crisis stability and the role cruise missiles might play in our strategic force posture.

Crisis instability refers to a situation in which both sides believe a decisive advantage can be gained by striking first against the other side's forces. Air-breathing systems are not particularly destabilizing, since they make poor first strike weapons because of their long flight times—about ten hours for intercontinental missions and two to three hours for theater missions. Thus, if detected, bombers and cruise missiles give adequate time for an opponent to launch its forces before they are attacked. This conclusion also holds even for supersonic cruise missiles. If cruise missiles or bombers could sneak under early-warning radars, attacking without warning, the situation would be very different.

A related scenario, the "decapitation" strike, arises if Soviet cruise missiles attack Washington, D.C., from submarines. The point to keep in mind here is that SLCMs do not pose a new threat, since SLBMs can also be used for decapitation strikes, especially if they are launched on a depressed trajectory. If SLCMs are launched 100 nautical miles from shore, they will take approximately fifteen minutes (the nominal flight time for SLBMs, if they are not on a depressed trajectory) to reach Washington, D.C. If such a threat developed, it would be relatively easy to enforce a keep-out zone 100 nautical miles around Washington, D.C., or other vital coastal cities by using antisubmarine warfare. Again, this conclusion rests on the assumption that SLCMs cannot evade early-warning radars or other detectors. Thus, the recent Soviet threat to deploy SLCMs within striking range of Washington, D.C., is a political move intended to counter NATO INF deployments, rather than a significant military threat.[18]

In sum, air-breathing systems do not contribute to crisis instability to the same degree as MIRVed ICBMs. To the extent that air-breathing systems pose a lesser threat to the United States, concern with potential treaty violations might be reduced. For example, surreptitious aircraft deployments would not enhance Soviet ability to strike first successfully. Nor would any offensive advantage necessarily arise if the Soviets covertly deployed nuclear cruise missiles among indistinguishable conventional systems. In fact, insofar as deployments (overt or covert) on either side contribute to a secure reserve, confidence in a successful first strike diminishes, thus enhancing crisis stability.

To appreciate the role of cruise missiles in our strategic force posture, we should consider the following three missions: the role of cruise missiles as a secure strategic reserve force, their ability to saturate air defenses, and the role of conventional cruise missiles in theater and strategic warfare. The requirements for adequate verification depend, in part, on likely missions for Soviet cruise missiles. Moreover, the enthusiasm with which the U.S. military will embrace arms control constraints on cruise missiles depends on the military utility of these forces.

The merits of cruise missiles as an addition to our strategic reserve are debatable.[19] On the positive side, their mobility, ease of concealment, and large deployments make them difficult to target (this is also why they are hard to monitor). This enhances their prelaunch survivability, thus providing a larger force with which to retaliate. Since cruise missiles are capable of striking hard targets (for example, missile silos and hardened C^3 posts) and a wide range of other military targets, their role need not be confined to countervalue retaliation alone. On the negative side, if circumstances allow cruise missiles to be located and attacked before they disperse, they are relatively easy to destroy. Several other factors combine to make them less attractive than other reserve forces (SLBMs and penetrating bombers)—namely, the problem of penetrating Soviet air defenses (especially terminal defenses), though bombers suffer similar problems; poor cruise missile effectiveness against mobile targets; and a relatively inflexible retargeting capability.

Cruise missiles might provide a cost-effective means for saturating local air defenses if they are deployed in large numbers, since they are relatively inexpensive. Such deployments could significantly influence the dynamics of the offense/defense competition in an environment with unconstrained strategic defenses.

The proliferation of conventionally armed cruise missiles will affect theater, if not strategic, warfare. Theater missions will feel the impact first, since conventional cruise missiles have shorter ranges (approximately 700 nautical miles for current-generation U.S. conventional cruise missiles).[20] In the

European theater, cruise missiles might enhance conventional deterrence/ defense by providing viable "deep strike" options against Soviet or Warsaw Pact targets. With increasingly accurate guidance systems and specialized conventional warheads, conventional cruise missiles may perform certain missions previously relegated to nuclear weapons—for example, limited nuclear options or demonstrations of resolve.

Whether the proliferation of conventional cruise missiles reduces the likelihood of nuclear war depends on the scenario. For theater missions, conventional cruise missiles may reduce the likelihood of conventional conflict by strengthening conventional deterrence. Furthermore, if deterrence fails, the likelihood that nuclear weapons will be used diminishes if effective conventional weapons exist. Obviously, a detailed analysis is required to determine whether cruise missiles do, in fact, enhance one's conventional options. As a means to accomplish strategic missions, conventional cruise missiles appear less attractive. For example, though limited strategic strikes might appear less escalatory with conventional warheads, this is probably illusory, since it requires that escalation depend more on the warhead used than on the target struck. Furthermore, one's opponent may not wait until the weapon detonates before retaliating, in which case it hardly matters whether the warhead is conventional or nuclear. In fact, the greater willingness to use conventional weapons for strategic strikes might lead to nuclear war more quickly.

Insofar as cruise missiles become a new strategic reserve force, or can be used to saturate local air defenses, or will be an effective conventional weapon for theater warfare, they will likely be deployed in large numbers. Consequently, arms control ceilings for cruise missiles will probably be high. Although this may seem discouraging to some, it has the virtue that adequate verification becomes easier to accomplish, simply because small violations tend to be less significant. Therefore, high aggregate ceilings may be adequately verifiable despite our modest ability to monitor deployments.

Thus, although monitoring bomber and cruise missile characteristics and activities with high confidence appears to be difficult, the possibilities for adequate verification may not be hopeless. At this point, however, one cannot make any definitive statements about the prospects for adequate verification.

Notes

1. *SALT II Agreement, Vienna, June 18, 1979*. Selected Document No. 12B. U.S. Department of State.

2. "Cruise Missiles Deployed on Attack Submarines," *Washington Post*, June 28, 1984, p. A17.

3. *Verification: The Critical Element of Arms Control*, Publication No. 85, U.S. Arms Control and Disarmament Agency, March 1976.

4. Howard Stoertz, "Monitoring a Nuclear Freeze," and Steve Meyer, "Verification and Risk in Arms Control," *International Security* 8(Spring 1984).

5. Stoertz, "Monitoring a Nuclear Freeze," p. 95.

6. J.W.R. Taylor, ed., *Jane's All the World's Aircraft: 1983–84* (London: Jane's, 1983), pp. 234–240.

7. U.S. Department of State, *SALT II Agreement,* Article II-3, pp. 12–13.

8. J.W.R. Taylor, ed., *Jane's All the World's Aircraft: 1980–81* (London: Jane's, 1980), p. 203.

9. Taylor, *Jane's All the World's Aircraft: 1983–84,* pp. 234–240.

10. U.S. Department of State, *SALT II Agreement,* Article II-3, Fourth Agreed Statement.

11. *Aviation Week and Space Technology,* September 5, 1977, p. 17.

12. P.G. Hill and C.R. Peterson, *Mechanics and Thermodynamics of Propulsion* (Reading, Mass.: Addison-Wesley, 1965), p. 145.

13. *The Military Balance, 1983–84* (London: International Institute for Strategic Studies, 1983), p. 121.

14. Taylor, *Jane's All the World's Aircraft: 1983–84,* p. 269.

15. J.W.R. Taylor, ed., *Jane's All the World's Aircraft: 1982– 83* (London: Jane's, 1982), p. 260; and Ray Braybyook, *Battle for the Falklands: Airforces* (London: Osprey, 1983), pp. 17–18.

16. Kosta Tsipis, "Cruise Missiles," *Scientific American,* February 1977, pp. 20–29.

17. John C. Toomay, "Technical Characteristics," in *Cruise Missiles: Technology, Strategy, Politics,* ed. R.K. Betts (Washington, D.C.: Brookings Institution, 1981), p. 39.

18. "Soviet Subs Off U.S. Bear Cruise Missiles," *Washington Times,* January 27, 1984, p. 1.

19. Bruce Bennett and James Foster, "Strategic Retaliation Against the Soviet Homeland," in *Cruise Missiles: Technology, Strategy, Politics,* ed. R.K. Betts (Washington, D.C.: Brookings Institution, 1981).

20. Toomay, "Technical Characteristics," p. 46.

7

Verification of Compliance in the Areas of Biological and Chemical Warfare

F.R. Cleminson

As a Canadian, I find the subject of chemical warfare verification opportune for two reasons. First, chemical warfare, in all of its guises, holds a special significance for Canadians. Canada entered both world wars on a European, not an American, timetable. That meant that in World War I, Canadian troops were in France before Christmas 1914. Consequently, when the first massive military use of chemical weapons was initiated on April 22, 1915, at Ypres, elements of the First Canadian Division were in the line and Canadian soldiers were among the first victims in the world of this new type of warfare. Nevertheless, they succeeded that day in holding their ground. Although this action is remembered with pride by the Canadian Army, it probably produced a psychological effect on generations of Canadians, and, in part at least, it accounts for a seeming Canadian preoccupation with the issue. Canadian interest in arms control verification is of more recent origin. In 1979, the Departments of External Affairs and National Defence, having identified verification as a subject for study in the generic sense, undertook a modest cooperative research effort in this regard. The Compendium of Arms Control Verification Proposals, the Conceptual Paper on Arms Control Verification, and associated studies are the result of that basic research. In June 1982, at the Second UN Special Session on Disarmament, Prime Minister Trudeau focused on the subject and cited verification as probably the single most significant issue in the arms control and disarmament process in the decade of the 1980s. He pledged an expanded effort on the part of the government of Canada on this issue. As a result, the deputy prime minister and secretary of state for external affairs, the Honorable Allan J. MacEachen, announced on October 20, 1983, a verification program, interdepartmental in scope, with substantial new funding and additional personnel to coordinate the program and to develop an in-house verification research capacity. Thus, from the Canadian perspective, verification and chemical warfare are subjects that, particularly when combined, attain more than immediate concern.

Background

Perhaps it would be useful at this point to review very briefly the background of the chemical warfare issue. Although some historians claim to have been able to trace chemical use back to the Carthaginians, it is safe to say that serious international attempts to limit the use of chemicals in war date back only to the late 1800s. In 1874, representatives of fourteen leading European governments, meeting in Brussels at the invitation of the Russian czar, adopted the "International Declaration Concerning the Laws and Customs of War," which, inter alia, prohibited the use of poison or poisonous weapons. Although the declaration was never ratified, it served as a progenitor for the 1899 and 1907 Hague Peace Conferences. The 1899 Hague Conference proposed a resolution "to abstain from the use of projectiles the sole object of which is the diffusion of asphyxiating or deleterious gases." By 1914, however, research and development of both gases and means of delivery had gone far beyond the narrow wording of the resolution. Effectiveness of means of delivery, of types of gases, and, of course, of protective measures improved, but by war's end, an estimated 1.3 million casualties had been created, of whom almost 10 percent were fatalities. The remainder returned home to lead haunted lives and to serve as living examples of the horror of that type of warfare.

The Versailles Treaty of 1919 developed stringent restrictions on the part of Germany. Article 171 said:

> The use of asphyxiating, poisonous or other gases and all analogous liquids, materials or devices being prohibited, their manufacture and importation are strictly forbidden in Germany. The same applies to material specially intended for the manufacture, storage and use of the said products or devices.

This provision went well beyond simple use of chemicals in war, although it was this aspect that became the single objective of the Geneva Protocol. Article 171 included manufacture and importation as well, though it applied in this instance solely to Germany. Verification in this context was not difficult to visualize, given the powers assumed by the occupying forces. The 1921 Washington Conference on the Limitations of Naval Armaments dealt briefly with chemical aspects of warfare, and the 1925 Geneva Protocol was accepted by the international community as the cornerstone of arms control of chemical weapons. The Geneva Protocol dealt only with aspects of use, however, and the verification requirement was met by conveniently ignoring it. Many nations, Canada included, attached reservations to their ratification of the protocol. The United States remained aloof from the protocol until December 17, 1974, when it became the 104th nation to ratify.

Post–World War II

World War II ended, as we know, with no military use having been made of chemical weapons, although they were stored in large quantities on both sides.

In 1962, under the cochairmanship of the Soviet Union and the United States, the Eighteen-Nation Disarmament Committee (ENDC) in Geneva took up disarmament negotiations, including the chemical and biological warfare issue. In 1969, President Nixon unilaterally announced that the United States would divest itself of biological weapons (later to include biotoxins) and agreed to non-first use of chemical weapons. He made a unilateral decision to cease production of chemical weapons as well. At the same time, the United States agreed to a United Kingdom–inspired approach in the Conference of the Committee on Disarmament (CCD, formerly the ENDC) that, in effect, split biological warfare considerations from the chemical warfare issue. By so doing, the verification aspect, which was and is of overriding importance in terms of chemical weapons, was downplayed, thus permitting agreement to the 1972 Biological Weapons Convention.

The 1972 Biological Weapons Treaty

The verification provisions of the 1972 Biological Weapons Treaty, which provides for the prohibition of the development, production, and stockpiling of bacteriological (biological) and toxin weapons and destruction of existing stocks, are contained in Articles 5 and 6. The method of verification provided for in Article 5 is cooperation and consultation. Provision was made in Article 6 for lodging a complaint with the UN Security Council that might result in an investigation.

It must have been clear at the time of negotiation of this treaty that the cooperation and consultation method of verification was, at best, symbolic. Ratification of the treaty by the major powers holding stocks could be seen as de facto recognition that this type of weapon was no longer required in their own arsenals and that the confidence-building effect of the treaty was assessed to outweigh the significance of possible retention of such weapons by others.

If proof of the ineffectiveness of these verification provisions was required, it was provided by the Sverdlovsk incident in 1979. When the U.S. government had reason to suspect a breach of the treaty because of a major outbreak of anthrax in the northern city of Sverdlovsk in the Soviet Union, the Soviet government denied the charge and refused to discuss the incident further. The explanations provided by the Soviet Union were not compatible with information available to the United States, and the result was unsatisfactory.

Unfortunately, the United States chose not to undertake to invoke the provision of Article 6. Although a Soviet veto in the Security Council might have resulted, as the United States maintained, it remains a fact that, from the legal standpoint, the full provisions of the treaty were not applied.

Chemical Convention Negotiations

In the preamble of the Biological Weapons Convention, the negotiators recognized the convention as a first step toward the possible achievement of agreements on effective measures to prohibit the development, production, and stockpiling of chemical weapons, and they continued negotiations to that end.

In 1974, Richard Nixon and Leonid Brezhnev signed a joint agreement that said, in part, that both nations agreed to consider a "joint initiative in the Conference of the Committee on Disarmament with respect to the conclusion, as a first step, of an international convention dealing with the most dangerous lethal means of chemical warfare." Bilateral talks, which commenced in 1977, brought forth little substantive progress until the signing of SALT II in Vienna. At that time, Presidents Carter and Brezhnev reaffirmed the intention of their respective governments to intensify the talks. In 1979 and 1980, the USSR and the United States submitted joint reports (CD/48 and CD/112) on the progress of their bilateral discussions to the Committee on Disarmament (CD). The talks broke off as a result of deterioration of U.S.–Soviet relations and the policy review by the Reagan administration. The U.S. government subsequently announced that it would pursue the negotiation of a chemical weapons convention only in a multilateral forum. The Committee on Disarmament in Geneva is the only international multilateral negotiating body on disarmament activities. In 1981, the CD modified its negotiating approach by establishing a number of ad hoc working groups. Within the group devoted to chemical weapons, there was general agreement that a verification system for the chemical weapons issue must blend national and international means. Behind this general recognition, however, there remained some very important differences in approach. Basically, the Eastern group underscored the principle of self-inspection. The West and, increasingly, members of the Neutral and Non-Aligned group recognized the essential character of international on-site inspection. In addition, the Soviet Union insisted that verification provisions should not be discussed before the basic negotiations had been completed. The West held the view that basic negotiations could not be undertaken if it was not known what methods of verification would be acceptable to the negotiating parties.

The 1983 CD Negotiating Session

On February 3, 1983, Vice-President Bush addressed the Committee on Disarmament and dedicated the United States to accelerating the negotiating process on a chemical weapons convention. His remarks centered specifically on the verification aspects of compliance. Subsequently, the United States tabled a working paper (CD/343) containing detailed views on the content of a convention. This paper complemented a Soviet paper (CD/294) that had been tabled too late in the 1982 session to be discussed. It had initially been introduced at UNSSOD II by Foreign Minister Gromyko. These two documents, taken together, constituted the most comprehensive and comparable statement by the superpowers since the 1979 and 1980 joint papers.

The Soviet draft, though couched in treatylike language, was not a draft treaty. It served as a relatively noncontroversial document to update Soviet views, and it reiterated certain Soviet views as elaborated in the 1980 joint progress report. While continuing to stress national verification means (that is, a type of self-inspection as the major thrust), the Soviet draft did include the possibility of "systematic international on-site inspection," which it suggested each country could consider favorably or otherwise. In apparent response, the United States in its submission used the same expression, "systematic international on-site inspection," but referred to it as mandatory. This seemed to be a clear difference in approach but, by the same measure, an obviously clear issue for negotiation.

It is generally agreed that the 1983 session of the CD moved the two sides appreciably closer. This could be attributed, in part, to the papers tabled by the superpowers and, in part, to the game plan implemented by the Western chairmanship. As the chairman of the 1983 Working Group, Ambassador D.S. McPhail of Canada, in presenting the results of the Working Group to the Committee on Disarmament in plenary session (CD/416), said:

> The Working Group agreed to set out, in one single document, the substance of provisions for a Chemical Weapons Convention. This document indicates the consensus reached earlier and during their session, and sets out remaining differences clearly where further work is needed, so as to reveal how best the Committee can proceed to the final elaboration of a Convention. We thus developed an integrated or internally consistent procedure whereby each provision is intended to be presented in a logical hierarchy, progressing from the general to the particular, and whereby each provision is accompanied by an indication of the control or verification measures appropriate to it.

Chemical Weapons Use in the CD Context

Prior to the 1983 session of the CD, chemical weapons use had been dealt with primarily in the UN General Assembly by a number of resolutions spanning several sessions. In the General Assembly, it had taken on a controversial nature, centering on the "yellow rain" issue and international investigation. Strangely enough, the inclusion of a ban on the use of chemical weapons as part of a comprehensive convention was accepted by all sides in the CD during the 1983 session with a distinct lack of acrimony, though the yellow rain issue featured prominently in the vice-president's February 3, 1983, address to the CD.

The Yellow Rain Experience

Although the handling of the yellow rain allegation by the United States, the United Nations, and indeed the world community has left something to be desired, this experience has been significant in terms of the development of international criteria pertaining to the investigation of allegations of chemical weapons use. The significance lies in two areas. First, the political dimension is that the United Nations did bring itself, through a number of resolutions, to establish an international group of experts that undertook inspections relevant to the allegation. The second significant aspect was a recognition of the amount of analysis required to undertake an investigation of one specific event. Even the controversy that has developed within the academic community is useful as a marker of what would finally be required in the establishment of an effective international verification mechanism.

The UN study (A/37/259, 1 December 1982), which has been maligned in some quarters, is indeed a report of considerable value. It would have been unrealistic to assume that, at this stage, such a report could have been more definitive. But this report does focus, in an international document, on several important problem areas in undertaking an investigation of chemical weapons use: (1) the lack of accessibility to areas of alleged attack; (2) the long delay between alleged attack and investigation; (3) the requirements for analytical support; and (4) the necessity for an internationally accepted methodology.

The UN report is also important because it represents a real-life attempt to apply a theory that has proved to be lacking in practical application. From the Canadian perspective, it is seen as the embryo stage of the development of an international verification capability. The Southeast Asia experience constitutes a useful prototype in terms of a probable requirement for other investigations if and when other allegations are made. For example, the January 6, 1984, edition of the *Ottawa Citizen* reported that Soviet and Angolan officials had charged South Africa, backed by Washington, with the bombing of a southern city with highly toxic nerve gas. It can only be regretted that the Soviet Union had not seen fit to support the UN resolutions calling for investigation of previous allegations of chemical weapons use. Had it done so, and had its Southeast Asian allies permitted UN investigators to visit the scenes of alleged attacks, an operationally effective international apparatus might have been in existence to investigate these first allegations in 1984. It is clearly in the interest of the United Nations to develop an international capability to investigate these and other allegations of noncompliance. It must also develop an ability to allocate proper weight to different types of evidence. There will always be those who will choose to ignore the overwhelming evidence in field investigations and attempt to reduce human tragedy to a laboratory exercise. Certainly, the defecating habits of bees has never assumed a higher profile than in the last twelve months.

1984 Prospects

The modest optimism that was engendered by the progress of the 1983 session has been considerably enhanced by two events: the January 10, 1984, Soviet proposal on a chemical weapons free zone in Europe (CWFZE) and the announcement by Secretary of State Schultz of the intention of the United States to submit a draft convention on chemical weapons early in the 1984 session of the CD.

The Soviet proposal for "freeing Europe from chemical weapons" is not new. It has surfaced in a number of ways (the Warsaw Pact 1983 Prague Declaration, for example), and it was initially broached in the Palme Commission Report in June 1982. The Palme Commission highlighted, at the same time, the necessity to declare existing depots and stockpiles with adequate verification, including on-site inspection. These aspects are not readily apparent in the Soviet draft. There is no attempt to explain why negotiation of a regional European chemical weapons free zone would be easier than a universal ban, particularly since the majority of chemical weapons are in Europe. It would, of course, leave the Soviets with stockpiles east of the Urals, which could easily be relocated, and it would address the political dimension of the issue while ignoring the technical aspects.

Nevertheless, there are positive elements on this proposal, not the least of which is the interest expressed by the Soviet Union in the chemical weapons issue and, in particular, the Soviets' desire to facilitate achievement of a comprehensive ban. Although the Soviet position on verification has not changed— that is, "it can be discussed as it becomes necessary"—nevertheless, verification must now be recognized by all as the single major obstacle to a convention. The current Soviet phrase is "mutually acceptable adequate forms of verification."

Though clearly inadequate in terms of a treaty, the Soviet proposal could be seen as extremely useful as an initial implementation plan following the successful conclusion of a comprehensive convention.

On April 18, 1984, Vice-President George Bush tabled the draft convention on the prohibition of chemical weapons (CD/500), which he characterized as the latest expression of the firm U.S. resolve to ban chemical weapons totally. Drawing not only upon American expertise but also from much of the work completed by the CD in past sessions, the U.S. draft represents the most comprehensive and detailed proposal yet tabled in the CD. Its format and language should serve as excellent models upon which negotiations in the CD can be based.

Not unexpectedly, the areas likely to be the most controversial are those relating to compliance and verification. Although Articles VIII, IX, and XI are likely to form the basis for serious and strenuous negotiations, it is Article X, which deals with special on-site inspection or what Mr. Bush referred to as a new "open invitation" concept, that has drawn the greatest criticism. On October 25, for example, in the UN General Assembly First Committee debate, Soviet Ambassador Petrovsky referred to this provision as having been drawn in such a way as to make it unacceptable.

Article X provides for special on-site inspection of any military location or facility or any other location or facility owned or controlled by the government of a party to the convention. It has been criticized because of the obligatory nature of the provision as well as the timeframe (24 hours) within which such an inspection can be initiated. Although these provisions are unprecedented, there are a number of factors that critics must recognize. First, this is an initial draft of a convention on a particularly complex issue. It represents a first attempt to provide a detailed matrix of interacting methodologies designed to provide an acceptable level of confidence in compliance. Second, by submitting these verification proposals to the conference, the United States is the only nation to have committed itself to the provisions on a reciprocal basis. Indeed, to this time, no other nation has made so open a commitment. Finally, as U.S. Ambassador Fields has emphasized during each of his explanatory interventions in plenary sessions of the CD: (1) the United States has not submitted its draft on a "take-it-or-leave-it" basis, and (2) the United States is willing to consider any other formulation of words that will provide the same level of confidence of compliance.

It is anyone's guess as to the direction in which the Conference on Disarmament might move on this issue during its 1985 session. Traditionally, chairmanship of the chemical weapons ad hoc committee has been on a rotational basis, and it should fall in 1985 to the Socialist group. During the 1985 session, the U.S. draft treaty, in concert with certain other major conference papers, should stand as a significant document in the development of a convention. In line with the U.S. invitation for alternative wording, a parallel draft treaty by the USSR would not be inappropriate as a first order of business. Both drafts could provide the catalyst essential to the final process of achieving consensus in this most controversial area.

Conclusions

The invitation by the U.S. government to member nations of the Committee on Disarmament to visit the chemical agency destruction facility at Tooele, Utah, in November 1983 is likely to have a significant effect on chemical weapons negotiations as a theoretical problem. It is safe to say that all who visited went away from the event convinced, first, that chemical weapons munitions can be destroyed in large numbers safely and, second, that the destruction of stocks can be verified with minimum intrusive effects. This message is likely to be transmitted to the remaining twelve nations who, for one reason or another, were unable to attend the demonstration.

From the verification perspective, this means that destruction of stocks and, presumably, of dedicated production facilities—the *disarmament aspect* of a treaty—can be accomplished and verified effectively. The area in which verification is still to be proved is in the monitoring of the nonproduction of chemical weapons in the commercial or civilian segment of the chemical industry. This constitutes the *arms control* aspect of the treaty.

Depending on the scope of negotiations in 1985, the development of a full and comprehensive draft treaty may or may not be possible. If not, thought might be given to reworking the convention into two phased treaties. The first treaty might undertake the disarmament aspect of chemical weapons, including the declaration and destruction of existing stocks and dedicated facilities under a full verification regime. This process is estimated to require ten years for completion. The second treaty would concern the nonproduction and chemical weapons use aspects. Negotiations of these aspects of the overall treaty might continue concurrent with the actual destruction of declared stocks, with a target date of four years after the initiation of destruction of stocks. Presumably, the confidence-building effects of a successful implementation of phase 1 would impinge upon the negotiation of phase 2. Lack of success in either phase would have an adverse effect, of course, and would nullify both stages. Given the necessity of coming to grips with the problem, the Conference on Disarmament and its member nations must prepare to recast some of the theology of negotiation that has built up over the years and begin an innovative process. The responsibility rests mainly with the nations that possess the weapons.

8

The Political Dynamics of Verification and Compliance Debates

Michael Krepon

Public and congressional debates over verification have featured predictable arguments about the advisability of arms control agreements and the monitoring requirements needed for them. By the early 1960s, when attempts at comprehensive nuclear disarmament gave way to more limited goals, advocates of arms control argued for a degree of flexibility in monitoring requirements. There were several reasons for doing so. Arms controllers argued that the possibility of Soviet cheating had to be weighed against the probability of detection and the potential impact of undetected Soviet cheating on U.S. national security. Moreover, it was not reasonable to expect either perfect confidence in U.S. monitoring capabilities or treaty constraints that allowed absolute certainty in monitoring compliance.

In this view, U.S. detection capabilities provided a deterrent to Soviet cheating, since detection would, at the very least, be politically embarrassing. Detection could also prompt reactions that were very much inimical to the cheater. In addition, there were bureaucratic reasons to expect treaty compliance. As Abram Chayes argues:

> An agreement that is adopted by a modern bureaucratic government will be backed by a broad official consensus generated by the negotiating process, and will carry personal and political endorsement across the spectrum of bureaucratic and political leadership. These are exceedingly hard to undo or reverse, the more so since, once the treaty goes into effect, they are reinforced by the ponderous inertia of the bureaucracy.[1]

As a result of these factors, the United States could still enter into compacts with less than perfect assurance in monitoring capabilities, so long as U.S. security would not be jeopardized as a result. Since, for arms controllers, political

Sara Goodgame at the Carnegie Endowment for International Peace assisted in the research for this chapter, which was written under the auspices of the Carnegie Endowment's Verification Project, which is supported by a grant from the Ploughshares Fund.

compacts were the essence of security and an unfettered competition in nuclear armaments was not, standards of verifiability did not have to be overly stringent.

Jerome Wiesner suggested in 1961 that "the level or intensity of inspection required to monitor a disarmament agreement is in some way proportional to the degree of disarmament."[2] With offensive nuclear capabilities continuing to rise, the "Wiesner curve" should become more forgiving over time. In fact, it has not—a sad commentary on the political dynamics of the arms race. Monitoring requirements have become more severe with the introduction of new, hard-to-monitor forces such as mobile missiles and cruise missiles.

Advocates of arms control have again suggested avoiding rigid standards in handling hard-to-monitor systems. Bookkeeping solutions such as counting rules can be applied, in principle, to cruise missiles, just as they have been applied to MIRVed missiles in the past. Cooperative measures can be worked out at production facilities and central basing areas for mobile missiles, as was contemplated by the Carter administration for the MX missile. These approaches to difficult monitoring problems will not provide the greatest degree of precision in intelligence estimates nor as high a confidence against breakout as one would like. However, to advocates of arms control, they are acceptable, given the levels of offensive capabilities already deployed and the urgency of placing some restraints on continued deployments.

Imperfect monitoring capabilities pose risks with respect to Soviet compliance, but they are risks that arms controllers have long been willing to accept, especially when they are compared to the risks of not reaching agreement. For example, as Pentagon officials testified at the time, there were risks associated with Soviet compliance with a MIRV ban: the Kremlin could test single reentry vehicles from a postboost vehicle capable of multiple releases, or they could test MIRVs disguised as space launches.[3] But were these risks sufficiently great to foreclose a ban on MIRV testing and development? Before that, officials in the Kennedy administration did not argue with those who contended that monitoring capabilities for a comprehensive test ban could not detect all instances of Soviet noncompliance—only that these were risks worth taking in the light of the perceived benefits. As President Kennedy said in his transmittal message to the Senate:

> The risks in clandestine violations under this treaty are far smaller than the risks in unlimited testing. . . . No nation tempted to violate the treaty can be certain that an attempted violation will go undetected, given the many means of detecting nuclear explosions. The risks of detection outweigh the potential gains from violation, and the risk to the United States from such violation is outweighed by the risk of a continued unlimited nuclear arms race.[4]

Skeptics of the value of arms control had a very different calculus of benefits and risks. For them, the notion of negotiated agreements with a committed adversary was somewhat a contradiction in terms. Agreements could not alter long-term Soviet ambitions, but they could hinder U.S. defense programs necessary to foil the Kremlin's maneuvering for advantage.

In other words, underlying the familiar theme of "you can't trust the Russians" lay a deeper concern: arms control could not be trusted to protect and advance U.S. security interests. This belief was often unstated because of the widespread popularity of arms control, at least in the abstract. But it could be inferred from the specific proposals championed by those most skeptical of the process; proposals deemed worthy of support were also wholly unacceptable to our negotiating partner. At the heart of this deep skepticism toward arms control was a belief that negotiated agreements provided only the most diaphanous solutions to the hard competition of international politics.

This mindset naturally bred a far different approach to verification issues, since there were few incentives—bureaucratic or otherwise—for Soviet compliance with arms control agreements. To the contrary, the Kremlin's impulse was not to comply with agreements that constrained military forces needed to achieve national objectives—particularly when penalties were not forthcoming for noncompliance. Failure to detect Soviet noncompliance did not necessarily mean that the Kremlin was behaving itself; it meant only that violations had not yet been detected. Of particular concern was the Kremlin's high priority on the arts of secrecy, deception, and concealment. The potential for noncompliance was therefore great for most sorts of arms control agreements. In the view of Amrom Katz and his disciples, the United States has never found anything that the Soviets have hidden successfully.[5] In other words, the possibilities of cheating were endless. The best checks against nefarious Soviet practices were highly intrusive monitoring provisions and a forceful policy of sanctions and unilateral actions once detection had occurred.

The views expressed by advocates and skeptics of arms control on treaty verification have been far more varied than those ascribed here. However, the terms of political debate have been set by the most vocal partisans; their themes and the political dynamics resulting from them have remained fairly constant over time.

Adequate Verification, 1963–1979

From the Limited Test Ban Treaty to the SALT II Treaty, American presidents supported a flexible approach to verification requirements. Their operational construct was "adequate" verification. On occasion, such as during the public defense of the Biological Weapons Convention (BWC) in 1972, this standard was not employed. But the BWC was a special case, since the United States had no interest in pursuing biological weapons. For President Nixon and his advisers, verification and compliance procedures for the BWC seemed to be less important than having the Kremlin formally subscribe to a position we had taken unilaterally.

For nuclear arms control agreements, verification concerns were far more pressing. American presidents from Kennedy to Carter applied a remarkably similar formula: the United States had to be in a position to detect Soviet noncompliance of any consequence in time to take appropriate countermeasures. During the Limited Test Ban Treaty (LTBT) debate, this formulation was not explicit, but it could clearly be inferred from the presentations of treaty supporters. Speaking for the Joint Chiefs, General Maxwell D. Taylor acknowledged the possibilities of clandestine Soviet testing. He added:

> However, the dangers of detection and the cost and difficulty of testing in outer space would tend to impose severe restrictions upon such clandestine testing. Other clandestine tests in the atmosphere or under water, depending on their size, would involve a fairly high probability of detection by our conventional intelligence or our atomic detection system. Moreover, the Joint Chiefs of Staff consider the resulting progress which the Soviets might make clandestinely to be a relatively minor factor in relation to the overall present and probable balance of military strength if adequate safeguards are maintained.[6]

Those safeguards included strong laboratory nuclear test programs, improved monitoring capabilities, and preparations to resume atmospheric tests in the event of Soviet noncompliance. In sum, the limited test ban was defended and accepted on the basis that U.S. monitoring capabilities were deficient in certain respects but adequate when viewed in conjunction with other political and military factors.

At the outset of the SALT negotiations, President Nixon explicitly restated this formulation in his instructions to the SALT I negotiating team:

> No arms limitation agreement can ever be absolutely verifiable. The relevant test is not an abstract ideal, but the practical standard of whether we can determine compliance adequately to safeguard our security—that is, whether we can identify attempted evasion if it occurs on a large enough scale to pose a significant risk, and whether we can do so in time to mount a sufficient response. Meeting this test is what I mean by the term "adequate verification".[7]

In defending the SALT I accords, Secretary of Defense Melvin Laird flatly stated, "We have adequate means of verification."[8] Little debate ensued on Secretary Laird's conclusion, either in committee hearings or in congressional debate. Most agreed with Senator Jacob Javits, who stated at the conclusion of the desultory ratification debate over the ABM Treaty:

> I do not base my approval of the treaty and the agreements upon "trust" in the benign motives of the Soviet Union. No one is asked to do that. What I do base

it on is Dr. Kissinger's assurance that there is every likelihood that the agreements will be complied with because it is in the interests of the U.S.S.R. to do so.[9]

Verification issues were of far greater concern during the SALT II hearings because of the difficulty in monitoring the qualitative limits included in the SALT II Treaty and because of the compliance issues that arose from the SALT I accords. The Carter administration's defense of the "verifiability" of the SALT II Treaty was therefore similar to but more comprehensive and detailed than that of the Kennedy and Nixon administrations before it. In a State Department report on the treaty, the Carter administration presented its case in the following terms:

> The anticipated SALT II agreement is adequately verifiable. This judgment is based on assessment of the verifiability of the individual provisions of the agreement and the agreement as a whole. Although the possibility of some undetected cheating in certain areas exists, such cheating would not alter the strategic balance in view of U.S. programs. Any cheating on a scale large enough to alter the strategic balance would be discovered in time to make an appropriate response. There will be areas of uncertainty, but they are not such as to permit the Soviets to produce a significant unanticipated threat to U.S. interests, and those uncertainties can, in any event, be compensated for with the flexibility inherent in our own programs.[10]

During hearings on the SALT II Treaty, senior administration officials subscribed to these precepts, but public assurances, including those of the director of central intelligence and the chairman of the Joint Chiefs of Staff, did not alleviate congressional or public concerns. Unlike the SALT I debate, treaty opponents repeatedly raised numerous Soviet practices that could not be monitored easily. Events during the congressional review process heightened sensitivities over treaty verification, particularly the loss of Iranian monitoring stations after the fall of the Shah, and the "discovery" of a Soviet military brigade in Cuba. These specific incidents reinforced perceptions of presidential weakness, Soviet adventurousness, and disturbing trends in superpower fortunes and military capabilities.

Effective Verification, 1981–Present

Opponents of previous arms control agreements, including many in the Reagan administration, had long felt that "adequate" verification was not sufficient or, at the very least, that political judgments of adequacy in past agreements had been notably lax. Moreover, previous agreements had been poorly crafted, allowing Soviet exploitation of ambiguities in treaty provisions in ways that were injurious to U.S. national security and the strategic balance. In this view, tougher verification provisions and more exacting standards for determining adequacy would be required for future agreements.

President Reagan's first director of the Arms Control and Disarmament Agency (ACDA), Eugene Rostow, set this tone by citing the need to "construct a set of measures necessary to ensure verifiability. These may well include cooperative procedures between the United States and the Soviet Union, such as detailed data exchanges and provisions to enhance the confidence of each side in data obtained by national technical means.[11] The latter could be interpreted to include, among other things, a veiled reference to the need for on-site inspections, a possibility not ruled out by Rostow's colleague and U.S. START negotiator, Lt. Gen. Edward L. Rowny.[12]

The new watchword proposed by Reagan administration officials was "effective" verification.[13] No definition of what constituted effective verification or how it differed from adequate verification was forthcoming from President Reagan or his advisers. Clearly, the new standard was intended to be seen as tougher than the older one, but to what degree remained difficult to determine. U.S. "Verification Annexes" were in the process of preparation for both the START and INF negotiations, but neither had been completed when the talks came to a standstill in late fall 1983. In addition, no public attempt was made by Reagan administration officials to define what additional monitoring provisions were deemed necessary for a Comprehensive Test Ban Treaty. Administration officials based their opposition to resuming this negotiation on the need for an active nuclear weapon testing program, as well as on difficulties in verification.[14]

Opposition within the Reagan administration to resuming antisatellite weapons negotiations was likewise based on verification concerns, as well as on a military requirement "to prevent space from being used as a sanctuary for aggressive systems by our enemies."[15] As leaked to the United Press International (UPI), the Fiscal Year 1984–1988 Defense Guidance, a classified document, contained the following reference with respect to space warfare:

> We must ensure that treaties and agreements do not foreclose opportunities to develop the capabilities and systems contributing to strategic stability and deterrence. In particular, it must be recognized that agreements cannot protect our defense interests in space during periods of hostilities.[16]

As administration officials stated, comprehensive antisatellite (ASAT) agreements could not assure the total dismantlement and nonreconstruction of Soviet space warfare capabilities, since other military capabilities, such as ICBMs or ABM interceptors, could be used for ASAT missions. The verifiability of even a modest agreement banning tests of dedicated ASAT systems was also questioned by the Reagan administration. In its report to the Congress on ASAT arms control, administration officials argued that such tests could be concealed, just as some Nixon administration officials argued with respect to MIRV testing.[17] Moreover, even a relatively modest ASAT capability could alter the strategic balance in unacceptable ways. Given the multiple possibilities of hiding ASATs or of conducting ASAT missions by other means, it was difficult for those who adhered to the dictum that "we have never found anything that the Soviets have successfully hidden" to conceive of an effective verification system governing ASAT capabilities. Nevertheless, the Reagan administration agreed to include discussions on ASAT limitations in umbrella talks during 1985.

While the Reagan administration resisted formal ASAT negotiations, it entered into negotiations for a comprehensive ban on the development, production, and possession of chemical weapons. For these purposes, effective verification required the right to special and ad hoc on-site inspections at military locations and facilities throughout the Soviet Union.[18] The administration's report discussing the difficulties of ASAT verification and announcement of its proposal for a comprehensive ban on chemical weapons were disclosed within the same week. To critics of the Reagan administration, this suggested, at best, an inconsistency in applying standards for effective verification or, at worst, a disingenuousness about the pursuit of arms control in both cases.

Compliance Diplomacy, 1973–1979

In congressional debates from the Limited Test Ban Treaty to SALT II, supporters of arms control argued that Soviet leaders would be unlikely to violate agreements that were in their interest as well as ours; that U.S. capabilities to detect violations of any consequence would also serve as a deterrent; and that if violations took place, the United States could take appropriate action, including abrogation of the agreement in question.

During the LTBT debate, several potential compliance issues were raised by committed treaty opponents. Nuclear weapon tests in Lake Baikal, in deep space, behind the moon, or under a few feet of earth during periods of heavy cloud cover were deemed possible by those who foresaw a determined Soviet effort to foil U.S. national technical means of verification. The possibility of Soviet nuclear weapon tests at or just over the Chinese border was also raised.[19]

These concerns were brushed aside by Kennedy administration officials, who pointed out the cost and extraordinary difficulties involved in these evasion measures. A treaty amendment offered by Senator John Tower calling for on-site inspections was easily defeated by those who felt they were unnecessary, given the limited scope of the treaty and the impressive detection capabilities either in place or soon to be there.[20] Although the LTBT contained no mechanisms to handle compliance issues, none appeared to be needed; if the Soviets reneged on their commitments, the United States could follow suit. After all, this was what happened in 1961 when the Soviets resumed atmospheric testing after a moratorium of almost three years' duration.

During the Senate Foreign Relations Committee's consideration of the SALT I accords, compliance questions were not addressed in any detail or substance. The Armed Services Committees in both the House and the Senate did delve into these issues, however. Senator Henry Jackson raised concerns about the fuzziness of Soviet baseline forces allowed under the Interim Agreement, suggesting difficulties in monitoring additions to these forces.[21]

A far more serious matter was the extent to which the Kremlin would be able to increase the military potential of new ICBMs replacing existing forces. In the SALT I negotiations, the United States first tried to place direct limits on the volume of new Soviet ICBMs, then tried to do so indirectly by limiting increases in silo dimensions. The United States and the Soviet Union agreed that "in the process of modernization and replacement...dimensions of land-based ICBM silo launchers will not be significantly increased." Moreover, both sides agreed that the term "significantly increased" meant an increase of 10 to 15 percent over existing dimensions of ICBM silos. But did this mean that calculations were to be based on existing silo diameter, depth, or both? The negotiating record left no agreed interpretation. When calculated on the basis of two dimensions rather than one, the resulting increase in volume could be quite considerable—on the order of 50 percent.

During congressional hearings on the Interim Agreement, skeptical members of Congress were primarily interested in pinning down favorable interpretations of what would constitute permissible increases in missile volume. There was no shortage of witnesses to endorse the U.S. view that 10 to 15 percent increases calculated on the basis of one silo dimension, not both, were consistent with the terms of the Interim Agreement.

Later, this issue became the springboard for considerable debate over Soviet violations of the Interim Agreement. During the final stages of congressional consideration of the SALT I accords, however, debate centered on safeguards associated with any subsequent agreement, rather than on prospective Soviet noncompliance. The prevailing concern of Senator Jackson and his allies was not that the Soviets would cheat, but that they could do so much harm without resort to cheating. Thus, any future agreement signed by an American president had to be in conformity with the Jackson amendment, requiring U.S. levels of intercontinental strategic forces not inferior to the limits provided for the Soviet Union.

When the Nixon administration acceded to this formulation, the Interim Agreement was assured a smooth passage in both houses of Congress. President Nixon was in a strong position to counter concerns about potential Soviet noncompliance in any event. He had no need to defend his hard-line credentials, and he freely supported a wide range of strategic modernization programs to accompany the new SALT accords. In addition, the agreements created a new forum, the Standing Consultative Commission (SCC), to implement the accords and to iron out compliance questions arising from them.

The SCC was almost immediately faced with the contentious issue of new Soviet ICBMs that did not adhere to assurances provided by Nixon administration officials or congressional testimony expressing the view that such Soviet actions would constitute a violation of the Interim Agreement. Other U.S. complaints included the construction of what initially appeared to be new missile silos, the possible testing of a surface-to-air (SAM) radar in "an ABM mode," and Soviet concealment practices associated with new weapons systems.

The Nixon, Ford, and Carter administrations adopted a common approach to such compliance questions. They all agreed to work quietly and patiently within the SCC to clear up ambiguities in the agreements, to "fence in" problems when they occurred, and to work out "implementing understandings" to prevent the agreements from being undermined. Their approach during this period has been described by a former U.S. commissioner at the SCC in the following terms:

> The essence of the S.C.C. implementation task is to head off gross dislocations or irretrievable circumstances by acting early enough and finding mutually-acceptable measures to sustain intact the agreements within its field of responsibility.
>
> The initial requirement of this task is to raise potential problems for resolution before they get out of hand and become causes for undesired reconsideration of an entire agreement. Lying in the grass and building a comprehensive case for eventually jumping up and shouting "gotcha" might be fun for some of the grass-dwellers, but it would not be a sensible way to sustain a desired agreement.[22]

Presidents Nixon, Ford, and Carter were reasonably satisfied with the work of the SCC. Compliance problems could be ironed out during this timeframe because both nations recognized that this forum was being used to maintain the viability of previous agreements rather than to prosecute cases of noncompliance. Compliance questions raised during this period were resolved in a variety of ways. For example, on the question of new types of Soviet ICBMs that were appreciably larger than their predecessors, the United States did not make headway at the SCC since the new deployments were prohibited by a unilateral U.S. interpretation of the Interim Agreement, an interpretation the Soviets rejected during the SALT I negotiations and afterward. On the question of new ICBM launchers, the Kremlin's position at the SCC was borne out over time; the construction begun in 1973 turned out to be for new launch control centers, not for prohibited missile silos. After raising questions of Soviet concealment practices at the SCC in 1974, this pattern of expansion stopped. The questionable SAM radar operations also stopped within three weeks after the United States raised this issue at the SCC. The two delegations subsequently worked out an implementing agreement governing these practices.

In a report issued in conjunction with the SALT II debate, the Carter administration concluded that in every instance when the U.S. raised SALT I compliance questions in the SCC, "The [Soviet] activity has ceased or subsequent information has clarified the situation and allayed our concern."[23] Still, the Nixon, Ford, and Carter administrations all noted a disturbing Soviet pattern of testing at the margins of negotiated agreements.

Compliance Diplomacy, 1981–Present

Critics of the SALT process reached far different conclusions about the work of the SCC and the record of Soviet compliance. These concerns were fully aired during the bitter SALT II debate and were reflected in positions subsequently taken by the Reagan administration.

During the Senate Foreign Relations Committee's SALT II hearings, Paul Nitze was asked if he knew of any compliance issues not resolved at the SCC. He responded: "No, but how were they resolved? They were resolved by accepting that which had been done in violation."[24] To buttress this view, hard-line critics of the SALT process compiled lists of Soviet "violations and circumventions" of arms control agreements, while leaks of new violations appeared periodically in newspapers and journals with a strong editorial stance against Soviet "cheating." The willingness of the Carter administration to acknowledge these violations was also called into question. During the SALT II debate, Richard Perle wrote:

> From a political point of view, the last thing we will desire is to catch the Soviets in a violation—and especially in a violation of a provision that careless negotiating had rendered unenforceable.... In the real world we would face a choice between precipitating a political crisis of enormous proportions or ignoring evidence of the Soviet violation. If past history is any guide, our officials will find an endless list of excuses to justify doubtful Soviet behavior.[25]

Perle also criticized the Carter administration for poor drafting of the SALT II Treaty, which, for example, made it difficult to monitor compliance with the provisions regarding production or operational deployment of SS-16 missiles. A more serious problem, in Perle's view, related to the "new types" provisions of SALT II:

> We have, for example, persuaded ourselves that the SALT II treaty will prevent the Soviets from deploying new types of ICBMs. Over and over Administration spokesmen have pointed to the limitation on new types of ICBM as a central achievement of SALT II. The fact is, however, that the Soviets have succeeded—with cooperation from our negotiators—in getting a

definition of the term "new type" that will permit them to complete the development of all the ICBMs we believe they intend to complete during the period of the treaty—the so-called "fifth generation."[26]

Concerns such as these resonated deeply among those advising Ronald Reagan in his presidential campaign. The Republican party's platform during the 1980 campaign formally pledged "to end the Carter cover-up of Soviet violations of SALT I and SALT II."

In many instances, agreements are purposely vague because both sides may not wish to foreclose military options or because they cannot reach a mutually agreeable limitation. If both sides wish to maintain the viability of negotiated agreements, compliance diplomacy can succeed. Compliance diplomacy cannot succeed, however, when one or both parties question an agreement's worth or its future viability.

The questioning process begins when treaty signatories take steps that are not expressly prohibited by agreements but that undermine agreed limitations. These steps erode the political, if not the military, benefits of arms control agreements. Both the United States and the Soviet Union have hedged their bets in this way, although the Kremlin has been, by far, the worst offender. The Soviet military places considerable stock in achieving marginal advantages in gray areas, and there are few internal political or bureaucratic checks against their doing so.

The SCC succeeded in ironing out compliance questions during the Nixon, Ford, and Carter administrations because neither side questioned the other's basic intentions toward the SALT agreements. Successes were possible despite the ups and downs of superpower relations and despite all the hedges, because both nations had shared perceptions of the benefits of the SALT accords and the risks of their unraveling. In both capitals, these calculations have changed dramatically over the last three years, symbolized by the release of U.S. and Soviet reports of each other's noncompliance. What makes the current situation so unsettling is that both Washington and Moscow are now asking fundamental questions about each other's basic intentions toward previous agreements. Hedges, both past and prospective, are accumulating to the point where both sides are questioning the value of the negotiating relationship.

Reagan administration officials have long held the view that the Soviets could be expected to reap the benefits of the SALT process only until they could gain more by breaking out of treaty restraints. Numerous public statements by these officials could only raise similar Soviet concerns about U.S. intentions toward SALT agreements. Former secretary of state Alexander Haig declared: "We consider SALT II to be dead. We have so informed the Soviet Union and they have accepted and understood that." Secretary of Defense Caspar Weinberger declared that U.S. defense programs were in conformity to SALT I and II restraints as a matter of coincidence rather than design, and the president's White House Counselor, Edwin Meese III, stated that the Reagan administration had no moral or legal commitment to abide by expired or unratified SALT agreements. When challenged by State Department and Arms Control Agency legal experts on this assertion, the White House issued a defense of Meese's position, calling it "entirely accurate." Subsequently, Secretary of State George Shultz expressed reservations about extending SALT II constraints after their expiration in 1985.[27]

Several military initiatives of the Reagan administration telegraphed this ambivalence toward the SALT agreements, since they could not be pursued within the confines of existing arms control agreements. The ill-conceived dense-pack deployment scheme for the MX would have required digging holes for new missiles, an activity prohibited by the SALT I Interim Agreement and the SALT II Treaty. Administration officials explained that the excavations would be allowed because they were for new "hardened capsules" rather than silos, and they would be completed after the expiration of SALT II in any event. Later, the president agreed to press ahead with a second new ICBM— the Midgetman—to complement the MX. Again, its deployment would begin after the terms of the SALT II agreement—which permitted only one new type of ICBM—were to expire. Then the president endorsed a "Star Wars" defense against nuclear attack, which could not be tested in space or deployed without violating the ABM Treaty. More conventional ABM research projects continued, which would also pose treaty compliance problems.

In contrast to U.S. military programs suggesting prospective compliance problems, Soviet activities were of immediate concern. Questions of Soviet compliance with the Geneva Protocol and the Biological Weapons Convention were generated by evidence that Soviet troops and Soviet-equipped Vietnamese forces used "yellow rain" in Afghanistan and in Southeast Asia. Some knowledgeable observers contend that yellow rain can be explained by natural causes—that it is the result of honey bee feces that have become infected with toxigenic fungi. However, this theory is inconsistent with eyewitness reports of chemical warfare, at least one physical sample that includes a synthetic industrial chemical, and other information gathered by diverse intelligence sources and methods. This evidence supports the theory that yellow rain is a chemical agent that is biologically produced. If so, then its use in Afghanistan, Laos, and Kampuchea is a reprehensible form of chemical warfare inconsistent with the Geneva Protocol, although allegations of Soviet and Vietnamese treaty violations are clouded by the fact that the victimized states are not parties to the treaty. (The USSR and Vietnam have ratified the Geneva Protocol with the reservation that its terms would be binding only for other signatories.) These legal distinctions seem far less important than the evidence suggesting chemical and biological weapons attacks and casualties, although evidence of such attacks has dried up since 1983.

Concerns over Soviet compliance with the Biological Weapons Convention (BWC) have also been raised by an accident at a suspected biological weapons facility in Sverdlovsk in 1979. This incident resulted in an outbreak of what appears to be pulmonary anthrax. The BWC bars development, production, and stockpiling of biological warfare agents in undefined quantities that have "no justification for prophylactic, protective or other peaceful purposes." The Kremlin has blamed infected meat for the events that transpired at Sverdlovsk, an explanation that does not seem plausible in light of available evidence.

Reports of Soviet chemical and toxic warfare activities magnified concerns over SALT compliance questions. Initially, the Reagan administration declined to endorse the long list of "violations and circumventions" prepared by bitter critics of the SALT I accords. As new compliance issues relating to the unratified SALT II agreement arose, pressures from conservative members of Congress mounted for a public accounting of Soviet transgressions. As was the case after the Interim Agreement was signed, the flight-testing of new Soviet ICBMs became a highly contentious issue, fueled this time by assurances from Carter administration officials that only one "new type" of ICBM would be allowed under SALT II. The high level of encryption associated with these missile flight tests was inconsistent with the SALT II provision barring these practices when they impede verification of treaty constraints. Of greater concern was the unexpected discovery of a new phased-array radar under construction in Siberia, confirmed in the summer of 1983.[28]

When SALT II questions arose, protracted debates took place within the Reagan administration over whether and how these questions should be discussed in the Standing Consultative Commission. Some reportedly argued against using the SCC channel, since to do so would sanctify the SALT II Treaty.[29] Initially, the acting chairman of the U.S. delegation at the SCC was instructed to raise concerns about encryption and missile force reconstitution with the Soviets but to refuse to become engaged in discussions on these subjects. Other diplomatic channels were also used to convey U.S. concerns.

Finally, the United States revised its concerns over new ICBM types in the spring 1983 session of the SCC; discussions concerning the new radar began in the fall round. Not surprisingly, these sessions concluded without resolution of the radar and "new types" issues; complex compliance problems have never been ironed out quickly in the SCC, where the process of consultation is no less time-consuming than in arms control negotiations. Both sides agreed to meet again in the spring 1984 round, when the Soviets would presumably respond to further questions raised by the U.S. side.

During the winter recess of the SCC, the Reagan administration published its report of Soviet noncompliance. Included in the administration's findings were citations of new Soviet ICBM types and the SS-16 deployments previously considered by SALT critics to be either unverifiable or within the permissive boundaries of the SALT II Treaty. Also included was a citation on underground nuclear weapon tests above the 150 kiloton limit provided by the Threshold Test Ban Treaty (TTBT). Working from the same evidentiary base, the Carter administration declined to assert such a violation, given the ambiguous nature of the evidence.

Administration officials defended the release of the president's January 23, 1984, report on Soviet noncompliance as mandated by a congressional requirement. Nothing in that reporting requirement, however, mandated the particular timing of the report's release nor findings of probable violations in ambiguous cases. All of the Reagan administration's concerns over SALT compliance related to problems of treaty definitions and concealment practices. In this sense, the issues in dispute have many antecedents. In previous cases, however, Presidents Nixon, Ford, and Carter were able to hammer out new agreed definitions and to curtail Soviet concealment practices at the SCC. The objective for these presidents was not necessarily to reestablish the status quo ante but to maintain the viability of the SALT I accords. In their view, and in the view of Pentagon officials at the time, they succeeded; no compensating U.S. military actions were deemed necessary to counter the Kremlin's crowding at the margins.

President Reagan's public report on Soviet noncompliance reflected a different approach to compliance diplomacy than that practiced by his predecessors—one no less important than the difference between "adequate" and "effective" verification. To begin with, the president and his advisers were extremely ambivalent about upholding arms control agreements negotiated by previous administrations. Reagan administration officials further believed that the Soviets gained advantage from their previous record of SALT "compliance" and that the status quo ante, or something close to it, should be the outcome of SCC deliberations. As a consequence, it followed that if solutions could not be reached that met these requirements, the president should go public quickly with findings on Soviet violations, even in ambiguous cases.

President Reagan partially endorsed this course of action. His report on Soviet noncompliance was released before diplomatic remedies were exhausted, but it was also handled without fanfare, and it was couched in conditional language. Nevertheless, the act of going public with presidential findings of violations and probable violations—and the predictable Soviet countercharges—made the prospects of ironing out these difficulties in private negotiations more remote. Public disclosures of this kind—particularly with exchanges of information on outstanding compliance issues incomplete—inevitably raised questions for the Kremlin about U.S. intentions and the utility of trying to revise presidential judgments.

When treaty signatories do not believe arms control agreements have a bright future, it should not be surprising that compliance problems mount and compliance diplomacy fails. With bilateral relations under considerable strain, current agreements are unraveling, as both sides define their treaty obligations in more permissive ways. For those strongly opposed to previous arms control agreements, this turn of events might be deemed a success, but most Americans and their elected officials will hardly judge the progressive decontrol of strategic armaments as a welcome development.

In this context, official reports citing compliance problems confirm the downturn in U.S.–Soviet relations but do nothing to secure treaty compliance or to improve mutual security. In an article written over two decades ago, Fred Iklé proposed "restorative measures" in response to compliance problems that were unwanted, unfavorable, and costly to the violator. Restorative measures could mean selective abrogation of parts of an agreement and additional penalties, as appropriate. The key to an effective policy of sanctions was to disabuse the Soviet Union of the notion that it could, in Iklé's words, "discourage, circumvent or absorb" our reaction.[30]

In the wake of the U.S. and Soviet reports of noncompliance, domestic critics of SALT were left with a political landscape that could not be readily altered to suit their restorative measures. As the Reagan administration stated along with its report, treaty abrogation was not contemplated, at least in the near term. Selective nonobservance of treaty provisions also appeared difficult to accomplish, unless subsequent Soviet activities provided the basis for far more conclusive judgments about noncompliance or injury to U.S. national security. Indeed, the president's report stipulated that the United States would continue "to carry out its own obligations and commitments under relevant agreements."[31]

Defense spending has already risen considerably since 1978. Further boosts in spending as a result of questionable Soviet violations of dubious military utility would be difficult to carry out over strong congressional opposition. Multilateral initiatives would be even more difficult to coordinate in response to findings of noncompliance by the Reagan administration. Economic sanctions against far more clearcut instances of Soviet misbehavior, such as the invasion of Afghanistan or the pressures placed on Poland, seemed more injurious to the West than to the Soviet Union. Political sanctions would be equally difficult to enforce, given the strong desire on the part of NATO countries to maintain lines of East–West communication in the face of deteriorating superpower relations.

Seen in this light, the Reagan administration's report on Soviet noncompliance, unaccompanied by a coherent strategy to deal with compliance issues, constrains U.S. options more than Soviet misbehavior. Until U.S.–Soviet relations improve, and until both nations reaffirm their commitments toward the SALT accords, little progress can be expected in ironing out existing disputes at the SCC or in handling new ones that are bound to arise. Allied concerns about the course of U.S.–Soviet relations will increase, as will their reluctance to become partisans in prospective disputes. Future arms control agreements are likely to be more difficult to arrive at and to defend for presidents to the left of Ronald Reagan.

For those who seek national security through unilateral actions, these concerns are overdrawn. From this perspective, success is measured by new military capabilities, not by future progress in arms control. However, arms control agreements continue to have broad popular support. Treaty abrogation or selective nonobservance of negotiated restraints will be a bitterly contested and politically painful step to take for any president.

In the wake of the Reagan administration's report on Soviet noncompliance, the domestic political dynamics of verification and compliance issues appear more intractable than ever. Advocates of arms control will face formidable obstacles in ironing out compliance issues, while skeptics will continue to contemplate the difficulties of extraction from negotiated restraints.

Notes

1. Abram Chayes, "An Inquiry into the Workings of Arms Control Agreements," *Harvard Law Review* 85(1972): 968.

2. Jerome B. Wiesner, "Inspection for Disarmament," in Louis B. Henkin, ed., *Arms Control: Issues for the Public* (Englewood Cliffs, N.J.: Prentice-Hall, 1961), p. 113.

3. These were concerns raised by Director of Defense Research and Engineering John Foster and Assistant Secretary of Defense G. Warren Nutter. See Alton Frye, *A Responsible Congress, The Politics of National Security* (New York: McGraw-Hill, 1975), p. 62.

4. "Nuclear Test Ban Treaty," Hearings before the Committee on Foreign Relations, U.S. Senate, 88th Cong., 1st sess., 1963, p. 4.

5. See Amrom H. Katz, "The Fabric of Verification: The Warp and the Woof," in William C. Potter, ed., *Verification and SALT: The Challenge of Strategic Deception* (Boulder, Colo.: Westview Press, 1980), pp. 193–221.

6. "Nuclear Test Ban Treaty" hearings, p. 274.

7. President Nixon's instructions appeared in "The SALT II Treaty," Hearings before the Committee on Foreign Relations, U.S. Senate, 96th Cong., 1st sess., 1979, part 2, p. 241.

8. "Strategic Arms Limitation Agreements," Hearings before the Committee on Foreign Relations, U.S. Senate, 92nd Cong., 2d sess., 1972, p. 64.

9. *Congressional Record*, August 2, 1972, p. 26691.

10. "SALT I Compliance and SALT II Verification," Selected Documents No. 7, U.S. Department of State, Bureau of Public Affairs, 1978, p. 12.

11. Eugene Rostow, Statement before the First Committee of the Thirty-sixth General Assembly of the United Nations, October 21, 1981.

12. *Washington Post*, January 6, 1983, p. A22.

13. Ronald Reagan, letter of transmittal to Congress, "U.S. Arms Control and Disarmament Agency: 1982 Annual Report," February 9, 1983.

14. Former ACDA director Rostow explained: "We do not believe that, under present circumstances, a comprehensive test ban could help to reduce the threat of nuclear weapons or to maintain the stability of the nuclear balance." Mimeographed statement to the Committee on Disarmament, Geneva, February 9, 1982, p. 16.

15. See joint statement of Air Force Secretary Verne Orr and Chief of Staff Charles Gabriel in "Defense Department Authorization and Oversight Hearings on

H.R. 2287, Department of Defense Authorization of Appropriations for Fiscal Year 1984," Hearings before the Committee on Armed Services, House of Representatives, 98th Cong., 1st sess., part 1, p. 1072.

16. UPI wire story, January 17, 1983.

17. "Report to the Congress, U.S. Policy on ASAT Arms Control" (mimeo), March 31, 1984, p. 4.

18. See draft "Convention on the Prohibition of Chemical Weapons," United States of America, April 18, 1984, Articles X and XI.

19. "Nuclear Test Ban Treaty," Hearings before the Committee on Foreign Relations, U.S. Senate, 88th Cong., 1st sess., 1963, pp. 241–242, 461; *Congressional Record*, September 13, 1963, pp. 17099–17100; September 19, 1963, pp. 17511–17515; September 20, 1963, pp. 17605–17606, 17638.

20. *Congressional Record*, September 19, 1963, p. 17456; September 20, 1963, pp. 17605–17606; and September 23, 1963, pp. 17733–17734.

21. "Military Implications of the Treaty on The Limitation of Anti-Ballistic Missile Systems and the Interim Agreement on Limitation of Strategic Offensive Arms," Hearing before the Committee on Armed Services, U.S. Senate, 92d Cong., 2d sess., 1972, pp. 207–208, 211.

22. R.W. Buchheim, "The U.S.-U.S.S.R. Standing Consultative Commission (SCC) and Its Work," Prepared remarks before an Arms Control Association press briefing, April 22, 1981, p. 7.

23. "Verification of SALT II Agreements," Special Report No. 56, U.S. Department of State, Bureau of Public Affairs, August 1979, p. 3.

24. "The SALT II Treaty," Hearings before the Committee on Foreign Relations, U.S. Senate, 96th Cong., 1st sess., 1979, part 1, p. 493.

25. Richard N. Perle, "What Is Adequate Verification?" in *SALT II and American Security* (Cambridge, Mass.: Institute for Foreign Policy Analysis, 1980), p. 58.

26. Richard Perle, "SALT II: Who Is Deceiving Whom?" in Robert L. Pfaltzgraff, Jr., Uri Ra'anan, and Warren Milberg, eds., *Intelligence Policy and National Security* (Hamden, Conn.: Archon Books, 1981), pp. 151, 154.

27. Presidential press conference, January 29, 1981; "Nuclear Arms Reduction Proposals," Hearings before the Committee on Foreign Relations, U.S. Senate, 97th Cong., 2d sess., 1982, p. 118; "Strategic Weapons Proposals," Hearings before the Committee on Foreign Relations, U.S. Senate, 97th Cong., 1st sess., 1981, part 1, p. 15; *Los Angeles Times*, May 21, 1981; *Washington Post*, March 30, 1984.

28. Testimony of the Honorable Richard Perle, Assistant Secretary of Defense (International Security Policy), before the Subcommittee on Defense Appropriations, Senate Appropriations Committee, March 28, 1984.

29. Michael R. Gordon, "Can Reagan Blow the Whistle on the Russians While Saying No on Salt II?" *National Journal*, May 7, 1983, pp. 953–957.

30. Fred Iklé, "After Detection—What?" *Foreign Affairs*, January, 1961, p. 208.

31. "The President's Report to The Congress on Soviet Noncompliance with Arms Control Agreements," The White House, Office of the Press Secretary, January 23, 1984.

9

The Politics of Verification

Mark M. Lowenthal
Joel S. Wit

T reaties are commonly thought of as the end product of a process, the end of a war, the codification of a relationship—in general, the conclusion of a negotiation. In the case of arms control agreements, however, the actual signing and enactment of treaties are largely transition points in the negotiations. Unlike many other treaties, arms control agreements require constant supervision regarding compliance—called *monitoring*—about which policy assessments, judgments, and decisions are made, called *verification*.

Verification, which has become a shorthand expression both for alleged instances of Soviet noncompliance and for U.S. reactions or inaction, has now taken on a political life and importance of its own, one that threatens to overwhelm other aspects if not the whole of arms control. Verification has become a hotly contested political issue, played out both within and between the executive and legislative branches of the U.S. government, although not necessarily in such a way as to clarify U.S. policy decisions or requirements. Indeed, one could argue that the current controversies over Soviet compliance and the significance for the future of arms control has served to confuse U.S. policy goals in verification even further. As we will argue here, a vagueness in the U.S. government regarding the likely expectations and issues involved in arms control verification means that attempts to better define these questions would come only under the extreme pressure of events. Obviously, this would not be the best time to resolve these issues.

The still vague requirements levied on verification have become a very fine-grained but indeterminate filter through which all arms control agreements —current and future—must pass. Although originally intended as a means of deterring or catching violations and as a way of building public support for arms control, the politics of verification are elevating this single component of arms control into virtual opposition to the broader goal. As it is debated today at both ends of the arms control–verification spectrum of opinion, an either/or

The views expressed in this chapter are those of the authors, not of any other agency or group. This chapter is adapted with permission of the MIT Press from an earlier version which appeared in the *Washington Quarterly*, Summer 1984.

equation has arisen: there is a choice between arms control agreements or necessarily stringent verification, but we cannot have both.

This juxtaposition is widely cited. Opposing factions can be found in the arms control community in the executive, and they are not confined by agency or administration. In Congress, a majority probably exists in favor of arms control as a general goal at any time and in favor of many specific proposals or agreements. Nonetheless, there are many members of both houses who have doubts not only about Soviet behavior and compliance but also about the record of successive administrations in responding to questionable activities or events. Witness the 1983 passage in the Senate, by 93–0, of an amendment requiring the administration to submit a report on Soviet compliance with existing agreements. A similar requirement was enacted into law by both houses in 1983 as part of the ACDA authorization. This pattern is replicated among the public at large. Public opinion polls indicate that an extremely high percentage of those questioned favor some kind of comprehensive arms control measure, such as the nuclear freeze; at the same time, however, an equally high percentage anticipate that the Soviets will cheat.

Unease about verification has grown in disproportionate measure to equally important arms control issues. Although the importance of verification is self-evident, it actually threatens to overshadow other major questions that should be posed regarding effects of agreements on force structure, constraints on systems we desire or those we wish to block, and the effect of agreements in channeling competition into new technologies. As the Reagan administration has learned, arms control is a policy that each administration must be seen to be pursuing actively. Given this fact of American political life, too much concentration on verification could well weaken the fullness of the national debate required before any agreement is accepted.

The Historical Context

In tracing the evolution and politicization of verification, it is important to go back before the advent of nuclear weapons to appreciate certain preconceptions and perceptions of the early nuclear age. The outbreak of World War II was seen, in part, as the failure of an entire regime of interwar treaties and agreements, among them such arms control agreements as the Washington Naval Treaty and the Anglo-German Naval Agreement. Indeed, both of these exhibited the flaw of any arms control agreement—either one party intends to violate the treaty, or a party's perceived national interests change, undercutting the reasons for complying. A notable omission in these agreements was any verification provisions, although the nature of the weapons involved minimized the immediate threat of covert noncompliance.

The perceived shortcomings of the pre–World War II arms control agreements appeared magnified in the nuclear age. First, few U.S. policymakers doubted the inimical intent of their adversary and potential partner in arms control, the Soviet Union—a state that, according to one high-ranking U.S. official, would not hesitate to violate any accord or pursue any course of action which it feels serves the Communist cause. Second, the weapons at issue were capable of inflicting devastating damage, even in relatively small numbers. Thus, based on "lessons" learned from earlier agreements, perceptions of the adversary and potential partner, and the nature of the weapons, verification of compliance was seen as a sine qua non of any arms control agreement.

Early U.S. proposals reflected this philosophy. In the Baruch Plan of 1946, the United States offered to relinquish its nuclear monopoly to an international control authority, provided that the organization was able to conduct unimpeded inspections and to enforce sanctions. President Eisenhower's "open skies" proposal of 1955 was just that—a proposal to allow the United States and the USSR to inspect one another's military establishments by air. The Comprehensive Test Ban Treaty negotiations, conducted during the late 1950s and early 1960s, included elaborate U.S. proposals for on-site monitoring of any agreement.

These proposals and others of the same period evidenced one of the ironies of the arms race. The very fear and distrust that prompted efforts to isolate and control these weapons also dictated means of verification that were unlikely to be acceptable. At a certain level, the problem was technological. Individuals on site or in planes overhead were the only means available for monitoring, and both seemed too intrusive. The advent of artificial satellites offered two advantages. The satellites were too remote to be seen as directly intrusive, but their surveillance could not be prevented or tampered with. The fact that, in 1957, the Soviets launched the first satellite to transgress national boundaries in space undercut whatever objections they might raise to others doing the same. Khrushchev admitted as much at the 1960 Paris summit meeting, when he allowed that any nation that wanted to photograph the Soviet Union by satellite was completely free to do so. If verification had been a stumbling block, breakthroughs in technology might have facilitated agreements. But this meant that the technology of monitoring could also shape, if not dictate, the scope of agreements.

Although it did not result from advances in monitoring technology, the first major postwar nuclear agreement, the 1963 Limited Test Ban Treaty (LTBT), was a harbinger of things to come. The agreement was made possible largely by earlier technological developments that were more modest. Beginning in 1947, the United States had deployed a network of ground detection stations and radioactive debris-collecting aircraft. The main purpose of this network—called the Atomic Energy Detection System (AEDS)—was to monitor and gather intelligence on Soviet nuclear testing. The existence of this readily available, effective, comparatively nonintrusive system made the LTBT relatively easy to consummate. Indeed, in terms of arms control and verification, the LTBT was an exemplary agreement; it was simple, dealing directly with the question at issue, and it was easily monitored and verified. But it was also a relatively minor agreement in terms of the arms race itself. To control the actual weapons, new surveillance technologies were necessary.

By the late 1960s, further advances in monitoring technology, mostly in the form of satellites, combined with the efforts to place U.S.-Soviet relations on a more even keel allowed the United States to pursue strategic arms control. The ABM Treaty and the SALT I Interim Agreement, largely shaped by surveillance capabilities, set a number of important precedents for verification. First, unlike the 1963 LTBT, these agreements were weapon-specific. Second, unlike the test ban, SALT I was a complex package, recognizing asymmetries in the U.S. and Soviet strategic forces and attempting to create a sense of parity by accepting these asymmetries. Third, both agreements recognized the role of national technical means (NTM) for monitoring; although this was generally assumed to mean space-based sensors, NTM was not precisely defined. Fourth, although the agreements recognized the principle of noninterference with NTM, this principle also was not precisely defined. Finally, the agreements created an ongoing forum for resolving compliance issues—the Standing Consultative Commission (SCC).

In retrospect, however, it is clear that the Nixon administration oversold the ABM Treaty and SALT I and that the Congress and the public all too willingly bought them. Despite the aforementioned achievements, legitimate and important questions about verification either were not raised (with the notable exception of efforts by Senator Henry Jackson) or were answered glibly and pursued no further. The use of unilateral statements, their standing within the treaty and agreement, and even the hasty nature of the final negotiations were issues that should have been addressed more pointedly. The net effect of this somewhat cursory examination was to underplay the potential for post-agreement verification issues to arise, thus raising the expectations of Congress and the public for a postsignatory regime like any other. This, in turn, magnified the political damage wreaked by the verification issue once it did surface.

Again, hindsight suggests that Congress and the public could have been better prepared. This assumes, however, that U.S. negotiators knew what sort of verification issues would arise, when in fact this was not necessarily the case. The creation of the SCC indicated an expectation of some problems, but these were more on the level of bookkeeping—schedule delays and similar discrepancies that were likely to occur given uncertainties regarding the nature and definition of some of the provisions. Although some policymakers anticipated the more disturbing questions regarding Soviet behavior, they did not foresee the effect these questions would have on arms control as a whole, nor did they express their qualms. If they had, it is doubtful that the agreements would have been approved by Congress. One may also argue that differences in the utility of NTM for compliance tasks rather than for strategic intelligence gathering were not fully appreciated. Although practitioners of both monitoring and verification stress that NTM are used not to find violations but to keep track of Soviet actions across a wide spectrum, it would be naive to argue that the two tasks are wholly identical. The very existence of an arms control treaty raises the political stakes considerably, adding stress to both NTM and the arms control intelligence evaluation process. Thus, a lack of past experience in this area, combined with executive and congressional eagerness for the agreements and new stresses on NTM, led to a minimization of the verification issue, allowing initial approval of the two agreements but aggravating the effect of later noncompliance issues.

Questions about Soviet compliance began surfacing publicly in the spring of 1975. According to a 1978 Department of State report to Congress, the United States raised eight different issues in the SCC, six of which were resolved satisfactorily. In three instances—testing an SA-5 surface-to-air missile (SAM) radar in an ABM mode, covering ICBM launchers under conversion, and exceeding the SALT I limits because of insufficient speed in dismantling old ICBMs—the Soviet activity ceased after the United States raised the issue. In one case—the question of whether new installations near existing launch facilities were new launchers or launch control centers— subsequent intelligence led the United States to conclude that they were the latter and to close discussions. In another instance—involving the dismantling of excess ICBM launchers—Washington noted the inadequacy of Soviet reporting and notification procedures. In two instances—the conversion of single-warhead SS-11 ICBMs to MIRVed SS-19s and the installation of ABM radar at the Kamchatka ICBM test site—the issues went unresolved, at least to U.S. satisfaction, because of ambiguities in the agreements themselves and differences in the negotiating record that were overlooked at the time, such as the Soviet refusal to define heavy ICBMs and thus limit their impending SS-19s.

Given the types of issues that were raised, it became increasingly clear that the SCC would have greater responsibilities in the future. Only two of the foregoing instances—the ICBM dismantlement and the excess ABM launchers —fell into the bookkeeping category. The rest represented more complex issues that were not so easily resolved, although most were resolved to U.S. satisfaction. Indeed, it is arguable that almost all of these issues did not directly affect the strategic balance. The one exception may have been the conversion of SS-11s to SS-19s, which was one of the factors exacerbating the Minuteman vulnerability problem in the late 1970s. In all fairness, however, even these conversions were not clear violations. Rather, they were the most visible manifestation of what was going to be standard Soviet operating procedure—namely, to abide by agreements while exploiting their ambiguities. Nevertheless, many found the Soviet behavior disillusioning, which contributed to the political significance of compliance issues.

Prior to the ABM Treaty/SALT I experience, arms control was generally seen as a laudable goal, though considerable skepticism was voiced regarding its practicality. The verification experience now gave critics a solid issue. Melvin Laird, who had defended the agreements as secretary of defense in 1972, wrote in 1975 that they were a "calculated risk" gone bad.[1] Henry Kissinger, whose views on verification had been tortuous at best, later accused the Soviets of "sharp practice" and admitted that the unilateral statements were unwise. The bloom was off the arms control rose, and verification was the major cause of the blight.

These issues were technical in nature, though it is also worth noting one bureaucratic issue that heightened unease over verification. In hearings held in 1975, the House Intelligence Committee examined Kissinger's role as both chief negotiator and controller of the verification process. As expressed by a number of former Nixon administration officials, the negotiator had an obvious and inherent interest in proving the success of his agreements, which clouded his objectivity. Although the solution in this instance was obvious and bureaucratic, the raising of this issue highlighted the distrust now endemic to arms control and largely expressed through verification issues.

In addition to the ABM Treaty/SALT I experience, the other major nuclear agreement of the Nixon-Ford years, the 1974 Threshold Test Ban Treaty (TTBT), also proved to be a verification hot potato. Banning all weapons tests over 150 kilotons, the treaty's threshold was intended to allow continued testing at lower levels; it had little relationship to monitoring capabilities. U.S. intelligence could detect explosions in the 150 kiloton range and much lower, but estimates of exact yields were subject to wide discrepancies, which was hardly desirable from a political standpoint for the verification of an arms control agreement. The treaty did allow for cooperative measures to narrow these discrepancies. It also resorted to a rather unique formulation—a "mistake" clause that allowed "one or two slight unintended breaches per year." Although it was perhaps necessary, given the inexactitudes of testing and monitoring, the clause proved to be political dynamite. As a result, one ACDA official who worked on the agreement sardonically labeled it "the mistake's mistake."

Verification problems became evident as the TTBT went to the Senate for approval in the summer of 1976. High-yield Soviet tests triggered an avalanche of press reports that the USSR was violating the pending treaty. The Ford administration, in the throes of a presidential campaign, made matters worse by announcing the tests officially nearly a month after the first one occurred, in contrast to the previous policy of immediate announcements. In addition, it was disclosed that yields would no longer be announced, again in contrast to previous policy. Finally, the administration was forced to admit publicly to significant monitoring uncertainties—President Ford himself stating that the blasts could be between 100 and 300 kilotons. Granted, the treaty's cooperative measures had not been in force, but coming on the heels of the SALT/ABM verification debate, the TTBT experience could not help but further aggravate the political situation for verification and arms control.

The heightened concern regarding verification spilled over almost immediately into the Carter administration. The debate once again centered on government organization for monitoring arms control agreements. President Carter's controversial choice as chief SALT negotiator and director of the ACDA, Paul C. Warnke, disbanded his agency's Verification and Analysis Bureau, which contained some of the most ardent critics of Soviet compliance behavior. Warnke argued that having a central bureau was less useful than parceling out these analysts to the specific subject areas. His critics in Congress and the press, most of whom opposed Warnke's nomination, charged that he hoped to weaken the faction at ACDA that favored stringent verification. Central to their argument was the perceived bifurcation noted earlier—that verification and arms control were somehow incompatible.

In 1979, the completion of the SALT II agreement set the stage for a major debate over arms control and verification. Regardless of the actual content of the agreement, SALT II was bound to face a more probing inquiry than its predecessors. In part, this was one of the central lessons of the SALT experience; in part, it reflected the growing polarity of verification and arms control. Moreover, in attempting to move into qualitative constraints on weapons, such as MIRVed systems and modernization limitations, the agreement moved beyond the ability of national technical means alone to monitor compliance. Verification now required a number of aids—such as counting rules, type rules, and functionally related observable differences (FROD)—to ensure its effectiveness. Thus, at the same time verification was becoming an increasingly controversial political issue, the technical requirements were also becoming more demanding.

As was the case with so many issues in the Carter administration, SALT II and its verification regime became hostage to international events. The loss of two key U.S. intelligence installations in Iran after the fall of the Shah undercut the U.S. ability to monitor treaty clauses dealing with ICBM modernization. Moreover, the administration handled the issues poorly. In January 1979, President Carter attempted to minimize the effects of the loss. Yet, in April, Director of Central Intelligence Stansfield Turner stated in secret testimony that the lost capabilities could not be replaced until 1984, one year before the agreement expired. Secretary of Defense Harold Brown issued an immediate clarification, stating that a substantial portion of the capabilities needed to monitor SALT could be recovered in a year. However, coinciding with the completion of the negotiations, the statements of Brown and Carter seemed self-serving. The Senate Intelligence Committee, in reviewing the president's release of a CIA report on Soviet oil production in 1977, had already chided him for making political uses of intelligence.

The actual debate over SALT II proved inconclusive, eventually ending with the Soviet invasion of Afghanistan. However, a number of Senate documents revealed a different attitude toward verification from that evidenced in the early 1970s. The Senate Intelligence Committee warned that the Soviet Union would push for any advantages or use any ambiguities in the treaty; that adequate U.S. monitoring systems and analytic capabilities would be required; and that, in certain instances, intelligence on Soviet activities had been kept from pertinent executive officials. The Senate Foreign Relations Committee noted the Soviet practice of probing ambiguities, agreed on the need for redundant monitoring capabilities, and concluded that SALT II was verifiable in that any Soviet cheating could be detected in time to prevent the USSR from gaining a significant military advantage. Also, a number of amendments dealing with verification were introduced in the relevant committees; eight concentrated on nonbinding efforts to ban interference with national technical means, and five involved imposing congressional oversight on the verification process, particularly the SCC. These amendments represented a broad, bipartisan spectrum of senators—Birch Bayh (D-Ind.), John Chafee (R-R.I.), David Durenburger (R-Minn.), John Glenn (D-Ohio), Walter D. Huddleston (D-Ky.), and Patrick Leahy (D-Vt.)—reflecting the degree of skepticism of the issue.

Looking closely at the Senate reports and the proposed amendments to SALT II, one observes an interesting division. Although concerns over the verification of the treaty itself appear to have been allayed, the issue of the post-ratification compliance process remained. This division suggests that critics were satisfied with the technical requirements for verification as they related specifically to SALT II, an area for which the executive branch provided a wealth of information. To skeptics, however, such information seemed self-serving. Having negotiated the treaty, an administration had to be able to claim that it could be adequately or effectively verified. But uncertainty remained over what is essentially an international process in which the incumbent administration was seen as a subjective political actor.

In sum, the arms control experience of the 1970s had led to a sense of wariness, at best, and had instilled deep doubts in many. Expectations of future Soviet behavior were more realistic, but these doubts meant that the postsignatory phase of treaties would remain politically charged and difficult to isolate from the wider tenor of U.S.–Soviet relations. Remarks from the Senate Foreign Relations Committee report regarding the ability to catch violations before they became militarily significant were cold comfort to those who were already dubious of Soviet motives, U.S. capabilities, and U.S. responses. The debate over SALT II and its verification neither defused the verification issue nor resolved the doubts. Indeed, given the combined effects of Iran, the 1980 election, and the odd limbo into which the treaty slipped, verification probably became even more politicized.

With the election of the Reagan administration, conservative Republicans and Democrats who had criticized the verification provisions of the 1970s arms control agreements now held the most important foreign policy positions in the new government. Eugene Rostow, in his first public statements as director of the ACDA, emphasized that the administration was troubled by very grave questions concerning Soviet compliance behavior. More important, the administration's approach to arms control and verification seemed to foreshadow a return to the postwar era, when verification was the paramount arms control issue. Indeed, its initial preference seemed to be to delay arms control negotiations—to a large degree because of efforts to find new approaches for the strategic arms negotiations—while holding talks with the Soviets on past, present, and future verification issues.

Domestic political pressure for progress in arms control and the administration's success in gaining congressional support for its strategic modernization program helped move the Reagan administration to advance new arms control proposals. At the same time, however, the administration created new verification problems by its policy toward the "fatally flawed" SALT II Treaty. Having foresworn ratification, the president offered a policy of restraint: if the Soviets would observe the terms of the SALT I and SALT II accords, the United States would do the same. Although it seemed preferable to discarding these agreements, the United States was now pledged to two accords—one expired and one never enacted—with U.S. compliance tied to that of the Soviets. Tactically, this created at least three problems. First, the legal status of the agreements, and thus of restraint on the Soviets and the United States, was questionable. Second, given past Soviet exploitation of ambiguities without clearly violating the agreements, there was little hope that future Soviet activity would be so clearcut as to make possible U.S. initiatives in response. Finally, this policy underestimated the compliance controls on U.S. policy. Barring some outright and obvious Soviet violation, there was, and is, little that any administration could do beyond the bounds of the agreements. New programs or weapons would require additional funding, and it is unlikely that Congress would support such moves, knowing that they meant the demise of the only strategic arms control available.

The alternative to this unbalanced compliance dilemma would be to air publicly the entire catalog of Soviet behavior in order to build a consensus for the United States taking positive initiatives. In response to Soviet tests of two new ICBMs, seemingly in violation of SALT II limits on missile modernization, President Reagan appeared to be inching toward doing just that in the spring of 1983. In a press conference on May 18, however, he retreated, arguing that although he believed the Soviets were cheating, better evidence was needed.

Nonetheless, verification issues continue to surface in public. The most recent allegations have concerned considerable Soviet encryption of test telemetry, the continued testing of two new IBCMs, and the construction of a radar that could contravene the limits on early-warning radars set by the 1972 ABM Treaty.

In 1983, Congress requested that the president report to it on Soviet compliance with arms control agreements. After a long interagency effort, this report was issued on January 21, 1984. It covered Soviet compliance with five agreements—those customarily referred to as the Chemical and Biological Weapons (CBW) Agreements (1925 and 1975), the 1975 Helsinki Final Act, the ABM Treaty, SALT II, and the TTBT. The report found Soviet violations in the area of CBW and in the notification of military exercises as called for by the Helsinki Final Act—both areas in which the United States had already made identical public charges. A violation was also charged in the case of Soviet encryption practices. In other cases—the ABM radar, limits on new ICBMs, SS-16 deployment—probable violations were found. In the case of the TTBT, no definitive conclusion was reached. It is questionable how far the compliance report advanced or resolved the verification debate. Although the report made it clear that Soviet practices were disturbing and even potentially threatening to the arms control process, it also underscored the uncertainties involved. Some of the uncertain or "probable" cases remained disturbing, but the report probably did little to affect perceptions at either end of the verification political spectrum, and it was too complex to be easily assimilated by the public at large.

Coupled with the increased politicization of the verification issue are indications that the relationship between verification and arms control will again resemble that of the immediate postwar era, when verifiable compliance was deemed essential. However, the technological revolution that made such agreements possible during the past two decades may now have run its course—as much a victim of an increasingly comprehensive arms control process as of new weapons systems, such as mobile ICBMs and cruise missiles, that are harder to monitor. Moreover, pessimistic assessments of Soviet intentions and practices have made verification increasingly important, encouraging policymakers to seek supplemental, perhaps unacceptable, on-site measures. As a result, the whole arms control process may grind to a halt. A case in point is the intermediate nuclear component of the arms control negotiations, where, beyond the matter of even agreeing on weapons totals, a long, arduous, perhaps intractable process of negotiating stringent verification measures lies ahead. If there is to be a solution—and if verification is to be brought to proper context in the arms control debate—then, at the very least, the basic lines taken in the debate thus far will have to be changed.

The Politics of Verification

Two different criteria are involved in assessing allegations or instances of noncompliance. The first—military significance—refers to noncompliance that could give some sort of discernible advantage to the noncomplying power. It is a fairly narrow term, given the array of forces and weapons on both sides and the likelihood that any activity aimed at changing the military situation would be detected over time. The second criterion—political significance—is a much broader term; it refers to the intentions of the noncomplying power, regardless of the military significance of the violation. Although the military significance of any violation may be small, there remains a political significance. In fact, the smaller the military significance, the more troubling the political significance becomes. Violating a treaty for some military advantage may make sense, depending on the calculation of risks and benefits. Risking a treaty, or perhaps an entire regime of treaties, for a small military advantage sends a troubling message about the intentions of that party. In essence, then, all cases of noncompliance have political significance; some also have military significance. The amount of importance attached to these two factors is a function of political orientation.

The polarization engendered by this issue has resulted in two schools of thought, at either extreme, which we will call *strict constructionists* (of verification) and *loose constructionists.* The strict constructionists downplay military significance and stress political significance, although they may raise fears about an impending strategic imbalance. Nevertheless, they are realistic enough to know that, barring some hitherto unpredicted weapon or hidden "breakout" program (that is, a weapons program capable of clandestine development and then such rapid expansion that it would unilaterally upset the strategic balance), any violation of military significance will be detected long before it reaches fruition. Rather, they find probes of ambiguities or taking advantage of loopholes disturbing, regardless of their military significance. Their concern is that the Soviets are using the agreements to pursue, incrementally and cumulatively, certain programs that will further their own ends, while a self-constrained United States is held to strict compliance. Regardless of the net military effect, goes the argument, the Soviets are deriving a unilateral advantage that should cause us to rethink our arms control policy.

Underlying this approach is the basic assumption that Soviet intentions toward the United States are obviously inimical. Do we want to be bound to treaties with the USSR, given their current behavior? Strict constructionists are prone to make public the case that the Soviets are "cheating" and to argue for more and better verification, even if it delays reaching agreements. Here, unfortunately, the strict constructionists face an interesting dilemma. If we had perfect verification, how would we know? Would the absence of noncompliance mean that nothing was happening or that we were not seeing it?

The most visible strict constructionists can be found in the U.S. Senate. Following some recent Soviet missile tests, which were viewed by these senators as clear violations of SALT II, one spokesman urged the president to publicize Soviet arms control violations. This included not only the recent tests but also a long list of Soviet "violations" of the SALT I, ABM, and SALT II accords, as well as the TTBT. Recalling that the arms control efforts of the

1930s actually contributed to the outbreak of World War II, one senator asserted that U.S. compliance with arms control treaties, while the Soviets cheat, can be dangerous to world peace and U.S. national security. The solution to this problem would not involve abandoning arms control, although many in this group are opponents of the SALT agreements for reasons other than verification. Enforcement of compliance would be "of the highest priority."

The second school, the loose constructionists, downplays political significance and stresses military significance. Loose constructionists agree that Soviet behavior is disturbing and argue that they are not blind to Soviet intentions. Some in this group argue that Soviet behavior in arms control reveals nothing new. Loose constructionists argue that arms control is about weapons and, therefore, that the military significance must be paramount. This group maintains that, given our ability to detect violations before they become militarily threatening, and given that no violations of such significance have yet occurred, it is important to take some risks. Progress in arms control is more important than a totally clean slate of Soviet behavior. Although their actions may be disturbing, the Soviets have as much to lose as we do; therefore, they will not take actions that ultimately risk the agreements. The loose constructionists are willing to take larger verification risks for the sake of achieving arms control agreements. However, they have been accused of excusing Soviet behavior as they dismiss each individual case while avoiding looking at the total picture. Finally, loose constructionists are less inclined to go public with alleged Soviet violations, fearing the effect of such a policy on the arms control process.

This philosophy closely resembles official U.S. policy on verification from 1969 to 1980. Each successive administration pledged to seek "adequate verification"—that is, to ensure that "the United States will be able to detect any Soviet violations before they could affect the strategic balance."[2] This criterion closely resembles the "threshold of evasion" philosophy behind the 1963 test ban. As then director of defense research and engineering Dr. Harold Brown stated, "a comparison of the detectability of various kinds of tests ...leads to the conclusions that attempted violation carries high risks of detection wherever there is significant motivation for violation."[3]

These two positions are admittedly extremes, but what is striking about the current politics of verification is the virtual absence of any middle ground. If one were to construct a "centrist" position, it would take the following lines: By its very nature, and by the nature of the weapons systems and Soviet society, verification will always be imperfect. There will always be compliance issues; however, even if we accept the inevitability of such issues and acknowledge likely Soviet behavior, it would be foolhardy simply to dismiss these problems. At every opportunity, regardless of the military significance, the United States should make it clear to the Soviets that even behavior that is ambiguous but technically in compliance runs the political risk of undermining the arms control consensus in the United States and disrupting the entire process. It should be made clear to the Soviets that although a sizable consensus exists in the United States in favor of arms control, this is not a static situation, and other outcomes are also possible, especially if the public feels that our good faith has been exploited. Finally, we must take a hard look at aggregate Soviet behavior. Although each of the individual instances may be acceptable on both the military and political level, there is a threshold of tolerance that should be defined.

The need to foster a more informed public debate on the issue of verification could become more pressing in the near future. The Soviets have continued their practice of exploiting what seem to be ambiguities in existing arms control agreements. The actual military significance of the most recent compliance issues is open to debate, at the very least, but they are potentially more troubling than many of the past issues. For example, the recent discovery of a new large radar under construction in the south central region of the Soviet Union but oriented toward the northeast, seemingly a violation of the ABM Treaty, could be a first step in deploying a ballistic missile defense system around crucial ICBM fields. The military significance of the SS-X-25 may not be so great, but the idea of the Soviets deploying a new ICBM, which may violate the terms of the SALT II agreement, is likely to have greater importance in the minds of many than having a few excess ICBM launchers. This, combined with a fragile arms control regime consisting of informal agreements and the continuing high tension in U.S.–Soviet relations, makes it all the more important that any public debate on verification be well reasoned and well informed. Few people genuinely involved in arms control would want to see the entire regime unravel over an ambiguous but potentially important issue. Conversely, if the weight of evidence became so overwhelming as to warrant action, a well-informed public would provide a solid base of support for any such policy.

Depoliticizing Verification

A national consensus on verification—in terms of both internal policy goals and external tolerance limits—would also make it possible for a U.S. administration to press compliance issues with the Soviet Union with a firm sense of purpose and public support and without fearing that pressure for progress in arms control might overwhelm legitimate concerns about Soviet activities. The executive branch, Congress, and the public all have roles to play in this process.

A first step for the executive branch would be to negotiate a change in the regulations of the Standing Consultative Commission that keep deliberations totally private. Undertaken at Soviet insistence, this requirement undercuts any representations made by the United States regarding Soviet behavior. Although public statements need not go into great detail, and likely would not, they would serve to assure Congress and the public that the United States is defending its interests. This may also offer a means of affecting Soviet behavior, although it is more likely to engender further Soviet accusations regarding alleged U.S. violations. In this instance, the United States would have an advantage, given the generally more open nature of our defense programs.

It is worth noting, however, that the Soviets may be justified in lodging complaints in some cases. For example, in the mid-1970s, the Soviets complained about the U.S. use of shelters over Minuteman silos during construction and modernization to protect workers from harsh weather conditions, a practice the United States had complained about when the Soviets did it. According to the Soviets, this practice violated Article V of SALT I, which dealt with measures of deliberate concealment. By early 1977, in response to Soviet protests, the United States modified the size of the shelters by 50 percent, apparently resolving the problem. The open airing of such incidents, not necessarily in great detail, could have a sobering, beneficial effect on the verification debate, showing that instances of noncompliance are not always one-sided and involve more than "good guys" and "bad guys." It has been the Soviets' practice in the SCC to counter any noncompliance issues raised by the United States with issues of their own, largely for the sake of balance. Still, the Soviets would undoubtedly object to any revisions allowing for public reporting of SCC proceedings. However, this may be the price they have to pay for dealing with a democracy.

Future administrations would also be well advised to recognize that there remains sufficient support for arms control in this nation to make an arms control policy mandatory. The nature of the proposals might vary widely, but it is unlikely that any administration will be able to avoid the process of engaging in arms control negotiations with the Soviets, barring some sudden negative change in relations. This has become a fact of political life in the United States, and using verification as an excuse for avoidance is not going to change it.

The tendency in strategic arms control has been toward increasingly comprehensive and thus complex agreements. It may be advisable to reverse this trend and seek smaller, simpler agreements that are well matched to available monitoring capacities, such as the Limited Test Ban Treaty. These should result in fewer verification problems. But comprehensive proposals, such as SALT II or the nuclear freeze, are more likely to encounter verification problems and thus run the risk of eventually undermining support for arms control. This is not a simple undertaking, and it may not be possible, given the complexity of the weapons involved and their interrelationship in the strategic triad or (in the case of intermediate and strategic weapons) in the theoretical ladder of escalation. We must also recognize that even simpler treaties, such as the ABM Treaty, can run into problems, especially as weapons technology continues to advance. But there is little support at present for such an approach to future arguments. The one such proposal made in November 1982, President Reagan's "zero-option" for INF talks, has met with derision. Nonetheless, simpler may be better in terms of arms contrtol and verification.

Finally, when agreements are achieved, the tendency to oversell them must be resisted. This tendency is understandable, given the political value of any agreement and the sense of accomplishment after so many years of arduous negotiations. If possible, the presentation of agreements to Congress and the public should be forthright in pointing out possible verification problems, although this would have to be done carefully to avoid indicating to the Soviets where U.S. monitoring is weak. The tendency to downplay verification difficulties only exacerbates the problems when they inevitably arise, making responsible officials look like knaves or fools.

As indicated by the SALT II debate, one of the major concerns of Congress is the lack of information on SCC deliberations and on other compliance issues and verification in general. Although public reporting is a first step in the right direction, another important step would be for the executive branch to provide Congress with more detailed classified reports. These reports could be given to Congress as a whole or to the foreign relations, armed services, and intelligence committees. The provision of such information, however, would limit the freedom of members of Congress to raise allegations about Soviet behavior. This would not necessarily mean that Congress would be coopted. Congress now receives a great deal of information concerning proposed intelligence operations, but this has not resulted in a blind acceptance of such operations, as House action on Nicaragua indicates. Increasing available information would help foster a greater appreciation of the ambiguity of most cases of noncompliance, particularly regarding nuclear arms control agreements. To date, few if any cases have been simple enough to allow a firm answer one way or the other. Aside from making this ambiguity clear, greater sharing of information would also force the strict constructionists to temper their rhetoric and the loose constructionists to reevaluate their assumptions.

Underlying both of these recommendations is the assumption that the key to creating a well-informed Congress and public and to attaining the middle ground is to provide more information, particularly on the compliance process. The lack of information to date has only led to hysteria or indifference. Also, there have been few efforts to explain both the nature of verification issues and their ambiguity, as well as the nonjudicial nature of the SCC. The popular conception of the verification process appears to be something like a Perry Mason case: the Soviets are in the dock, the United States presents the damning evidence, and the judge declares the Soviets guilty. Nothing could be further from the truth. The SCC is a forum for continuing negotiations. The United States is very careful about the evidence it presents, always trying to preserve intelligence sources and methods so as to keep the Soviets uncertain about what we know and what we do not know and how the information was obtained. The United States has rarely made outright accusations of violations. Finally, there is no third party to whom to appeal or to pronounce sentence. There are only two parties: the United States and the Soviet Union.

Both strict constructionists and loose constructionists will be suspicious of any effort to achieve this middle ground, to depoliticize verification. That is the nature of a polarized situation; both poles will suspect those who are attempting to create this new consensus of belonging to the other camp. Both poles also have something to lose in creating this middle ground. Strict constructionists will have to give up their glib talk about violations and face the fact that some risks must be taken if arms control agreements are to be consummated. Loose constructionists will have to accept that even small or ambiguous noncompliance issues have some political effect that cannot be discounted and that arms control can be viable only if it survives in a highly political world.

Beyond the provision of more information, the depoliticization of verification may require a broader national debate in the United States on arms control. After decades of paying lip service to the general goal of arms control, the United States too hurriedly accepted agreements without recognizing likely problems or the nature of the Soviet Union. The continuing politicization of verification threatens to overwhelm the broader whys and wherefores of nuclear arms control. There is no denying that verification is an important issue in assessing any arms control proposal or agreement. But it is not necessarily the most important or even first among equals, except in an increasingly politicized atmosphere.

One way to depoliticize verification, thus bringing both this issue and the rest of arms control back into the proper perspective, is to ask ourselves publicly what we expect from arms control, how much risk we are willing to accept, and how much uncertainty we can tolerate. To date, these questions have tended to be answered only after agreements have been fashioned. Engaging in such a national debate now not only could bring the verification issue back into proper perspective but could also strengthen the U.S. position vis-à-vis the Soviets when dealing with these issues.

Notes

1. Melvin Laird, "Arms Control: The Russians Are Cheating," *Readers Digest*, December 1977, p. 97.
2. Cyrus Vance, Senate Foreign Relations Committee, *SALT II Hearings*, July 1979, p. 92.
3. Harold Brown, Senate Foreign Relations Committee, *Nuclear Test Ban Treaty Hearings*, August 1963, p. 539.

10
Technical Collection and Arms Control

Jeffrey Richelson

S ince 1963, the United States has entered into several major arms control agreements with the Soviet Union. These agreements have placed restrictions on nuclear testing, on the deployment of nuclear weapons in space and on the seabed, and on the size and characteristics of each nation's strategic forces. Some of these treaties have been ratified by the United States; in other cases, the United States and the USSR have each declared its intention of abiding by the unratified treaties so long as the other nation does.

A major concern with respect to all such arms control arrangements has been the ability of the United States to "adequately verify" Soviet compliance with the provisions of each treaty. The main, though not exclusive, means of verification is each nation's national technical means (NTM)—the array of reconnaissance satellites, strategic intelligence aircraft, ground stations for signals intelligence, space surveillance and nuclear monitoring, and ocean surface and subsurface intelligence collection systems.

This chapter explores the national technical means of the United States that are employed to collect intelligence relevant to U.S. participation in arms control agreements. I use the phrase "collect intelligence relevant to U.S. participation in arms control agreements" rather than "verify Soviet compliance with arms control agreements" to emphasize two points I will return to later. First, virtually all technical collection of military intelligence concerning the Soviet Union is relevant to U.S. willingness to enter into arms control agreements. This thesis, expanded upon in the concluding section, links U.S. ability to adequately evaluate the significance and desirability of treaty provisions that are intended to constrain Soviet strategic arms programs with the collection of intelligence on *all* aspects of strategic arms programs—whether they are covered by treaty or not. Further, intelligence on a multitude of nonstrategic programs may also prove relevant to the evaluation process. Second, verification is simultaneously too demanding a goal and not a sufficiently demanding goal. The correct question to ask with regard to technical collection capabilities is whether the intelligence produced is sufficient (when combined with other considerations) to make the cost-benefit calculus of entering into a particular arms control treaty positive. The other considerations include not just nontechnical collection capabilities but also the environment (domestic and international) in which Soviet strategic decisions are to be made and U.S. assumptions concerning the Soviet cost-benefit calculus.

For these reasons, I will examine the set of technical collection systems employed for the collection of military intelligence about the Soviet Union. While I will mention the utility of certain types of collection for monitoring of specific treaty provisions, such observations should not be interpreted as complete specifications of the utility of the systems with respect to arms control.

I will focus on five different categories of technical collection (photographic reconnaissance/imaging, signals intelligence, ocean surveillance, space surveillance and nuclear monitoring) relevant to the following treaties or agreements: the Limited Test Ban Treaty (1963), the Outer Space Treaty (1967), the Seabed Treaty (1971), the ABM Treaty (1972), the Threshold Test Ban Treaty (1974), the Peaceful Nuclear Explosions Treaty (1976), and the SALT II Treaty (1979). The technical collection systems to be examined are also relevant to the proposals for a nuclear freeze, a comprehensive test ban, and a treaty banning or limiting antisatellite (ASAT) weapons.

Subsequent to a review of the provisions of the treaties and the capabilities of the technical collection systems, I will discuss the limitations of those systems and the role of technical collection in arms control.

The Treaties

The Limited Test Ban Treaty (LTBT—formally the Treaty Banning Nuclear Weapons Tests in the Atmosphere, in Outer Space, and Under Water) was signed in Moscow on August 5, 1963, and entered into force on October 10, 1963. Although initial negotiations had focused on a comprehensive ban of all tests, the final agreement committed each party to the treaty not to carry out any nuclear explosions:

(a) in the atmosphere; beyond its limits, including outer space; or underwater, including territorial waters or high seas; or

(b) in any other environment if such explosions cause radioactive debris to be present outside the territorial limits of the state under whose jurisdiction or control such explosion is conducted.[1]

The Outer Space Treaty (formally, the Treaty on Principles Governing the Activities of States in the Exploration and Use of Outer Space, Including the Moon and Other Celestial Bodies) was signed at Washington, London, and Moscow on January 27, 1967, and ratified by the U.S. Senate on April 25, 1967. Among the many provisions of the treaty, Article IV states that parties to the treaty "undertake not to place in orbit around the Earth, any objects carrying nuclear weapons or any other kinds of weapons of mass destruction, install such weapons on celestial bodies or station such weapons in outer space in any other manner."[2]

Similarly, the Seabed Treaty (formally, the Treaty on the Prohibition of the Emplacement of Nuclear Weapons and Other Weapons of Mass Destruction on the Seabed and the Ocean Floor and in the Subsoil Thereof), signed on February 11, 1971, and entered into force May 18, 1972, provides that parties to the treaty not "emplant or emplace on the seabed and ocean floor and in the subsoil thereof" outside each nation's twelve-mile limit any nuclear weapons or launchers for such weapons.[3]

The Antiballistic Missile (ABM) Treaty (formally, the Treaty Between the United States of America and the Union of Soviet Socialist Republics on the Limitation of Anti-Ballistic Missile Systems) was signed in Moscow on May 26, 1972, and entered into force on October 3, 1972. The treaty requires each party to refrain from the deployment of an ABM system for the defense of the territory of its country and not to provide a base for such a defense.[4] Article II defined an ABM system as consisting of the following:

1. ABM interceptor missiles
2. ABM launchers
3. ABM radars (radars constructed and deployed for an ABM role or of a type tested in an ABM mode)

In addition to operational ABM components, the treaty restrictions apply to components under construction, undergoing testing, undergoing overhaul, repair, or conversion, or mothballed.[5]

Article III of the ABM Treaty permitted each nation to have one ABM system with a radius of 150 kilometers, centered on the nation's capital, with the restrictions that there be a maximum of 100 ABM launchers and 100 ABM interceptors at the launch sites and that there be no more than 6 ABM radar complexes, with the area of each complex being circular with diameters not greater than 3 kilometers.[6] A second provision of Article III allowed one ABM system with identical restrictions concerning launchers and interceptors around ICBM launch sites. This provision allowed two phased-array ABM radars comparable in potential to corresponding ABM radars operational or under construction and not more than eighteen ABM radars, each having a potential less than the potential of the smaller of the phased-array radars.[7]

Two further provisions of importance are contained in Articles V and VI. Article V specifies no development, testing, or deployment of ABM systems or components that are sea-based, air-based, space-based, or mobile land-based, and Article VI provides that "each party undertakes not to deploy in the future radars for early warning of strategic ballistic missile attack except at locations along the periphery of its national territory and oriented outward."[8] A protocol agreed to in 1974 reduced the permitted number of ABM sites to one—a Soviet site around Moscow and a U.S. site around the Grand Forks ICBM site.[9]

The Threshold Test Ban Treaty (TTBT—formally, the Treaty Between the United States of America and the Union of Soviet Socialist Republics on the Limitation of Underground Nuclear Weapons Tests) was signed on July 3, 1974. Although it was never ratified by the U.S. Senate, both the United States and the USSR are pledged to obey its provisions. The crucial provision of the treaty, contained in Article I, requires each party to "prohibit, prevent, and not to carry out" any underground nuclear weapons test with a yield of over 150 kilotons.[10]

As with the TTBT, the Peaceful Nuclear Explosions Treaty (PNET—formally, the Treaty Between the United States of America and the Union of Soviet Socialist Republics on Underground Nuclear Explosions for Peaceful Purposes) has not been ratified by either party since it was signed at Washington and Moscow on May 28, 1976. Both sides have pledged to honor its provision that prohibits all underground nuclear explosions for peaceful purposes that exceed 150 kilotons.[11]

Finally, the SALT II Treaty (formally, the Treaty Between the United States of America and the Union of Soviet Socialist Republics on the Limitation of Strategic Offensive Arms) was signed on June 18, 1979, but was never ratified by the U.S. Senate because of concern about verification capabilities and the Soviet invasion of Afghanistan.[12] As with the TTBT, however, each party has pledged to abide by the provisions of the treaty if the other side does.

Unlike the SALT I Agreement, the SALT II Treaty contains provisions limiting aggregate delivery vehicles, bombers, MIRVed ICBMs, and warheads per missile. Aggregate strategic offensive arms were to be limited to 2,250 by January 1, 1981, while MIRVed ballistic missile launchers were to be not greater than 820. In addition, the United States agreed not to deploy more than seven MIRVs per Minuteman III, not more than fourteen MIRVs per Poseidon C-3, and not more than seven MIRVs per Trident C-4. Likewise, the USSR was restricted to four warheads per SS-17, six per SS-19, ten per SS-18, and seven per SS-N-18. With respect to this restriction on warhead numbers, it was also agreed that "during the flight testing of any ICBM, SLBM or ASBM after May 1, 1979 the number of procedures for releasing or dispensing [warheads] may not exceed the maximum number of reentry vehicles established for missiles of corresponding types."[13]

Furthermore, the USSR agreed not to produce, test, or deploy ICBMs of the SS-16 type, and both parties agreed not to develop, test, or deploy systems for the rapid reload of ICBM launchers. Both parties also agreed that in the process of modernization, they would not increase the internal volume of an ICBM silo by more than 32 percent. In addition, both parties agreed that they would not test or deploy more than one new type of light ICBM.[14]

This overview of arms control agreements negotiated by the United States indicates the need for technical collection systems for photographing missile silos and for intercepting missile telemetry to ascertain warhead loadings, nuclear monitoring systems for detecting and evaluating possible tests in any environment, space surveillance systems for detecting potential weapons in space, and ocean surveillance systems and photo reconnaissance systems for determining the number of modern ballistic missile submarines.

Collection Systems

Imaging/Photographic Reconnaissance

In theory, imaging satellites can be employed to obtain visible light, infrared, or radar imagery of a variety of military related activities—many of which are constrained by arms control agreements.[15] Such satellites can be used to identify mobile and fixed ICBM launchers, SSBNs, and aircraft; to identify changes in the characteristics of such systems—in their length, diameter, and volume; and to detect activity at a test site or production facility.

Three treaties with provisions that can be directly monitored by imaging satellites are the LTBT, the ABM Treaty, and the SALT II Treaty. Thus, imaging satellites can detect activity associated with an aboveground nuclear test site and capture the effects of the test on film. Specific provisions of the ABM and SALT II treaties that can be monitored by imaging satellites involve the limitation of ABM system deployment area radius, the limitations on the number of ABM launchers and interceptor sites at a complex and on the numbers of ABM radars and the numbers of ABM launchers, the ban on the SS-16 missile, the ban on the rapid reload of ICBMs, the ban on conversion of light ICBM launchers to heavy ICBM launchers, and the dismantling of fractional orbital missiles near Tyuratam.

The ultimate utility of any imaging satellite is a function of several factors, the most prominent of which is *resolution*. Resolution may be defined as the minimum size that an object must be to be measurable and identifiable by photo analysts.[16] The smaller the resolution, the greater the detail that can be extracted from a photo. It should be noted that resolution is a product of several factors, including the optical or imaging system, atmospheric conditions, and orbital parameters.[17] The resolution requirements for various photographic interpretation tasks are given in table 10–1.

In addition to resolution, other factors that are considered significant in evaluating the utility of an imaging satellite include coverage speed, readout speed, analysis speed, reliability, and enhancement capability. Coverage speed is the area that can be surveyed in a given time; readout speed is the speed with which the information is processed into a form that is meaningful to photo

Table 10–1
Target Resolution Required for Interpretation Tasks

Target	Detection	General Identification	Precise Identification	Description	Technical Intelligence
Bridge	20 ft	15 ft	5 ft	3 ft	1 ft
Communications radar/radio	10 ft/10 ft	3 ft/5 ft	1 ft/1 ft	6 in/6 in	1.5 in/6 in
Supply dump	5 ft	2 ft	1 ft	1 in	1 in
Troop units (bivouac, road)	20 ft	7 ft	4 ft	1 ft	3 in
Airfield facilities	20 ft	15 ft	10 ft	1 ft	6 in
Rockets and artillery	3 ft	2 ft	6 in	2 in	.4 in
Aircraft	15 ft	5 ft	3 ft	6 in	1 in
Command and Control Headquarters	10 ft	5 ft	3 ft	6 in	1 in
Missile sites (SSM/SAM)	10 ft	5 ft	2 ft	1 ft	3 in
Surface ships	25 ft	15 ft	2 ft	1 ft	3 in
Nuclear weapons components	8 ft	5 ft	1 ft	1 in	.4 in
Vehicles	5 ft	2 ft	1 ft	2 in	1 in
Land minefields	30 ft	20 ft	3 ft	1 in	—
Ports and harbors	100 ft	50 ft	20 ft	10 ft	1 ft
Coasts and landing beaches	100 ft	15 ft	10 ft	5 ft	3 in
Railroad yards and shops	100 ft	50 ft	20 ft	5 ft	2 ft
Roads	30 ft	20 ft	6 ft	2 ft	6 in
Urban area	200 ft	100 ft	10 ft	10 ft	1 ft
Terrain	—	300 ft	15 ft	5 ft	6 in
Surfaced submarines	100 ft	20 ft	5 ft	3 ft	1 in

Source: Adapted from Senate Committee on Commerce, Science, and Transportation, *NASA Authorization for Fiscal Year 1978, Part 3* (Washington, D.C.:U.S. Government Printing Office, 1977), pp. 1642–1643; and Bhupendra Jasani, ed., *Outer Space—A New Dimension in the Arms Race* (Cambridge, Mass.: Oelgeschlager, Gunn & Hain, 1982), p. 47.

interpreters; and reliability is the fraction of time that the system produces useful data. Enhancement capability refers to whether the initial images can be enhanced to draw out more useful data.[18]

U.S. reconnaissance satellites come in three varieties—area surveillance, close-look, and real-time. At present, the United States is operating its fourth-generation area surveillance satellite and third-generation close-look satellite, although both are used only intermittently and are soon to be phased out. The fourth-generation area surveillance satellite, introduced in 1971, has been nick-named Big Bird, but it is officially the Keyhole-9 (KH-9).

The first launch of a KH-9 took place on June 15, 1971, and had a lifetime of fifty-two days. The present lifetime of the KH-9 satellite is in the neighbor-hood of nine months. The spacecraft is reported to weigh approximately 30,000 pounds and to be 50 feet long and 10 feet in diameter.[19] In addition to a conventional photographic camera, it has been reported to also carry infrared and multispectral scanners.[20] It carries four returnable film capsules, which are recovered either during descent or by frogman recovery.[21]

KH-9 satellites are launched into a north-south polar orbit with an apogee of approximately 155 miles, a perigee of about 100 miles, and a lifetime of approximately nine months. Its inclination is approximately 96.4 degrees, taking it over the Soviet Union and China.[22] The north-south polar orbit is also a sun-synchronous orbit; hence, each daylight pass over an area is made at an identical sun angle, thus avoiding differences in pictures of the same area that result from different sun angles. Each area is overflown twice a day—once in daylight and once in darkness.[23] The ground track repeats every 3.5 days; that is, Big Bird passes over the same territory every 3.5 days.[24]

Initial reports concerning Big Bird suggested that it was to be a signals intelligence (SIGINT) satellite.[25] Subsequent reports suggested that it was equipped with both close-look and area surveillance cameras in addition to the infrared and multispectral scanners.[26] The most recent reports, however, des-cribe it as purely an area surveillance satellite.[27]

KH-9 satellites have overflown areas of interest at times of particular concern: May 16–25, 1974, during which time the Indian nuclear test occurred; July 14–28, 1974, during which a crisis over Cyprus occurred; and July 1977, when South Africa was possibly planning a nuclear test.

The oldest of the presently operational U.S. imaging satellites, the KH-8, is the one with the greatest resolution. It has a significantly shorter lifetime than the KH-9—approximately eighty days. Its orbit has a 77-mile perigee and a 215-mile apogee, with a 96.4-degree inclination. Thus, it flies along the same path as Big Bird but closer to the ground. Film is returned in at least two reentry vehicles, which are recovered in midair by Lockheed C-130s stationed at Hickam Air Force Base, Hawaii. The resolution of its photographic images has been estimated at 6 inches.[28]

Two of the most recent KH-8 launches are interesting in different respects. The launch of February 28, 1981 (1981–19A) corresponded to a buildup of Soviet forces near the Polish border that was reaching its peak.[29] The launch of January 21, 1982 (1982–6A) has been *assumed* to be a close-look satellite, since it was launched on Titan 3B/Agena D and entered into 88 by 332 miles orbit with a 97.32-degree inclination—indicative of a close-look satellite. The satel-lite's mission has been reported to include producing pictures of a suspected Libyan troop buildup and of TU-22 Blinder bombers amassed along Libya's borders with Chad and the Sudan.[30] However, after its initial orbits, the satellite subsequently moved in sharp leads to an orbit of 350 by 415 miles, far higher than the orbit for a photoreconnaissance satellite and more typical of an electronic ferret.[31]

Apparently, both the Big Bird and the close-look systems recently have been or soon will be phased out. The decision to terminate them is due largely to the successful development and operation of the KH-11 spacecraft, first introduced in December 1976. As with the Big Bird, the KH-11 is launched by a Titan 3D booster and flies in a north-south sun-synchronous polar orbit that covers each area twice a day with an inclination of 97 degrees.[32] Unlike the pictures of the Big Bird or close-look satellites, KH-11 pictures are transmitted in real time, probably either to a facility at Fort Belvoir, Virginia, or to the Defense Special Missile and Astronautics Center at Fort Meade.[23] Instead of film, the KH-11 pictures are converted into digital radio pulses and transmitted immediately to a Satellite Data System (SDS) spacecraft and relayed to the Washington-area ground station.[34] Although the KH-11 has high resolution, it is not as good as that of the close-look satellite. Lower resolution results from a combination of factors—its higher orbit and the transmission of pictures rather than use of a film-based system.

Although the KH-11 has inferior resolution to the close-look satellite, it has an important advantage over both film-based systems with regard to lifetimes. The lifetime of the first KH-11, launched on December 19, 1976, was 770 days—three times greater than that of the longest Big Bird lifetime. The second KH-11, launched on June 14, 1978, had a lifetime of 760 days. The third KH-11, launched on February 7, 1980, had a lifetime of 555 days, the shortest of any KH-11. Its shortened lifetime may have been a result of its being maneuvered to cover aspects of the Iran-Iraq war in 1980, during which time it malfunctioned.[35] Subsequent KH-11 launches occurred on September 3, 1981, and November 17, 1982.

Several accomplishments of the KH-11 have been noted in the press. According to one report, a KH-11 revealed that the USSR was constructing a new super submarine and a new miniaircraft carrier and disproved reports of a new Soviet CBW center by showing that it actually was a reserve arms storage facility. A KH-11 also apparently discovered an SS-20 ballistic missile in its canister alongside an encapsulated SS-16 ICBM. It has been suggested that the Soviets were seeking to have Soviet reconnaissance satellites compare the two so that steps could be taken to increase the similarity and, hence, increase the chances for successful disguise.[36] Finally, the KH-11 was also used to try to determine exactly where in the U.S. embassy compound in Teheran the U.S. personnel were being held.[37]

With two systems on the verge of elimination, there appear to be at least two imaging systems under development. One, the KH-12, is a 32,000-pound follow-on to the KH-11. It will have resolution equal to the present close-look satellite and is scheduled for launch early in 1986.[38] Once these new spacecraft are operational, plans calls for launch of an individual satellite into about a 150 nautical mile polar orbit. The same shuttle mission then would retrieve another spacecraft that had been in orbit for some time and return it to earth for refurbishment.[39]

In addition, there are plans for an imaging radar satellite.[40] Such a satellite has been considered in the past; in 1962, the Air Force planned to develop a recoverable-payload satellite equipped with high-resolution radar for ground mapping.[41] The presently planned system is to be directed at Soviet and Warsaw Pact targets—targets that are often obscured by cloud cover.[42] Intelligence gathered will be relayed through the Tracking Data and Relay System Satellite to a ground station in White Sands, New Mexico.[43]

Satellites are the most productive of the U.S. photoreconnaissance/imaging collection systems in terms of being able to overfly any location without hindrance and, in the case of the KH-11, in terms of being able to provide information almost instantaneously. However, satellites possess certain limitations. Even if they are already in orbit, they cannot be dispatched to cover events on short notice. Furthermore, such systems are extraordinarily expensive, and priorities must be set; inevitably, some areas are neglected. Aircraft reconnaissance systems can supplement satellite coverage and provide a quick-reaction capability.

The United States relies on two aircraft for strategic photoreconnaissance collection activities: the SR-71 and the U-2. Built by Lockheed, the SR-71 (SR for Strategic Reconnaissance), originally known as the A-12, first became operational on January 7, 1966.[44] It is capable of Mach 3 speed (over 2,000 miles per hour) and it can attain a height of 85,000 feet. The plane is armed with a radar detector and a variety of electronic countermeasures (ECMs). At present, nine SR-71s are operational.[45]

Flying at 85,000 feet, the SR-71 can film 60,000 square miles in one hour. It is equipped with three high-power cameras that can map the United States in three passes and three-dimensional filming equipment that can cover 150 square miles so precisely that it could locate a mailbox on a country road.[46] It is reportedly also equipped with a synthetic-aperture radar for high-altitude night imaging.[47]

An SR-71 photographed the entire first Chinese nuclear test.[48] Until 1971, it was used constantly to conduct surveillance operations over China, but these operations were suspended as part of the agreement to open up relations with the People's Republic of China. Along with China, other prominent Southeast Asian targets have included North Korea, Vietnam, and Laos. The SR-71 was used to gather photographic intelligence concerning the Sontay prisoner-of-war (POW) camp in preparation for the raid that was designed to rescue the POWs.[49] Outside Asia, the SR-71 has been used for reconnaissance over Cuba and the Middle East. Thus, during the 1973 Arab-Israeli war, an SR-71 was sent to overfly the Negev desert on the basis of information that Israel was preparing to arm its Jericho missiles with nuclear warheads.[50] SR-71s based at RAF Mildenhall in England fly peripheral to Soviet territory bordering the Baltic. Using oblique photography techniques, an SR-71 can gather imagery on targets up to 60 miles inside the Soviet Union.[51]

The SR-71 is the second strategic reconnaissance aircraft built by Lockheed. Prior to the 1966 deployment of the SR-71, the primary U.S. strategic reconnaissance aircraft was the U-2. More than 55 U-2s in various versions are believed to have been built.[52] At present, there are eight U-2s in the arsenal, and at least two more are expected to be built over the next two years.[53]

Development of the U-2 by the CIA and Lockheed Aircraft began in 1954 at the urging of the Eisenhower Surprise Attack Panel. It became operational in 1956 and began overflying the Soviet Union that year. The U-2 brought back significant intelligence on airfields, aircraft, missile testing and training, nuclear weapons storage, submarine production, atomic production, and aircraft deployment.[54]

It was the flight of May 1, 1960—which began in Peshawar, Pakistan, and was to conclude 3,788 miles later in Bodo, Norway—that brought the U-2 to world attention.[55] The plane was shot down, but its pilot, Francis Gary Powers, survived to stand trial. Powers's plane contained a camera with a rotating 944.6-millimeter lens that peered out through seven holes in the belly of the plane. It would take 4,000 paired pictures of a 125-mile-wide, 2,174-mile-long strip of the Soviet Union.[56]

The U-2R (the primary present version) has a range of 3,000 miles and a maximum speed of 528 knots at an altitude of 40,000 feet. Its operational ceiling is more than 70,000 feet.[57] Like the SR-71s, U-2Rs are capable of slant photography.[58]

U-2s have been flown from bases in Cyprus, Turkey, Pakistan, Japan, Formosa, Okinawa, the Philippines, Alaska, West Germany, and England.[59] The flights provided photographic intelligence coverage of not only the Soviet Union but China, North Korea, and the Middle East. With the advent of satellite reconnaissance capabilities and the SR-71, reliance on U-2 coverage was reduced. However, U-2s still provide coverage in some areas; for example, the U-2s photographic capabilities have been used to document the buildup of military forces in Nicaragua, and U-2s have been making regular flights to take pictures of military construction and arms depots.[60] U-2s are also used for overhead reconnaissance of other targets in the Caribbean and Central America, such as Cuba and Grenada.

Signals Intelligence

Signals intelligence (SIGINT) is a term that encompasses a wide variety of technical intelligence. The most general division between types of signals intelligence distinguishes between communications intelligence (COMINT) and electronic intelligence (ELINT).

COMINT is technical and intelligence information derived from the interception of encrypted or unencrypted communications.[61] These communications may include diplomatic, commercial, political, and military communications conducted by a variety of means—telephone, radiotelephone, radio, or satellite, landline, or undersea cable.

Electronic intelligence (ELINT)—technical and intelligence information derived from foreign noncommunications electromagnetic radiations emanating from other than atomic detonations or radioactive sources—also encompasses a wide variety of technical intelligence.[62] One prominent example of ELINT is radar intelligence (RADINT)—the intelligence derived from monitoring the electronic emanations of the radars of foreign nations, particularly those of the Soviet Union and China. The intelligence derived allows for the mapping of locations and hence targeting of early-warning stations, air defense systems, ABM systems, airfields, air bases, satellite tracking and control stations, and ships at sea. Recording their frequencies, signal strengths, pulse lengths, pulse rates, and other specifications allows for the ability to jam the transmitters in the event of war.

Electronic intelligence also includes the intelligence derived from nonimaging radar systems. Such systems do not have adequate resolution for producing images, but they can detect the presence of an object and determine the distance between the radar and the object and the object's altitude, size, speed, and directional data.[63]

Another subcategory of ELINT is telemetry intelligence (TELINT). Telemetry is the set of signals by which a missile, a stage of a missile, or a missile warhead sends back to earth data about its performance during a test flight. The data relate to such features as structural stress, rocket motor thrust, fuel consumption, guidance system performance, and the physical conditions of the ambient environment. Intercepted telemetry can provide intelligence on such questions as the number of warheads carried by a given missile, the range of the missile, its payload and throw-weight, and hence the probable size of its warheads and the accuracy with which the warheads are guided at the point of release from the missile's postboost vehicles.[64]

TELINT is also a subcategory of foreign instrumentation signals intelligence (FISINT). Foreign instrumentation signals are electromagnetic emissions associated with the testing and operational deployment of aerospace, surface, and subsurface systems that may have military or civilian application. FISINT includes, but is not limited to, telemetry, beaconing, electronic interrogators, tracking-fusing-aiming-command systems, and video data links.[65]

In addition to the foregoing standard subcategories of signals intelligence/electronic intelligence, two further subcategories were listed in the proposed National Security Agency (NSA) charter of 1980: information derived from the collection and processing of nonimaging infrared and coherent light signals. The former involves sensors that can detect the absence or presence and movement of an object or event via temperature. *Coherent light* is another expression for laser and hence refers to the interception of laser communications, such as future communications between Soviet satellites and submarines using blue-green laser communications techniques.[66]

Signals intelligence provides pertinent information with regard to Soviet compliance with the ABM and SALT II treaties. Specific provisions whose violation might be detected by SIGINT include the prohibition of testing of radars not designated as ABM radars as such, the limitation of radar potential, the prohibition of mobile land-based ABM systems, the limitation on the number of new missile systems that can be developed and deployed, the restriction on the number of warhead release maneuvers for specific missiles, and the limitation of the throw-weight of new missiles.

Collection of signals intelligence is achieved by a multitude of means, including satellites, aircraft, ships, submarines, and ground facilities. There are basically two types of SIGINT satellites: high-orbiting satellites, with apogees over 20,000 miles, and low-orbiting satellites, with apogees under 1,000 miles.

The high-orbiting SIGINT satellite about which the most is known—and which is most important in terms of arms control monitoring—is known as Rhyolite; it is controlled from ground stations at Pine Gap, Australia, and Buckley Air National Guard Base, Colorado. Rhyolite, developed by the CIA and built by TRW Incorporated, was described in a TRW briefing as being a "multipurpose covert electronic surveillance system."[67]

Rhyolite is capable of being targeted against telemetry, radars, and communications. Rhyolite's communications-intercept capability against Soviet and Chinese telephonic and radio communications extends across the very high frequency (VHF), ultra high frequency (UHF), and microwave frequency bands.[68] With respect to microwave frequencies, Robert Lindsey has written that the Rhyolite satellites "could monitor Communist microwave radio and long-distance telephone traffic over much of the European land mass, eavesdropping on a Soviet Commissar in Moscow talking to his mistress in Yalta or on a general talking to his lieutenants across the great continent."[69]

In addition, the Rhyolite radiotelephonic traffic intercepts may include early morning stock exchange and other business calls.[70] Interception of commercial communications may include those transmitted by INTELSAT satellites.[71] These satellites, first launched in 1965, have a capacity for simultaneous transmission of 11,000 two-way telephone conversations. In the VHF–UHF range, Rhyolite satellites regularly monitor the radio traffic between aircraft and air traffic controllers.[72]

The highest priority of the Rhyolite program has always been telemetry interception. The telemetry from Soviet missile tests is generally transmitted on about fifty channels. It is frequency modulated and ranges in frequency from 150 MHz in the VHF band to perhaps 3 GHz in the super high frequency (SHF) band, thus substantially falling in the microwave range.[73]

The Rhyolite program was quite successful initially. It was not until 1975, when it was informed of Rhyolite's capability by Christopher Boyce and

Andrew Daulton Lee, that (according to several sources) the Soviet Union abandoned the conventional wisdom that signals at VHF and higher frequencies could not be intercepted by satellites at geostationary altitudes. According to some sources, no attempt was made to encrypt the telemetry data until mid-1977—six months after the arrest of Boyce and Lee.[74] Presumably, the Soviets feared that encryption might give away the Soviet acquisition of material on Rhyolite. (However, it appears that telemetry encryption began prior to the Boyce-Lee disclosures and was related to the beginning of the Soviet MIRV program.[75])

According to a 1979 account, there were four Rhyolite launches as of May 1979—the first March 6, 1973, and subsequent launches on May 23, 1977, December 11, 1977, and April 7, 1978.[76] According to this account, two of the satellites are stationed near the Horn of Africa, primarily to intercept telemetry signals transmitted by liquid-fueled ICBMs launched from Tyuratam in a northeasterly direction toward the Kamchatka Peninsula; two stationed farther east are intended to monitor telemetry from the SS-16 and SS-20 missiles launched from Plesetsk in northern Russia.[77]

The Rhyolite project was described by former CIA official Victor Marchetti in the following terms:

> This was a very interesting project, a very much advanced project in terms of technology and a very desirable project because getting information of the type that we wanted and needed on Soviet ICBM testing, anti-ballistic missile programs, anti-satellite programs and the like, much of this activity of course takes place in the Eastern Siberia and Central Asia, getting information on the Chinese ICBM program.[78]

Rhyolite is not the only high-orbiting U.S. signals intelligence satellite. In June 1979, the existence was revealed of a satellite code-named Chalet, apparently in geosynchronous orbit, which was being reconfigured to give it a capacity against Soviet missile telemetry.[79] A modified Chalet launch occurred on October 1, 1979.[80] The initial Chalet launch appears to be that of June 10, 1978, and the most recent launch appears to be that of October 31, 1981.

In addition, it appears that the United States has another SIGINT satellite system under the cover of the Satellite Data System (SDS) program. The known functions of SDS include communications links for the Strategic Air Command (SAC) bombers flying over the poles and between the Air Force Satellite Test Center in Sunnyvale, California, and the other components of the Air Force Satellite Control Facility and the transmission of KH-11 photography.[81] In its highly elliptical orbit of 200 by 24,000 miles, SDS "hovers" over the northern Soviet Union/Arctic for long periods of time. At those times, it is ideally suited to receive and transmit photos from the KH-11 as it flies over Russia or to communicate with bombers flying over the Arctic.[82]

A SIGINT satellite with the same orbital parameters as a SDS satellite would hover over Soviet/Arctic staging bases for bombers and over Murmansk Naval Base, intercepting signals from those targets, among others. The first and second launches of this system apparently occurred on March 10, 1975, and August 6, 1976.

In the wake of the loss of Iranian ground stations, a revised version of the ARGUS system was approved.[83] This version was placed in orbit by the space shuttle *Discovery* on January 25, 1985.

In addition to high-orbiting SIGINT satellites, the United States also has a low-orbiting ferret satellite. The purpose of this satellite has been to map Soviet, Chinese, and other radars.[84] The radars include Soviet air defense, surface-to-air missile (SAM), and early-warning radars that operate in the 1–50 GHz frequencies. The satellite operates in orbits that (with rare exceptions) are always distinctively higher than those for photoreconnaissance satellites but lower than all other U.S. military satellites.

In the midst of the original ferret satellite program, another type of ferret satellite was developed. This satellite was launched "piggyback" with another larger satellite, which was ejected in its own orbit. The first such launch occurred on August 29, 1963. The most recent version of these ferrets have been launched on board KH-9 photoreconnaissance satellites. With a 96–degree inclination and an orbit of 375 miles, these octagonal satellites continue to map Soviet and Chinese radars.[85]

Since the end of World War II, the United States has relied on aircraft for a significant portion of its SIGINT collection program. In the late 1940s, special electronic airborne operations were flown by Air Force bombers and transports and by Navy patrol planes. These operations had the objective of ferreting out Soviet radar capabilities for the purpose of developing electronic countermeasures and locating Soviet air defenses.[86]

With the development of ferret satellites and changes in the world situation, such provocative missions were curtailed. However the United States still relies on aircraft for a variety of SIGINT missions. Both the SR-71 and the U-2 aircraft have SIGINT as well as photographic capabilities. The SR-71's SIGINT capability includes equipment for monitoring radio and radar transmissions.[87] Some of the new SR-71As stationed at RAF Mildenhall in England have been configured for ELINT or COMINT surveillance and have flown missions at regular intervals. Many of these missions spanned more than 10 hours and involved peripheral flight work along the borders of the Soviet Union and other Warsaw Pact nations. The purpose of these peripheral intelligence missions is to pinpoint locations and characteristics of potentially hostile signal emitters.[88]

The U-2's SIGINT capability has been upgraded by the addition of the SENIOR RUBY ELINT system.[89] U-2s also fly from RAF Mildenhall and Akrotiri airfield in Cyprus, conducting signals intelligence missions on the periphery of the Soviet Union and Eastern Europe and in the Mediterranean area.[90] In 1979, there were plans to modify the U-2 to intercept missile telemetry.[91]

In addition to the U-2 and SR-71, planes used in SIGINT collection have included the EC-135, the EC-121, and the RC-135. The EC-121, which has recently been phased out, was for many years a significant SIGINT collection system. The EC-135 is a modified KC-135 Stratotanker. The EC-135C is equipped as a flying command post for SAC's airborne alert role. Seven EC-135Ns, also known as Advanced Range Instrumentation Aircraft (ARIA), were equipped as airborne radio and telemetry stations for the Apollo program and have also been used to monitor U.S. and Soviet missile tests and space activities. Eventually, the ARIA fleet will consist of six EC-18B and two EC-135E aircraft.[92]

The most important strategic intelligence collection aircraft devoted solely to SIGINT collection is the RC-135; it has assumed much of the work of the retired EC-121s. The RC-135, of which there are several versions, is a modified Boeing 707 that can stay aloft for 18 hours. It is packed with a variety of equipment for COMINT and ELINT gathering.[93]

At present, there are eighteen RC-135s in the U.S. inventory.[94] United States–based RC-135s include those at Offutt AFB, Nebraska, Eielson AFB, Alaska, and Shemya Island, Alaska. European-based RC-135s include those at RAF Mildenhall, England, and Hellenikon, Greece, while Asian-based RC-135s are stationed at Kadena AB, Okinawa.[95]

The RC-135s based in Alaska are used to monitor Soviet air exercises, military communications, missile tests, and the alert status of Soviet defenses. Thus, several RC-135s routinely patrol off the Soviet coast near Kamchatka and the Sakhalin Islands—flying in an elliptical pattern on an average of twenty days or nights a month.[96]

Under normal circumstances, the primary mission of the RC-135 is to document the electronic order of battle of Soviet radar stations, antiaircraft missile bases, and overall Soviet air defense procedures.[97] When a test of a new missile is believed imminent, the recording of telemetry from such a test becomes the primary goal. On the night of August 21, 1983, when the RC-135 from Eielson AFB flew a parallel course to the doomed KAL 007 flight, its objective was interception of telemetry from an anticipated test of an SS-X-24.[98]

An extremely important set of SIGINT collectors are the radars and antennas placed throughout the world—including on the periphery of the Soviet Union and China and on the paths of their ballistic missile test trajectories. The most important of these is the COBRA DANE radar on Shemya Island in the Aleutians—situated 480 nautical miles from Kamchatka Peninsula and the surrounding ocean area, which is the primary impact point for practically all Soviet missile tests.[99] COBRA DANE is a phased-array radar (that is, it electronically scans the field of view rather than moving an antenna dish across the field of view). COBRA DANE was designed to track Soviet reentry vehicles during ICBM tests and to track foreign satellites. Specifically, the primary purpose and value of COBRA DANE is as follows:

> ...to acquire precise radar metric and signature data on developing Soviet ballistic missile weapon systems for weapon system characteristics determination. The Soviet developmental test to Kamchatka and the Pacific Ocean provide the U.S. the primary source for collection of this data early in the Soviet developmental program.[100]

From Shemya Island, COBRA DANE can obtain data on missile trajectories, separation velocities, and payload maneuvers and signature data on reentry vehicles from missiles fired from both the Soviet land mass and the Soviets' primary SLBM launch site.

COBRA DANE can detect a basketball-sized object at a range of 2,000 miles and can simultaneously track more than a hundred objects. Processed data on objects being tracked are transmitted in real time to the continental United States via the Defense Satellite Communications System and distributed to the NORAD Space Defense Center and the Foreign Technology Division. In the event of a missile attack, the radar would function as an early-warning sensor. In this mode, COBRA DANE can detect and track up to 300 objects simultaneously and can provide predicted impact points for up to 200 objects.[101]

To supplement COBRA DANE, the United States recently deployed another phased-array radar, COBRA JUDY, on the Observation Island U.S. Naval Station. With its operational base at Pearl Harbor, COBRA JUDY operates in the Pacific Ocean to complement COBRA DANE. The COBRA JUDY system was designed to monitor the final near-earth trajectories of Soviet reentry test vehicles. That portion of their flight is not visible to COBRA DANE because of line-of-sight constraints imposed by the curvature of the earth.[102]

Also part of the COBRA series are the FPS-17 detection and FPS-79 tracking radars located at an INSCOM base near Diyarbakir, Turkey. These radars are targeted against missiles launched from Kapustin Yar and Tyuratam.[103]

In addition to the Turkish sites, SIGINT facilities in China and Norway also contribute significantly to U.S. information concerning the Soviet Union. In 1979, the United States and the People's Republic of China reached agreement on the establishment of two SIGINT stations in the Xinjiang Uighur Autonomous Region in Western China near the Soviet border. The stations were constructed by the CIA Directorate of Science and Technology's Office of SIGINT Operations but manned by Chinese under the command of their SIGINT agency. The information collected at the two sites includes data on the development of new Soviet missiles tested at Leninsk and Sary Shagan as well as Soviet military communications, and it is shared by China and the United States.[104]

Installations operated by the Norwegian Security Service in cooperation with the CIA and the NSA are located at Vadso, Kirkenes, Fauske (two installations), Namsos, Jessheim, and Randaberg.[105] The equipment at Vadso includes high frequency (HF) listening equipment and VHF/UHF antennas. The HF equipment can be used to monitor long-distance point-to-point radio communications and ship-to-ship, ship-to-shore, and air-to-ground communications. Four of the eight VHF/UHF antennas are pointed toward Murmansk and one toward the Barents Sea to monitor telemetry from Soviet test launches.[106]

At Randaberg, there are further circular arrays that are similar but not identical to the smaller Vadso arrays. These arrays are probably used mainly to intercept HF communications from Soviet ships, submarines, and long-range ocean surveillance aircraft in the Norwegian sea.[107] At Jessheim, there is an array identical to the one at Vadso.[108]

A large radome at one of the Fauske sites (Vetan) is situated in a valley surrounded by mountains—the typical layout for satellite ground control stations. This station apparently is either intercepting telemetry beamed down from a Soviet military satellite to a ground station at Murmansk or is a ground station for an electronic reconnaissance satellite.[109]

A second system used for a variety of SIGINT missions is the AN/FLR-9 system, also known as Wullenweber or Circularly Disposed Antenna Array (CDAA). This system is designed to locate and intercept signals from the low to high frequency bands. Low-band traffic includes submarine traffic, whereas radiotelephone traffic falls in the high band.[110] The United States maintains CDAAs at bases in the Philippines, England (Menwith Hill and Chicksands), Japan, Korea, Germany (Augsburg), and Italy (San Vito dei Normanni).[111]

The United States also maintains, either at its own bases overseas or in cooperation with several foreign governments, VHF–UHF–SHF receivers that are capable of intercepting telemetry from Soviet launch sites. Telemetry from missiles launched from Kapustin Yar and Tyuratam are intercepted by the VHF–UHF–SHF receivers at the Karamursel facility. Such receivers may also be present at Iraklion Station, Greece, for the same purpose.[112]

In the very early 1960s, the United States began to use a variety of naval vessels for the collection of signals intelligence—converted World War II vessels as well as modern submarines and Advanced Range Instrumentation Ships (ARISs). The latter two types of ships had a significant role with regard to strategic intelligence collection. The United States has employed two ARISs for the collection of strategic military intelligence. The primary missions of the ships are to provide tracking data on U.S. missile and space launches; they are normally deployed off the Eastern and Western Test Ranges (Cape Canaveral and Vandenberg AFB). As a secondary mission, they have been deployed for 45-day periods off the Kamchatka Peninsula to collect data on Soviet ballistic missile tests.[113]

In addition to surface vessels, the United States has also employed submarines for the collection of signals intelligence. In 1975, it was revealed that the United States had been conducting intelligence collection activities via submarine, near Soviet coastlines for over fifteen years.[114] The program apparently began in the last years of the Eisenhower administration.[115] The ships employed were Sturgeon 637-class submarines with electronic gear and a special NSA unit aboard. The project was code-named, at various times, Holystone, Pinnacle, and Bollard.[116]

Holystone missions collected a variety of valuable intelligence by several means. The submarines were able to plug into Soviet land communications cables that were strewn across the ocean bottom and thus were able to intercept high-level military messages and other communications considered too important to be sent by radio or less-secure means. They also took photos of the underside of an E-class Soviet submarine, apparently in Vladivostok harbor. In addition, they observed missile launches of Soviet SLBMs inland and obtained voice autographs of Soviet submarines.[117]

In addition to whatever Holystone missions are still being performed, there are also two U.S. nuclear submarines, code-named Watchdog and Tomcat, on station on the floor of the Sea of Okhotsk to follow their Soviet counterparts and monitor military communications.[118]

Ocean Surveillance

Watching the Soviet fleet has long been a major activity of U.S. intelligence—particularly of the technical intelligence community. In addition to their military combat uses, Soviet ships (whether military or "civilian") have for many years been employed for intelligence collection purposes and for arms shipment. Although it is less sophisticated than the present Typhoon, the Soviet Union has had a significant SSBN fleet—over 60 boats—for several years. Hence, tracking the Soviet Navy has been a major intelligence requirement—the goal being to know the location of every Soviet naval vessel at any time.

As with signals intelligence, ocean surveillance data is collected by a wide variety of collection systems—satellites, aircraft, ground stations, and surface ships. In addition, since underseas activities are also a major target of intelligence collection, several underseas collection systems are employed. All of these systems constitute the Ocean Surveillance Information System, and the data they produce are transmitted to regional Fleet Ocean Surveillance Information Centers and to the Current Operations Department of the Navy Operational Intelligence Center.

The connections between ocean surveillance information and the monitoring of treaty provisions are less direct and more numerous than those for imaging and signals intelligence. Such information contributes, both directly and indirectly, to monitoring the Seabed Treaty and to monitoring Soviet compliance with the SALT II limits on SLBM launchers. Also, as discussed in more detail later, ocean surveillance information concerning Soviet programs such as antisubmarine warfare (ASW) has an impact on the U.S. evaluation of strategic arms control provisions.

Until 1976, the U.S. Navy did not have a dedicated overhead reconnaissance system for ocean surveillance. Apparently, ocean surveillance data were obtained from U.S. photoreconnaissance satellites, with the Air Force and Navy cooperating on reconnaissance matters.[119] Thus, it was suggested at the time that the April 18, 1975, launch of a high-resolution KH-8 satellite was intended to acquire data on the massive Soviet naval exercise then taking place.[120]

Initial studies for a dedicated ocean surveillance satellite system began in 1968.[121] In 1970, the Chief of Naval Operations ordered a study of overall ocean surveillance requirements, resulting in the five-volume *Ocean Surveillance Requirements Study* by the Naval Research Laboratory.[122] Such studies were initiated by the Navy in response to the significant buildup that was occurring in Soviet naval forces and capabilities. Designated Program 749, the ocean surveillance satellite study focused on the development of high-resolution, phased-array radars that would allow all-weather ocean surveillance monitoring as well as detection of low-trajectory sea-launched missiles.[123] In addition, the possibility of equipping the satellites with an infrared scanner was explored.[124]

Despite the emphasis of these initial studies, the ocean surveillance satellite system, Classic Wizard, lacked any radar capability. Instead, White Cloud, the satellite portion of the Classic Wizard system, is a passive interceptor.[125] White Cloud is apparently equipped with a passive infrared scanner and millimeter-wave radiometers as well as radio-frequency antennas capable of monitoring radio communications and radar emissions from Soviet submarines and ships.[126] Apparently, passive interferometry techniques are used to determine the location of Soviet vessels; the craft computes a ship's position from data provided by several antennas that measure the direction from which the vessel's radar or radio signals arrive.[127]

The satellite system consists of a mother ship and three subsatellites. The present satellites are launched from the Western Test Range (Vandenberg AFB) into a near-circular 63-degree inclined orbit at an altitude of approximately 700 miles, employing an Atlas F booster.[128] The three spacecrafts are dispersed from the main vehicle into three parallel orbits, with latitude separation as well as time/distance separation along their orbital paths. At the 700-mile altitude, the spacecraft can receive signals from surface vessels more than 2,000 miles away, providing overlapping coverage on successive passes.[129]

Five operational satellite clusters have been placed into orbit since 1976. The ground segment of the Classic Wizard system consists of five ground stations at the Naval Security Group facilities at Diego Garcia; Guam; Adak, Alaska; Winter Harbor, Maine; and Edzell, Scotland.[130]

As was the case with photographic and signals reconnaissance activities directed at land-based targets, the United States employs several aircraft in the ocean surveillance role, including the EP-3E, the EA-3B, the P-3, and modified U-2s. The EP-3E Orion and the EA-3B Skywarrior are operated by the Fleet Air Reconnaissance Squadrons and detachments in Rota (Spain), Agana (Guam), and Atsugi (Japan). Both planes are employed to monitor signals emanating from Soviet vessels in the Atlantic and Pacific regions. In the case of the EP-3E, which is a modified P-3, some of its targets may also be land-based. The EA-3B is often employed on aircraft carriers for periods ranging from days to months in order to extend the range of coverage.[131]

The P-3 Orion is a four-engined aircraft capable of flying 1,560 miles, patrolling for four hours, and returning to base.[132] P-3s operated in two versions—the P-3B and P-3C—are engaged in surveillance on both surface and submersible vessels, although antisubmarine warfare functions would take precedence in wartime.[133] The P-3C is equipped with a general-purpose digital computer that coordinates the returns from sensor systems and presents them in visual form by means of cathode ray display tubes. Sensor systems include active or passive sonobouys, magnetic anomaly detectors, forward-looking infrared (FLIR) sensors, and radar.[134]

U.S. Orions are based at sixteen major bases throughout the world, including Clark AFB in the Philippines, Misawa and Kadena (Okinawa) in Japan, Alaska, Iceland, Hawaii, Guam, Spain, Italy, Ascension Island, and Diego Garcia. To provide occasional surveillance in remote areas, the Navy has initiated a program to provide an in-flight refueling capability for the P-3Cs.[135]

Two U-2s also serve in an ocean surveillance role. These are U-2 variants that have a long-loiter capability and are specially equipped with a Westinghouse high-resolution radar, infrared scanner, and ELINT and COMINT receivers designed for ocean surveillance purposes.[136]

In addition to the aerospace systems used for ocean surveillance, the United States also relies on ship- and land-based HF/DF systems. HF/DF equipment can be found on a large number of Navy destroyers, and land-based HF/DF systems include stations in Diego Garcia, Rota (Spain), Edzell (Scotland), Keflavik (Iceland), Japan, Guam, and Brawdy (Wales).[137] European stations such as those in Edzell, Brawdy, and Keflavik monitor passage of ships from the Soviet port of Murmansk through the GIUK (Greenland-Iceland-United Kingdom) Gap, while the Diego Garcia station performs similar duties for the Indian Ocean area.

Much of the subsurface ocean surveillance data that is gathered falls under the heading of acoustic intelligence (ACOUSTINT)—intelligence information derived from the analysis of acoustic waves radiated either intentionally or unintentionally by the target into the surrounding medium. This includes the underwater acoustic waves from ships and submarines that can be used to develop the "signature" of those vehicles.

The most important submarine detection and tracking system is a global network of large, fixed sea-bottom arrays of hydrophones that passively listen for sounds generated by submarines. These arrays are collectively known as the Sound Surveillance System (SOSUS), although, strictly speaking, only about two-thirds of the arrays are part of the SOSUS network proper, the other one-third being allied systems. SOSUS was described by one U.S. admiral in 1979 as "the backbone of ASW detection capability."[138]

In 1979, SOSUS was described by the Stockholm International Peace Research Institute (SIPRI) as follows:

> Each SOSUS installation consists of an array of hundreds of hydrophones laid out on the sea floor, or moored at depths most conducive to sound propagation, and connected by submarine cables for transmission of telemetry. In such an array a sound wave arriving from a distant submarine will be successively detected by different hydrophones according to their geometric relationship to the direction from which the wave arrives. This direction can be determined by noting the order in which the wave is detected at the different hydrophones. In practice the sensitivity of the array is enhanced many times by adding the signals from several individual hydrophones after introducing appropriate time delays between them. The result is a listening "beam" that can be "steered" in various directions towards various sectors of the ocean by varying the pattern of time delays. The distance from the array to the sound source can be calculated by measuring the divergence of the sound rays within the array or by triangulating from adjacent arrays.[139]

It was stated in 1974 that twenty-two SOSUS installations were located along the east and west coasts of the United States and at various choke points around the world, and the locations of a further fourteen similar installations have also been identified.[140] These thirty-six facilities are distributed around the world as follows: eight on the east and west coasts of the continental United States (including the AUTEC facility on Andros Island), two in the United Kingdom (one at Brawdy in Wales and the other at Scatsa in the Shetland Islands), two in Turkey, two in Japan, and one each in Alaska, Hawaii ("Sea Spider"), Puerto Rico, Bermuda, Barbados, Canada (Argentia, Newfoundland), Norway, Iceland (Keflavik), Santa Maria Island in the Azores (AFAR), Ascension Island, Italy, Denmark, Gibraltar, the Ryukus, Galeta Island in the Panama Canal Zone, the Philippines, Guam, Diego Garcia, and the northeastern part of the Indian Ocean.[141]

Data from these shore facilities are transmitted via FLTSATCOM and DSCS satellites to "a central shore station" at the Acoustic Research Center

(ARC) at Moffett Field, California, where they are integrated with data from other sources and processed by the Illiac 4 computer complex to provide a real-time submarine monitoring capability.[142] According to one report, the detection capabilities of SOSUS are sufficient to localize a submarine to within a radius of 80 kilometers at ranges of several thousand kilometers, but other reports suggest that localizations within radii of 15 kilometers are now possible.[143] In one test of an array deployed off the coast of Oregon, a submarine was detected off the coast of Japan some 6,000 miles away, but ranges up to about half this are more typical.[144] According to testimony submitted to Congress in May 1980:

> SOSUS has demonstrated a substantial capability to detect submarines patrolling or transmitting through SOSUS areas of coverage. . . . Since the first USSR deployment of SSBNs, a large fraction of the SSBN deployed force [was available] to SOSUS detection and tracking.[145]

Other reports have even more categorically claimed that SOSUS has been able to detect all Soviet submarine movements.[146]

Space Surveillance

Initially, U.S. concern for tracking and detection of space objects resulted from the requirements of the U.S. space program—the ability to monitor and control U.S. satellites. However, with the launch of Sputnik I in 1957, the United States came to place a high priority on developing a dedicated system for tracking of Soviet satellite systems.

Since that time, the military's use of space has become a major aspect of Soviet and U.S. military strategy. In addition to the reconnaissance and surveillance functions discussed earlier, satellites have come to play important roles in military communications, navigation, and weather reporting. Consequently, the significance of the space surveillance mission has grown sharply. The detection, tracking, and investigation of Soviet satellites, from their launch through their orbital lifetime and eventual reentry, provide the United States with several significant items of intelligence.

Space surveillance helps provide the United States with intelligence on the characteristics and capabilities of Soviet space systems and their contribution to overall Soviet military capabilities. Such data aid the United States in developing countermeasures to Soviet Systems, provide a database for U.S. ASAT targeting, and allow the United States to assess the threat represented by Soviet ASAT systems. The detection and tracking of Soviet satellites allow the United States to avoid coverage of certain sensitive U.S. military activities—such as the tests of Stealth aircraft—via the Satellite Reconnaissance Advance Notice (SATRAN) system.[147] U.S. military forces conducting sensitive activities are notified whenever Soviet reconnaissance satellites are due to pass overhead and are instructed to cease and camouflage such activities during the relevant period.

Space surveillance data also contribute to monitoring compliance with the provisions of the Outer Space Treaty, the ABM Treaty, and the SALT II Treaty. Specific provisions that can be monitored, directly or indirectly, are those prohibiting placement of weapons of mass destruction in space, space-based ABM systems, and fractional-orbital missiles. Clearly, if an ASAT treaty were to be signed, space surveillance data would also be applicable to the monitoring of its provisions. Tracking and detection of Soviet satellites might reveal ASAT-type maneuvering or actual detonations.

The means of detecting, tracking, and investigating foreign—especially Soviet—satellites are primarily ground-based, although the feasibility of space-based surveillance has been demonstrated in several instances. During the initial space shuttle flight—that of the *Columbia*—the KH-11 was apparently maneuvered into position to examine the tiles damaged during the launch phase. The quality and content of those images convinced NASA that the damaged tiles would not interfere with reentry, allowing completion of the orbital phase of the shuttle's mission.[148] Thus, the KH-11 would appear to have the capability to photograph Soviet satellites in low earth orbit.

In addition, research and development is underway to give the United States a dedicated space-to-space reconnaissance capability. The Air Force is developing one such system, while the Defense Department's Advanced Research Projects Agency (DARPA) has conducted space infrared experiments (SIRE), as part of its Space Infrared Surveillance Program, to develop an infrared system for detecting hostile satellites. The system has been successfully tested on the ground.[149] Development of a space-based space surveillance system in the far term has been described by the Air Force Deputy Chief of Staff, Research, Development, and Acquisition as the "primary thrust of the Space Surveillance Technology Program." The system is intended to provide full earth orbit coverage, to reduce overseas basing of sensors, and to provide near-real-time "operationally responsive coverage of objects and events in space."[150]

Thus, the Air Force requested $22.6 million for Fiscal Year 1984 for research, development, testing, and evaluation of a space-based surveillance system, with a deployment goal of the early 1980s. The system would consist of four satellites in low-altitude equatorial orbit. The long-wave infrared sensor on each satellite would view the volume of space from approximately 60 nautical miles to geosynchronous altitude.[151]

At present, though, U.S. space surveillance activities are predominantly ground-based. The overall military system is known as the Space Detection and Tracking System (SPADATS); the Air Force portion of this system, devoted to tracking foreign satellites, is the Spacetrack system. SPADATS consists of three types of sensors—dedicated, collateral, and contributing. Dedicated sensors are Strategic Air Command (SAC) and Navy sensors whose primary mission is space surveillance; collateral sensors are SAC sensors with a secondary space surveillance role; and contributing sensors are non-SAC sensors with a secondary space surveillance mission.

Until recently, the main dedicated sensor system was a series of Baker-Nunn optical cameras located at Edwards AFB, California; Mt. John, New Zealand; Pulmosan, Korea; St. Margarets, New Brunswick (Canada); and San Vito, Italy.[152] These cameras, which are 10 feet tall and weigh 3 tons, can photograph, at night, a lighted object the size of a basketball over 20,000 miles in space.[153]

Despite its impressive photographic capability, the Baker-Nunn system suffers from several limitations. It operates only in clear weather and during those hours when satellites are still illuminated by the sun. It is slow in terms of data acquisition, rate, and response time; that is, it takes several minutes to get a fix on one satellite, and it takes an hour or more to process the film and measure image positions. Finally, it is useful for tracking but not detection; the approximate position of a satellite must be known beforehand, so that the Baker-Nunn camera can be pointed toward the satellite.[154]

The Baker-Nunn system is in the process of being replaced by the Ground-based Electro-Optical Deep Space Surveillance (GEODSS) system. As with the Baker-Nunn system, the GEODSS system will have five locations— White Sands, New Mexico; Maui, Hawaii; Taego, South Korea; Diego Garcia; and Portugal. By now, construction has been completed at the White Sands site and probably at the Maui, Taego, and Diego Garcia sites as well.[155]

The GEODSS system will provide the capability to track objects optically from above 3,000 nautical miles out to 22,000 miles. It will also be able to search up to 17,400 square degrees per hour. Furthermore, GEODSS installations will be close enough together to provide overlapping coverage as a means of overcoming poor weather at any one site.[156]

As with the Baker-Nunn system, the GEODSS system depends on the collection of light reflected by the objects under investigation, and it will be operational only at night during clear weather. In addition, sensitivity and resolution will be downgraded by adverse atmospheric conditions.[157] However, the GEODSS system will be able to provide real-time data, with a computer-managed, instantaneous video display of surveillance data. Furthermore, the computer will automatically filter stars from the night sky backdrop and then use its memory of known space objects to determine the existence of new or unknown space objects, alerting the user when such objects are found.[158]

The GEODSS system will consist of three telescopes at each site, which will work together under computer control. Two 40-inch telescopes, designed primarily for high-altitude object observation, will be capable of examining up to 2,400 square degrees of the night sky each hour. The 15-inch telescope will be employed mainly for low-altitude observations, searching up to 15,000 square degrees per hour. Each telescope will have a sensitive Ebsicon tube, which will register the image of an object for real-time processing, and a radiometer for optical signature characterization and identification.[159]

A second set of dedicated SPADATS sensors includes those that constitute the Naval Space Surveillance (NAVSPASUR) system. The NAVSPASUR system detects and tracks satellites that pass through an electronic fence, which consists of a fan-shaped radar beam with a 6,000 mile range that extends in an east–west direction from San Diego, California, to Fort Stewart, Georgia. The beam cannot be steered.[160] Detection results when the satellite passing through the beam deflects some of the beam's energy back to earth, where it is detected by several antenna arrays.

A third set of dedicated sensors includes those located at Cloudcroft, New Mexico, and Haleakala, Hawaii (Kaena Point), for the electro-optical observation of spacecraft. At Haleakala is an AN/FPS-2 "optical radar," which employs electronic detectors, as opposed to photographic film, and records the light collected by a telescope to produce an "optical signature" of any satellite.[161]

A planned addition to the set of dedicated sensors is the Pacific Radar Barrier (PACBAR)—three radars located on Guam, at San Miguel, Philippines, and on Kwajalein—which will provide the capability to determine the orbit of a satellite within its first revolution. The Philippines radar is an AN/GPS-10 search radar with a 60-foot dish that had been installed in Thailand in the early 1970s and code-named COBRA TALON.[162]

The collateral Spacetrack sensors are systems employed in either an early-warning or a strategic verification role. Early-warning systems that serve as Spacetrack collateral sensors are the Ballistic Missile Early Warning System (BMEWS) and the FSS-7, PAVE PAWS, Enhanced Perimeter Acquisition Radar Attack Characterization System (EPARCS), and FPS-85 radars. The main function of the BMEWS is the tracking of missiles and the determination of the quantity of missiles launched and the targets. The system consists of three sites—Clear, Alaska; Thule, Greenland; and Fylingdales, Great Britain—each with a pair of radars. Together, the radars provide a 3,000-mile detection and tracking range.[163]

Early warning of SLBM launches has been provided by the FSS-7's radars at six locations (Mt. Helo, Washington; Mill Valley, California; Mt. Laguna, California; MacDill AFB, Florida; Fort Fisher, North Carolina; and Charlestown, Maine) on the east and west coasts, which comprised the SLBM Detection and Warning System.[164] The system is being replaced by four PAVE PAWS (AN/FPS-115) phased-array radars at Otis AFB, Massachusetts; Beale AFB, California; Robins AFB, Georgia; and Goodfellow AFB, Texas.[165] The Otis AFB and Beale AFB radars are already operational, and the Robins AFB and Goodfellow AFB radars will become operational in 1986–1987. Each radar has two arrays, providing a total of 240 degrees of coverage.[166] Although the primary mission of the system will be SLBM detection, the Robins AFB site will support NORAD tracking of space objects.[167] The EPARCS is located in Concrete, North Dakota, with a 2,500-mile range; it is employed in both an early-warning and a space-tracking role.[168]

At Elgin AFB, Florida, a long-range phased-array radar, the AN/FPS-85, was constructed in 1967. The radar—thirteen stories high and as long as a city block—has its principal axis aligned due south across the Gulf of Mexico, and it is capable of receiving and transmitting over an arc extending 60 degrees on either side. Most satellites must pass through its beam, which has a range of 2,500 miles, twice a day.[169]

As with COBRA DANE, the AN/FPS-85 "consists of several thousand individual transmitters the power outputs of which are added together by controlling their phases to form a single beam which can be electronically swept across the sky in millionths of a second."[170] The radar can search for unknown objects across 1,200 degrees of azimuth, from horizon to zenith, while simultaneously tracking several aleady-acquired targets. In a typical 24-hour period, it makes 10,000 observations.[171]

When first established, this radar was the main U.S.-based active sensor of the Spacetrack system, with 30 percent of its operating time devoted to search and surveillance, 50 percent to tracking specific satellite targets requested by NORAD, and 20 percent devoted to its SLBM early-warning role. Today, one-third of its operating time is devoted to space surveillance; its remaining time is devoted to SLBM detection and other tasks.[172]

Strategic verification radars also used in a space surveillance role are the COBRA DANE (AN/FPS-108) and the AN/FPS-79 (Pirinclik/Diyarbakir, Turkey) radars, which have already been discussed.[173] With its coverage extending northward over an arc from Kamchatka to the Bering Strait, COBRA DANE can be used to track satellites in polar and near-polar orbits in addition to its role in observing Soviet missile test reentry vehicles.[174]

Contributing sensors provide inputs to the Spacetrack database on the basis of contracts or agreements negotiated by SAC with its governmental or nongovernmental operators. Included among the contributing sensors are the Millstone Hill and Haystack deep space tracking radars of MIT's Lincoln Laboratory.[175] The Haystack radar can resolve objects in low earth orbit down to 1 foot and has been described in congressional hearings as providing

> . . . images of orbiting satellites that we can get from no other location. [It is a] long range, high altitude capable radar which provides extremely good intelligence data and now has a real-time operational reporting capability.[176]

Nuclear Detonation Monitoring

The nuclear energy programs of foreign nations are a subject of considerable U.S. intelligence interest. Of greatest priority are the nuclear weapons aspects of these programs, particularly when actual nuclear detonations are involved.

The same collection systems that can be employed to monitor the nuclear detonation activities of the Soviet Union, France, China, and other nations can also be employed for monitoring compliance. Besides providing intelligence related to compliance with the Threshold Test Ban Treaty's 150 kiloton limit and the Limited Test Ban Treaty's prohibition of nonunderground explosions, nuclear detonation monitoring can provide data on the characteristics of the detonated devices that can be employed to develop countermeasures. As has been noted in congressional testimony:

> Another aspect [of the U.S. worldwide nuclear test detection system] is devoted to the general area of nuclear weapon diagnostics. As a general rule, the assessment of the sophistication of a foreign weapons development program and the estimation of the probable intent of the developing nation in the application of nuclear weapons require some knowledge of the internal details of the device.
>
> Such questions as yield, nuclear materials employed and the construction characteristics that determine size, weight and output of the device are all-important to determine the type of delivery system that might be required and the vulnerability of U.S. systems to the output of such devices. In other words, in order to determine the response of the U.S. to a foreign nuclear weapons development program, more information than the mere existence of a nuclear explosion is required.[177]

Thus, the Atomic Energy Commission (AEC) was able to announce a few days after China's first nuclear explosion on October 16, 1964, that the bomb used uranium-235, rather than plutonium, based on examination of the radioactive cloud.[178]

In 1960, the United States began a systematic research and development program for nuclear detection monitoring from different environments under the code name VELA.[179] The program, which had three components, was concerned with detection of underground nuclear explosions, ground-based detection of nuclear detonations in the atmosphere and space from the ground, and space-based detection of nuclear detonations in space.[180]

The VELA HOTEL satellite, developed by TRW, has become an important part of the overall U.S. nuclear detonation monitoring capability. The first pair of VELA satellites was launched on October 17, 1963, and the sixth and last pair on April 8, 1970.[181] Although originally designed to last for only six months, the last pair is still operational.

Weighing about 300 pounds each, the first VELAs were placed on opposite sides of the earth at altitudes of between 60,000 and 70,000 miles—making them the highest-orbiting military satellites.[182] They carried a variety of detectors that would be sensitive to the X-rays, gamma rays, and neutrons created by a nuclear explosion. The fourth pair of VELAs was launched with improved capabilities. This and following pairs weighed between 506 and 770 pounds and carried an enhanced command and control capability; more sensitive versions of the X-ray, gamma ray, and neutron sensors; optical and electromagnetic pulse (EMP) sensors; background radiation counters; and an "improved logic circuitry better to discriminate between natural events and man-made bursts of radiation."[183] The optical light sensors, known as Bhangmeters, were designed to detect atmospheric nuclear explosions by means of the detonation's very brief but intense burst of light. Each satellite possesses two Bhangmeters, each with a different sensitivity.[184]

The strategy for determining whether the data acquired by a VELA satellite indicate the occurrence of a nuclear detonation involves requiring "high-order coincidences" among the various detectors.[185] That the detectors can yield ambiguous results is illustrated by the still-disputed event of September 22, 1979. On that day, a VELA detected a flash of light, possibly indicating a nuclear explosion in the area of Prince Edward Island, South Africa, or Antarctica. Because of the lack of corroborating evidence and because one of the Bhangmeters recorded more light than the other, considerable debate resulted. A presidential panel concluded that it was most likely an anomalous signal resulting from the impact of a small meteoroid on the satellite or sunlight reflected off debris. However, both the Defense Intelligence Agency and the Naval Research Laboratory concluded that a nuclear explosion did occur.[186]

As the remaining functional VELAs come to the end of their useful life, U.S. space-based nuclear detection (NUDET) monitoring will be the secondary function of at least two satellite systems. Since its initial launch in 1971, the secondary function of the Defense Support Program (DSP) satellites has been the detection of nuclear explosions in space or the atmosphere. Modifications in DSP sensors are planned to improve atmospheric burst location and advanced radiation detection capabilities. The latter improvement would increase the detection range for nuclear detonations in space.[187]

The prime means for providing trans- and postattack nuclear detection monitoring will be the NUDET Detection System (NDS) carried on board the NAVSTAR Global Positioning System (GPS). Although the primary function of the GPS is to provide accurate locational data for targeting and navigation purposes, the NDS will represent a major secondary function. The GPS satellite constellation will consist of eighteen satellites in near-circular 17,610-mile orbits, with an inclination of 55 degrees. The eighteen satellites will be deployed in three or more planes, with each plane containing no more than six satellites, equally spaced. The arrangement will guarantee that at least four to six satellites are in view at all times from any point on or near the earth.

The entire GPS constellation is intended to be operational in 1988. Beginning in 1983 with the launch of GPS-8, the NDS will be on all subsequent GPS satellites.[188] The two NDS packages will include X-ray and optical sensors, Bhangmeters, EMP sensors, and a data-processing capability that, according to congressional testimony, will allow the detection of nuclear weapons detonations "anywhere in the world at any time and get its location down to less than a [deleted]."[189] A reasonable guess for the deleted word is *mile*. Data will be reported on a real-time basis, either directly to ground stations or first to airborne terminals or other GPS satellites for subsequent downlink transmissions.[190]

In addition to the nuclear detection packages on the VELA, DSP, and GPS satellites, there also appears to be a NUDET package on at least one other satellite system whose NUDET capability is considered classified. This may be the previously discussed Satellite Data System (SDS) satellites or the Defense Meteorological Satellite Program (DMSP) spacecraft. The latter are acknowledged to have "classified sensors" in addition to their weather sensors.[191]

Besides space-based detection systems, aerial sampling is employed to detect the atomic particles emitted by a nuclear explosion. Aircraft employed in aerial sampling operations include the U-2, the P-3, the C-135, and the B-52.[192] Aerial sampling operations are conducted over the United States, the Southern Hemisphere, and other areas under a variety of code names. One version of the C-130, the HC-130, is outfitted with a seawater sampler for sorties flown against possible foreign underwater nuclear tests.[193]

Detection of underground nuclear explosions depends on distinguishing between the seismic waves generated by a nuclear explosion and those created by an earthquake. In most cases, determining the location of seismic events eliminates the large majority of earthquakes from consideration as possible nuclear detonations. Otherwise, analysts may be able to distinguish earthquakes from detonations by the differing nature of the signals produced by each phenomenon; detonations are a point source, whereas earthquakes result from two bodies of rock slipping past each other. At distances less than 625 miles from an event, explosions greater than a few kilotons can easily be distinguished from earthquakes. At greater distances, such distinctions become far more difficult.[194] In addition, the actual recording of a seismic signal is disturbed by both instrumental and natural background noise, the latter setting a threshold of detectability.[195]

The foregoing limitations place a premium on locating monitoring stations or equipment in suitable locations and on developing techniques to enhance the signal-to-noise ratio obtained at any location. The simplest form of earth-based monitoring equipment is the seismometer, which is basically composed of a magnet fixed to the ground and a spring-suspended mass with an electric coil.[196] According to SIPRI:

> When seismic waves move the ground and the magnet attached to it, they leave the mass with the coil relatively unaffected. The relative motion of the magnet and coil generates a current in the coil which is proportional to their relative velocity.[197]

One means of enhancing the signal-to-noise ratio is the use of several seismometers in an array. Arrays increase the data set available for analysis in several ways, including providing different arrival times of the seismic waves at the different seismometers.

The seismic arrays and seismometers operated by the Air Force Technical Applications Center (AFTAC) are distributed throughout the world. Among AFTAC's nineteen detachments are detachments located in Torrejon, Spain; Crete, Greece; Lakenheath, United Kingdom; Okinawa, Japan; Alice Springs, Australia; Clark AFB, Philippines; and Misawa, Japan.[198] In addition, there are unmanned locations consisting of unattended sensors.

In addition to present systems for collection of nuclear intelligence and treaty monitoring, experimental work on both ground- and sea-based systems is continuing. For example, the Department of Energy has established the Regional Seismic Test Network (RSTN) for learning how an "in-country" system might be used for monitoring compliance with a comprehensive nuclear test ban treaty.[199] The RSTN consists of five transmitting stations in the United States and Canada, spaced about 2,000 kilometers apart—at Yellowknife, Northwest Territories; Red Lake, Ontario; Black Hills, South Dakota; Adirondacks, New York; and CPO Tennessee and Nevada Test Site—and three receiving stations. The receiving stations are located at Washington, D.C., the Lawrence Livermore National Laboratory, and the main System Control and Receiving Station (SCARS) at Sandia National Laboratory in Albuquerque, New Mexico.[200]

The goals of the RSTN experiment include providing engineering experience in the siting and operation of sophisticated seismic equipment under severe climactic conditions and evaluating the performance of an on-site detection system that could be deployed in the Soviet Union.[201] In addition, the network experiment is intended to help determine the number of seismic stations and the data-processing capabilities required to distinguish earthquakes and explosions of low magnitudes.[202]

With respect to undersea monitoring of nuclear explosions, research and development efforts that formed the Fiscal Year 1983 and Fiscal Year 1984 Nuclear Monitoring Programs include the testing of an ocean-bottom seismic sensor system, involving the deployment of seismometers in boreholes beneath the sea floor in international waters. The concept was tested in an experiment in the mid-Atlantic in which a seismometer was successfully installed and recovered from a borehole 2,000 feet below the sea floor in 15,000 feet of water, using the drill ship *Glomar Challenger*. Installation of a prototype station was attempted in September 1982, but unfavorable geological conditions prevented the *Challenger* from completing the drilling of the borehole.[203]

Limitations of Technical Collection Systems

Despite its employment of the technical collection systems described here, the United States still faces significant constraints on its ability to collect intelligence relevant to arms control. These constraints result from a variety of factors.

First, the United States possesses a limited number of collection systems, which cannot provide complete coverage of all interesting targets—even all targets related to arms control. For the last several years, the United States has had an imaging satellite of some sort in orbit every day of the year—but this is not the same as 24-hour coverage of every target or installation. The coverage provided—whether of a missile field, a naval base, or a border region—is intermittent. Although one could theoretically place enough spacecraft in orbit to monitor every point on earth continuously, the expense—in terms of processing and analysis as well as the cost of the spacecraft—would be prohibitive. Thus, U.S. plans to develop a system known as the KH-X, which would have provided an enormous increase in coverage, was canceled when the scale of processing and analysis requirements became apparent.[204]

Similarly, a SIGINT satellite such as Rhyolite can access only a limited number of targets in any particular time period. At any one time, such a satellite can monitor only a limited geographical area and a limited number of frequencies. Hence, although it may sweep through an enormous area and a large variety of frequencies over time, it cannot access everything at once. Furthermore, if a crisis occurs in an area near the Soviet Union, its target priorities may be altered, thus reducing coverage of the Soviet Union.

Even when they are functioning "perfectly," technical systems have limitations. Two major limitations of photographic systems are darkness and cloud cover. Theoretically, infrared sensors are capable of night photography. However, the resolution of these sensors is far poorer than that of the visible-light sensors, eliminating the possibility of obtaining the same level of detail obtained by daylight photography. For example, although the resolution of LANDSAT's visible-light photography is 90 feet, the normal resolution of its thermal infrared photography is 787 feet—a factor of almost nine.[205] This is particularly important with respect to areas in the northern Soviet Union (such as Murmansk Naval Base) where there are particularly short days for much of the year.

Cloud cover can be an even greater impediment to photography. As noted earlier, neither visible-light nor infrared sensors can penetrate cloud cover. This represents a rather serious limitation on the ability to monitor the Soviet Union and Eastern Europe. A good illustration of the difficulty created by cloud cover was an overhead photograph of the Point Salinas airstrip in Grenada, in which substantial portions of the airstrip were totally obscured by cloud cover.[206]

Eastern Europe is under cloud cover for about 60 to 70 percent of each year, thus providing only selected photographic opportunities. Likewise, the cloud cover situation in the Soviet Union prevents constant coverage. In some cases, a particular installation—such as the Kharkov tank factory—may be under cloud cover for the entire year.[207] In other cases, the cloud cover is such that imaging a particular area or target may require several *years*. Hence, it is possible for the United States to be "surprised" by the sudden discovery of a facility well under construction, such as the Abalakova radar.[208] Although the Defense Meterological Satellite Program satellites can provide information in the absence of cloud cover—avoiding film wastage—they cannot remove the cloud cover.

Signals intelligence collection systems also have limitations. Satellites at geosynchronous altitudes may be able to pick up signals only a small fraction in strength of those picked up on the ground, and they may be unable to pick up any signals during the initial boost phase of the launch. Thus, the strength of the signal picked up by Rhyolite satellites monitoring Soviet missile tests was only 1/1000 the strength of that picked up by the Iranian tracking stations.[209] Also, if the data are encrypted, whatever signals are intercepted will be of little value. There has been increasing Soviet encryption since 1977, with the Soviets using a one-time code for encryption and developing the capability to tape-record telemetry data on board and parachute the tapes to earth.[210] Thus, part of the data for the SS-N-20 were transmitted in code when it was first tested.[211]

There are also substantial uncertainties in assessing the yield of nuclear explosions. Thus, as one analyst has written:

> Estimating the yield of a nuclear test from seismic data alone is hard enough when we know exactly where the test took place (in what geologic surroundings) and what materials lie along the paths the seismic waves take in reaching our detectors. It is far more difficult when these factors are unknown.[212]

Specifically, variations in the geologic characteristics of the region surrounding the source can introduce changes of up to a factor of ten in the coupling of the explosion energy to the seismic wave. Furthermore, the depth of the explosion and the nature of the geologic structure within a few wavelengths of the source can alter the amount or azimuthal distance of seismic wave energy. In addition, the release of equivalent amounts of stored tectonic strain energy, resulting in the modification of the outgoing seismic signal, may also result from an explosion.[213]

Beyond these factors, considerable data indicate that there is significant regional variation in the degree to which seismic waves are attenuated as they pass through the upper mantle (31 to 62 miles). These variations are present both in the region where the explosion takes place and at the station used to measure the seismic signal.[214]

Such limitations have made it difficult to determine conclusively the validity of charges of Soviet noncompliance. The impact of the limitations is that there is an uncertainty factor of two in estimates of the yield of Soviet underground tests. A detonation with an estimated yield of 120 kilotons might (with 95 percent probability) have an actual yield of between 60 and 240 kilotons.[215]

Thus, one classified study found that the distribution of seismically measured yields of Soviet weapons is not inconsistent with Soviet observance of the 150–kiloton limit. However, the distribution is also not inconsistent with a distribution of actual yields in which there are some events above 150 kilotons.[216] Specifically, since 1974, the United States-estimated yield of eighteen Soviet underground explosions has exceeded 150 kilotons. However, according to an NSC report, no direct accusations were made because of "the uncertainties involved in our yield estimation process."[217] It is not surprising, then, that "seismic verification of a [comprehensive test ban treaty] will *not* provide absolute assurance that all underground nuclear explosions below some significant threshold will be identified."[218]

Technical collection systems are also subject to Soviet cover, concealment, and deception activities. Both the United States and the Soviet Union maintain extensive space-tracking and surveillance networks that provide detailed information on the ground tracks of the other nation's reconnaissance satellites, allowing each side to move indoors or dismantle objects they do not want the other side to "see." In addition, given the limitations imposed by cloud cover and darkness, the Soviets also have the option of conducting sensitive activities during long nights or under cloud cover.

According to several accounts, the Soviet General Staff has established a Chief Directorate of Strategic Deception to coordinate all such cover, concealment, and deception activities.[219] As Suvorov has written:

> Each Chief Directorate unit serving with a military district, a group of armies or a fleet makes use of data provided by the computer to carry out similar work for its own force and area. Each army division and regiment receives constantly up-dated schedules showing the precise times at which U.S. reconnaissance satellites will overfly their area, with details of the type of satellite and track it will follow.[220]

Of particular interest is his claim that "the Chief Directorate is constantly organizing flights by aircraft, test of rockets, troop movements and other operations to take place as the satellites' cameras pass overhead with the aim of emphasizing one aspect of activity while concealing others."[221]

Among the numerous charges of Soviet deception are those relating to missile accuracy. It has been alleged that the Soviet Union, given an understanding of the technical indicators and methods by which the United States estimates warhead accuracy, managed to sharply underrepresent the accuracy of some of its intercontinental ballistic missiles.[222]

In some cases, the opportunity for deception or cheating may hinge on mistaken assumptions concerning test requirements. Thus, as noted earlier, the SALT II Treaty placed restrictions on the number of release maneuvers. According to the belief that if a missile is to be MIRVed with a complement of *x* warheads, it must be tested with *x* maneuvers, such a provision would seem to provide a verifiable limitation on warheads per missile. However, if such a belief is incorrect, deception becomes a possibility. Similarly, the accounts alleging Soviet deception concerning missile accuracy assert that the CIA was operating under the belief that vital telemetry data could not be falsified because it was needed for guiding the missile.[223]

Furthermore, as the number of tests required to ensure system reliability decreases, the probability of successful cheating increases, since there will be fewer occasions when deception or concealment is required. The increase in computer capabilities has reduced the number of tests required for ballistic missiles. Thus, as Hussain has noted:

> Historically, it can be demonstrated that the number of tests required for the development of nuclear weapons and ballistic missiles has been reduced as alternative techniques of assessment have become available, and as the body of knowledge on which these innovations are based has increased.[224]

The limitations of technical collection systems have been concisely summarized by Howard Stoertz, Jr., who noted:

> National technical means of verification comprise a variety of sensors that are remote from the things they are monitoring. For the most part, such sensors cannot observe any given activity or location 24 hours a day and 365 days a year, let alone all activities in a large country. They cannot reliably observe what goes on inside buildings. They cannot instantly reveal the characteristics of a weapon or the size and pace of a program. What they can do is to obtain a series of snapshots and fragments that accumulate over time to permit the experienced analyst to reconstruct a weapon, program or process.[225]

Conclusions

The ability of the United States to verify Soviet compliance with the provisions of arms control agreements via technical collection systems, has been taken by many as a fundamental requirement for establishing that a treaty is in the interests of the United States. Quite often, *verify* is interpreted in its dictionary sense: "to establish the truth, accuracy, or reality of."[226] As Stephen Meyer has observed:

> Many in government and in the broader defense and foreign policy community have come to accept the proposition that arms control agreements that are not completely verifiable pose a potential threat to U.S. national security. The logical implication is that arms control treaties, or individual treaty provisions, that are less than 100 percent verifiable cannot be in the national interest.[227]

The focus on attaining absolutely verifiable treaty provisions is based on two fundamental misunderstandings concerning arms control. The first has been noted by Meyer, who has pointed out the fundamental difference between risk and uncertainty.[228] With regard to some provisions of a treaty or some entire treaties, the risk involved may be minimal; hence, the inability to monitor Soviet compliance directly, with a high degree of confidence, may be unnecessary. It may be that a combination of political and economic restraints and the limited (or negative) payoff that a violator might obtain from noncompliance makes a lower degree of confidence acceptable, particularly when it is combined with the capability to collect data from which inferences concerning compliance can be drawn. Thus, in regard to the Outer Space Treaty, an official statement made the following observation:

> While the United States does not, at present, possess a technical capability of assuredly determining whether or not a party to the Treaty has, in fact, placed, a nuclear weapon in orbit, this lack of certainty should not be equated to U.S. ignorance of foreign space activities. Corroboration that Treaty promises are being matched by conduct will have to rely on this class of information. Thus, while we cannot be *certain* that there are no bombs in orbit at the moment, for a variety of reasons, we are *confident* that there are none. . . .
>
> Were any foreign space power to violate its Treaty commitments, by launching an orbital bombardment system, the risks of detection would be great. To achieve a significant military advantage would require the placing of a number of nuclear weapons in orbit. Should such an event occur, our current technological capabilities are sufficient to alert us to the fact there are now space vehicles in orbit whose purposes might not be readily apparent.[229]

Similarly, as Amrom Katz has noted, there are many structures in the Soviet Union that could be used to hide missiles and launchers.[230] However, in the absence of a credible scenario explaining the utility of such an activity, the U.S. inability to determine the exact nature of the structures with a high degree of confidence is not considered a serious impediment to arms control agreements. (Whether such a scenario is credible or not will depend, rather significantly, on one's view of the robustness of the strategic balance. Those who believe that a Soviet decision to go to or risk war would be based on an expectation of an enhanced CMP advantage in the postattack world will be far more likely than others to find such scenarios credible.)

The second misconception that can be expected to result from a focus on absolute verification is that absolute verifiability is sufficient. Focusing on verification alone leads to an examination of technical collection capabilities only with respect to the monitoring of treaty provisions after the conclusion of negotiations. However, technical collection capabilities provide much of the information upon which negotiating positions are built and Soviet proposals assessed. Only if one has sufficient information on the entire range of Soviet military activities can the impact of a potential treaty be properly evaluated. The inability to assess the scope and direction of a program not covered by a treaty may be more threatening to U.S. security than the inability to monitor compliance with total confidence.

To illustrate these points, one need only go back to SALT I and note that the agreement placed no constraints on either warhead numbers or bombers. Yet without the ability to assess the number of warheads per missile or the number of bombers, no agreement would have been possible. It would have been impossible for the United States to come to an agreement limiting launchers if it was unable to determine whether those launchers had one or three or five or more warheads on them. Indeed, it was more important for the United States to have a high degree of confidence in its estimates of warhead per missile than its estimate of launcher numbers. In addition, U.S. estimates of Soviet missile accuracy and the resulting concern over Minuteman vulnerability have affected U.S. preferences concerning mobility and the composition of the Soviet strategic forces—two issues that were the subject of negotiations in SALT II.

Thus, there are at least two reasons why the United States does not want to specify the channels of telemetry that the Soviets are encrypting, whose data is required for verification purposes. One reason is the familiar protection of sources and methods—specifically, protection of the method of analysis.[231] A second reason is that all channels are relevant to the arms control process; complete knowledge of the weapons system enhances U.S. ability to determine which constraints would be acceptable and which would not.

Intelligence concerning intermediate-range weapons systems also is pertinent both to formulating proposals for a potential treaty and to monitoring compliance. The similarity of the SS-16 and the SS-20, noted earlier, creates a potential for cheating. Recently, it has been reported that U.S. officials fear that the Soviet Union has been hiding the deployment of SS-25 missiles under the cover of preparing bases for the deployment of additional SS-20 intermediate-range missiles.[232]

Furthermore, it is not only intelligence about Soviet nuclear weapons programs that is relevant to arms control. Arms control agreements are negotiated not only with the objective of assuring a peacetime balance but also with the objective of avoiding wartime asymmetries. Thus, the expected capability of U.S. SSBNs to survive Soviet antisubmarine warfare (ASW) forces and of the U.S. bombers to penetrate Soviet air defenses are factored into the evaluation of alternative arms control regimes. Therefore, the intelligence collected by technical systems on Soviet ASW and air defense capabilities is quite relevant to arms control—despite the fact that they are not constrained by an agreement, nor are nuclear weapons programs. Hence, distinctions between arms control monitoring and military intelligence are often arbitrary and misleading. Although certain technical collection activities are of little or no relevance to the monitoring of an agreement, it can be legitimately claimed that all collection relevant to the strategic capabilities of the nation constrained by the agreement is relevant.

It should be further noted that the ability to negotiate agreements concerning warhead numbers and other such provisions is based on previous experience in collecting intelligence about such characteristics. Without the experience and developmental work involved in the Rhyolite satellite and the various tracking radars, it would have been impossible to conclude a SALT II agreement containing warhead limitations. "Verification technology" is not developed after an agreement; rather, technical capabilities to some extent dictate the types of provisions that can be included in a treaty. Today's espionage is tomorrow's verification.

It has been argued that with regard to the agreements between the United States and the USSR limiting the deployment, construction, or employment of nuclear weapons, "the intelligence relevant to U.S. participation in such agreements" can legitimately be said to include the entire gamut of intelligence concerning Soviet strategic capabilities. Of course, such an argument can provide a rationalization for collection programs that might otherwise be considered too costly or risky—despite the fact that the *initial* rationale of collection programs is almost never truly to support arms control but rather to provide desired military intelligence. Thus, an anonymous U.S. official justified the Holystone program with the statement: "One of the reasons we have a SALT agreement is because we know of what the Soviets are doing, and Holystone is an important part of what we know about the Soviet submarine force."[232] Such a statement might have been an attempt to "sell" the requirement for a risky program by wrapping it in the mantle of arms control.

If the U.S. arms control policy is to obey the dictate of PD-50 and its successor and help support the U.S. defense posture, it must be based on as thorough an understanding of Soviet strategic (and even theater) military capabilities. Whether the terms of a particular agreement are advantageous to the United States will depend on the information produced by U.S. technical collection systems directed at Soviet strategic activities and on an assessment of the political, economic, and technical constraints facing the Soviet military establishment.

Notes

1. *Arms Control and Disarmament Agreements: Texts and Histories of Agreements* (Washington, D.C.: Arms Control and Disarmament Agency, 1980), p. 41.
2. Ibid., pp. 51–52.
3. Ibid., p. 102.
4. Ibid., p. 140.

5. Ibid.

6. Ibid.

7. Ibid.

8. Ibid., p. 141.

9. Ibid., p. 162. For a history of the ABM Treaty and the SALT I Agreement, see John Newhouse, *Cold Dawn: The Story of SALT* (New York: Holt, Rinehart and Winston, 1973).

10. *Arms Control and Disarmament Agreements,* p. 167.

11. Ibid., p. 174.

12. For a history of the SALT II negotiations, see Strobe Talbott, *Endgame: The Inside Story of SALT II* (New York: Harper & Row, 1979).

13. *Arms Control and Disarmament Agreements,* pp. 214– 218, 221.

14. Ibid.

15. The basic difference between alternative means of obtaining imagery— visible-light photography, infrared, and radar—is that they rely on different portions of the electromagnetic spectrum to produce images. Photographic equipment is sensitive to electromagnetic radiation with a wavelength between 0.0004 mm and 0.00075 mm— the visible-light portion of the spectrum.

Photographic equipment may be of either the film-based or television types. A conventional camera records on film the varying light levels reflected from a scene and all of the separate objects in that scene. An electro-optical camera works by converting the varying light levels into electrical signals. A numerical value is assigned to each of the signals—called picture elements, or pixels. The process transforms a picture (analog) image to a digital image, which can then be transmitted electronically to distant points. The signal can then be reconstructed from the digital to the analog format, and the analog signal can then be displayed on a video screen or made into a photograph.

Imagery may also be obtained by infrared photography, which uses radiation in a portion of the near-infrared segment of the electromagnetic spectrum to produce imagery. Unlike the portion of the spectrum used by photographic equipment, infrared photography is not visible to the human eye. However, infrared photography, like visible-light photography, depends on the reflective properties of objects rather than their emission of radiation.

Color infrared film is also known as "false color" film because the objects are recorded in colors that are different from the way they appear in nature. Thus, healthy vegetation appears in exotic magenta-red tones, while cut vegetation does not reflect infrared radiation at all. Such film can be used as a means of detecting camouflaged field installations, weapons, or vehicles; ordinary film will not distinguish real vegetation from cut vegetation used for camouflage purposes, but color infrared film will.

Other sensors are employed to obtain imagery from the mid- and far-infrared portion of the electromagnetic spectrum. Thus, thermal infrared scanners work at long wavelengths and produce imagery via the radiation (heat) emitted by objects. Such devices can detect buried structures (such as missile silos) or underground construction by measuring temperature differences between targets and the earth's surface. Since infrared photography and thermal infrared scanners do not depend on visible light to develop imagery, these techniques can be employed during darkness. However, as with visible-light photography, infrared imagery depends on the sky being relatively free of cloud cover. Furthermore, the resolution of infrared photography is substantially poorer than that of visible light photography.

Radar (radio detection and ranging) is a means of producing imagery in the presence of cloud cover. Radar imagery is produced by bouncing radio waves off an area or object. The data concerning the time required for the pulses to return is used to produce an image. Since radio waves are not attenuated by the water vapor in the atmosphere, they are able to penetrate cloud cover.

In addition to the basic sensors that can be used to produce imagery, there are several means of enhancing the effectiveness of the sensor-produced data. Multispectral scanners use separate lenses to shoot several pictures simultaneously, each in a different region of the visible-light and photographic infrared bands. Special coloring and combination of the multiple images reveals camouflaged military facilities that regular photos would conceal. Image enhancement pulls out more submerged detail. In this technique, computers disassemble a picture into millions of electronic Morse code pulses, then use mathematical formulas to manipulate the color contrast and intensity of each spot. Each image can be reassembled in various ways to highlight special features and objects that were hidden in the original image. A third technique is optical subtraction, whereby electronic optical subtraction of earlier pictures from later ones makes unchanged buildings or landscapes in a scene disappear and new objects, such as missile silos under construction, stand out.

16. Bhupendra Jasani, *Outer Space—Battlefield of the Future?* (New York: Crane, Russak, 1978), p. 12.

17. See James Fusca, "Space Surveillance," *Space/Aeronautics,* June 1964, pp. 92–103.

18. Ibid.; National Photographic Interpretation Center, *Problems of Photographic Imagery Analysis* (Washington, D.C.: CIA, 1968) in Declassified Documents Reference System (DDRS) 1981–13B.

19. "Big Bird: America's Spy in Space," *Flight International,* January 27, 1977.

20. Philip Klass, *Secret Sentries in Space* (New York: Random House, 1971), pp. 170–171.

21. "Space Reconnaissance Dwindles," *Aviation Week and Space Technology,* October 6, 1980, pp. 18–20.

22. Ibid.

23. Curtis L. Peebles, "The Guardians," *Spaceflight,* November 1978, pp. 381ff.

24. Jasani, *Outer Space,* p. 1.

25. "Perspective," *Space/Aeronautics,* February 1970, pp. 22–24; and "Industry Observer," *Aviation Week and Space Technology,* June 30, 1969, p. 13.

26. See, for example, Klass, *Secret Sentries in Space,* chapter 17.

27. "Space Reconnaissance Dwindles."

28. Ibid.

29. Mark Hewlish, "Satellites Show Their Warlike Face," *New Scientist,* October 1, 1981, pp. 36–40.

30. James B. Schultz, "Inside the Blue Cube," *Defense Electronics,* April 1983, pp. 52–59.

31. Anthony Kenden, "A New U.S. Military Space Mission," *Journal of the British Interplanetary Society* 35(October 1982): pp. 441–444.

32. "Space Reconnaissance Dwindles."

33. "The Military Race in Space," *Defense Monitor* 9(1980): 2.

34. John Pike, "Reagan Prepares for War in Outer Space," *Counter Spy* 7(September–November 1982): 17–22.

35. "CBS Evening News With Walter Cronkite," October 3, 1980.

36. "Missile Disguise," *Aviation Week and Space Technology,* September 29, 1980, p. 17.

37. "Inside the Rescue Mission," *Newsweek,* July 12, 1982, pp. 19ff.

38. "New Payload Could Boost Shuttle Cost," *Aviation Week and Space Technology,* August 14, 1978, pp. 16–17.

39. Gerald L. Borrowman, "Recent Trends in Orbital Reconnaissance," *Spaceflight,* January 1, 1982, pp. 10ff; Pike, "Reagan Prepares for War in Outer Space"; "New Payload Could Boost Shuttle Cost."

40. "Space Reconnaissance Dwindles"; "Navy Will Develop All-Weather Ocean Monitor Satellite," *Aviation Week and Space Technology,* October 6, 1980, pp. 18–20.

41. "Industry Observer," *Aviation Week and Space Technology,* December 14, 1962, p. 12.

42. "Space Reconnaissance Dwindles."

43. "Washington Round-up," *Aviation Week and Space Technology,* June 4, 1979, p. 11; Robert C. Toth, "Anaheim Firm May Have Sought Spy Satellite Data," *Los Angeles Times,* October 10, 1982, pp. 1, 32.

44. Jay Miller, *The Lockheed A-12/Y-12/SR-71 Story* (Austin: Aerofax, 1983), p. 2.

45. "Shaping Tomorrow's CIA," *Time,* February 6, 1978, pp. 10ff; "Radar Detector Aboard SR-71 Alerted to Missile Attack," *New York Times,* August 29, 1981, p. 3.

46. "Shaping Tomorrow's CIA."

47. Leslie Gelb, "Korean Jet: Points Still to be Settled," *New York Times,* September 26, 1983, p. A6.

48. Col. Asa Bates, "National Technical Means of Verification," *Royal United Services Institute Journal* 123(June 1978): 64–73.

49. Benjamin Schemmer, *The Raid* (New York: Harper & Row, 1975), p. 169.

50. Col. William V. Kennedy, *Intelligence Warfare* (New York: Crescent, 1983).

51. "U-2 Facts and Figures," *Air Force Magazine,* January 1976, p. 55.

52. Ibid.

53. "Lockheed Back Into U-2 Spy Plane Business," *Defense Week,* February 22, 1983, p. 16.

54. David Wise and Thomas B. Ross, *The U-2 Affair* (New York: Random House, 1962), p. 56.

55. Ibid., p. 11.

56. Ibid.

57. Bates, "National Technical Means."

58. Ibid.

59. Wise and Ross, *The U-2 Affair,* p. 58.

60. Howard Silber, "SAC U-2's Provided Nicaraguan Pictures," *Omaha World Herald,* March 10, 1982, p. 2.

61. House Permanent Select Committee on Intelligence, *Annual Report* (Washington, D.C.: U.S. Government Printing Office, 1978), p. 31.

62. Ibid., p. 36.

63. John Prados, *The Soviet Estimate: U.S. Intelligence Analysis and Russian Military Strength* (New York: Dial, 1982), p. 203. See also Richard G. Wiley, *Electronic Intelligence: The Analysis of Radar Signals* (Dedham, Mass.: Artech House, 1982).

64. Prados, *The Soviet Estimate,* p. 203; Farouq Hussain, *The Future of Arms Control: Part IV, The Impact of Weapons Test Restrictions* (London: International Institute for Strategic Studies, 1980); and Robert Kaiser, "Verification of SALT II: Arts and Science," *Washington Post,* June 15, 1979, p. 1.

65. House Permanent Select Committee on Intelligence, *Annual Report,* p. 38.

66. House Permanent Select Committee on Intelligence, *H.R. 6588, The National Intelligence Act of 1980* (Washington, D.C.: U.S. Government Printing Office, 1980), p. 521.

67. Robert Lindsey, *The Falcon and the Snowman* (New York: Simon & Schuster, 1979), p. 54.

68. *Frequency* is a term used to describe either the number of times an alternating current goes through its complete cycle per second or the vibration rate of sound waves in the air. One cycle per second is referred to as a hertz (Hz); 1,000 Hz is a kilohertz (kHz); 1 million Hz is a megahertz (MHz); and 1 billion Hz is a gigahertz (GHz). Frequencies may range from 0.001 Hz to 8×10^{21} Hz. The terms used in this chapter and the corresponding frequency limits are given in the following table:

Terms Used	Frequency Limits
Very low frequency (VLF)	3–30 KHz
Low frequency (LF)	30–300 KHz
High frequency (HF)	3–30 MHz
Very high frequency (VHF)	30–300 MHz
Ultra high frequency (UHF)	300 MHz–3 GHz
Super high frequency (SHF)	3–30 GHz
Extremely high frequency (EHF)	30–300 GHz

Microwave frequencies overlap the UHF, SHF, and EHF bands, running from 1 to 50 GHz. See Robert L. Shrader, *Electronic Communications* (New York: McGraw-Hill, 1980), pp. 64–65, 627.

69. Lindsey, *The Falcon and the Snowman,* p. 157.

70. Desmond Ball, *Secret Satellites Over Australia,* forthcoming.

71. Ibid.

72. Ibid.

73. Ibid.

74. Lindsey, *The Falcon and the Snowman,* pp. 345–346; Clarence Robinson, "Soviet Push Telemetry Bypass," *Aviation Week and Space Technology,* April 16, 1979, p. 14.

75. Jeffrey Richelson and William Arkin, "Spy Satellites: (Secret) But Much is Known," *Washington Post,* January 6, 1985, pp. C1–C2.

76. Philip J. Klass, "U.S. Monitoring Capability Impaired," *Aviation Week and Space Technology,* May 14, 1979, p. 18.

77. Ibid.

78. Victor Marchetti interview in the film *Allies.*

79. Richard Burt, "U.S. Plans New Way to Check Soviet Missile Tests," *New York Times,* June 29, 1979, p. A3.

80. Hussain, *The Future of Arms Control.*

81. "Washington Round-Up," *Aviation Week and Space Technology,* January 2, 1984, p. 13; Pike, "Reagan Prepares for War in Outer Space."

82. "Washington Round-up," p. 13; Pike, "Reagan Prepares for War in Outer Space." The existence of such a satellite and its early launch dates becomes apparent when one compares the launch data for SDS satellites in the *RAE Table of Earth Satellites* with testimony in House Committee on Appropriations, *Department of Defense Appropriations for Fiscal Year 1980, Part 6* (Washington, D.C.: U.S. Government Printing Office, 1979), p. 160; *DOD C³I Program Management Structure and Major Programs*, 10 December 1980; Senate Committee on Armed Services, *Department of Defense Appropriations Fiscal Year 1980, Part 5* (Washington, D.C.: U.S. Government Printing Office, 1980), p. 2663.

83. "Washington Round-Up," *Aviation Week and Space Technology*, June 4, 1979, p. 14.

84. Kenden, "A New U.S. Military Space Mission."

85. Ibid.

86. David Alan Rosenberg, "The Origins of Overkill: Nuclear Weapons and America Strategy 1945-1960," *International Security* 7(Spring 1983): 3–71.

87. Ted Greenwood, "Reconnaissance, Surveillance and Arms Control," *Adelphi Papers* No. 88, 1972.

88. Duncan Campbell, "Spy in the Sky," *New Statesman*, September 9, 1983, pp. 8–9.

89. Harry F. Eustace, "Changing Intelligence Priorities," *Electronic Warfare/Defense Electronics*, November 1978, pp. 85ff.

90. Dennis MacShane, "Spy Stations in Cyprus," *New Statesman*, June 30, 1978, p. 890; Miller, *The Lockheed A-12/Y-12/SR-71 Story*, p. 51.

91. Richard Burt, "Technology is Essential to Arms Verification," *New York Times*, August 14, 1979, pp. C1–C2.

92. "Reconnaissance and Special Duty Aircraft," *Air Force Magazine*, May 1978, p. 118; Charles W. Corddry and Albert Schistedt, Jr., "Planes' Covert Role Is to Monitor Soviet Space Flights and Missile Tests," *Baltimore Sun*, May 7, 1981, p. 1; Department of the Air Force, *Supporting Data for Fiscal Year 1984, Budget Estimates Submitted to Congress Descriptive Summaries, Research, Development, Test and Evaluation* (Washington, D.C.: U.S. Government Printing Office, 1983), pp. 862–863.

93. T. Edward Eshelon and Tom Bernard, "A Personal View: Former RC-135 Crewmen Question U.S. Version of Jet Liner Incident," *Baltimore News American*, September 14, 1983, p. 8.

94. House Committee on Appropriations, *Department of Defense Appropriations for Fiscal Year 1984, Part 8*, (Washington, D.C.: U.S. Government Printing Office, 1983), p. 394.

95. Brian Bennett, Tony Powell, and John Adams, *The USAF Today* (London: West Aviation Group, 1981), pp. 49–53.

96. Philip Taubman, "U.S. Says Intelligence Plane Was on a Routine Mission," *New York Times*, September 5, 1983, p. 4.

97. Campbell, "Spy in the Sky."

98. Michael Getler, "Soviets Held Test of New Missile Three Days After Jet Downed," *Washington Post*, September 16, 1983, p. A28.

99. For a history of COBRA DANE, see E. Michael Del Papa, *Meeting the Challenge: ESD and the COBRA DANE Construction Effort on Shemya Island* (Bedford, Mass.: Air Force System Command, Electronic Systems Division, 1979).

100. Ibid., p. 3.

101. Philip J. Klass, "USAF Tracking Radar Details Disclosed," *Aviation Week and Space Technology,* October 25, 1976, pp. 41ff.

102. Kenneth J. Stein, "Cobra Judy Phased Array Radar Tested," *Aviation Week and Space Technology,* August 10, 1981, pp. 70–73.

103. Stockholm International Peace Research Institute (SIPRI), *World Armaments and Disarmaments, SIPRI Yearbook 1980* (London: Taylor & Francis, 1980), pp. 296–297.

104. "Spying on Russia, With China's Help," *U.S. News and World Report,* June 29, 1981, p. 10.

105. F.G. Samia, "The Norwegian Connection: Norway, (Un)willing Spy for the U.S.," *Covert Action Information Bulletin* 9(June 1980): 4–9.

106. Owen Wilkes and Nils Peter Gleditsch, *Intelligence Installations in Norway: Their Number, Function and Legality* (Oslo: Prio, 1978), pp. 7–36.

107. Ibid.

108. Ibid.

109. Ibid.

110. James Bamford, *The Puzzle Palace: A Report on NSA, America's Most Secret Agency* (Boston: Houghton Mifflin, 1982), p. 162.

111. See Jeffrey T. Richelson and Desmond Ball, *The Ties That Bind* (London: Allen & Unwin, 1984), chapter 8.

112. SIPRI, *World Armaments, 1980,* pp. 296–297.

113. Senate Committee on Appropriation, *Department of Defense Appropriations FY 1973, Part 4* (Washington, D.C.: U.S. Government Printing Office, 1972), p. 363.

114. Seymour M. Hersh, "Submarines of US Stage Spy Missions Inside Soviet Waters," *New York Times,* May 25, 1975, pp. 1, 42.

115. George Kistiakowsky, *A Scientist at the White House: The Private Diary of President Eisenhower's Science Advisor* (Cambridge, Mass.: Harvard University Press, 1976), p. 153.

116. Hersh, "Submarines."

117. Ibid.

118. Geoffrey Murray, "Under Soviet Eyes, U.S. and Japan Hold Sea Exercises," *Christian Science Monitor,* September 22, 1983, p. 6.

119. "U.S. Launches Recon Satellite, Soviet Fleet Maneuvers May Be Target," *Aerospace Daily,* April 22, 1975, pp. 290–291.

120. Ibid.

121. Anthony Kenden, "U.S. Reconnaissance Satellite Programs," *Spaceflight,* July 20, 1973, p. 257.

122. Janko Jackson, "A Methodology for Ocean Surveillance Analysis," *Naval War College Review* 27(September/October 1974): 71–89.

123. "Navy Plans Ocean Surveillance Satellite," *Aviation Week and Space Technology,* August 30, 1971, p. 13; "Industry Observer," *Aviation Week and Space Technology,* February 28, 1972, p. 9.

124. "Navy Plans Ocean Surveillance Satellite."

125. "Industry Observer," p. 9.

126. The entire system consists of the satellite/spacecraft (White Cloud), ground terminals for data receipt from the satellite, and data-processing equipment.

127. "Navy Ocean Surveillance Satellite Depicted," *Aviation Week and Space Technology*, May 24, 1976, p. 22.

128. "Expanded Ocean Surveillance Effort Set," *Aviation Week and Space Technology*, June 10, 1978, pp. 22–23; Hewlish, "Satellites Show Their Warlike Face."

129. "Expanded Ocean Surveillance Effort Set"; "Satellites Show Their Warlike Face."

130. Defense Marketing Service, *Code Name Handbook* (Greenwich, Conn.: Defense Marketing Service, 1980), p. 78; House Committee on Appropriations, *Military Construction Appropriations for 1981* (Washington, D.C.: U.S. Government Printing Office, 1980), pp. 1474–1477, 1504–1509; House Committee on Appropriations, *Military Construction Appropriations for 1982* (Washington, D.C.: U.S. Government Printing Office, 1981), pp. 1231–1236, 1301–1306; House Committee on Appropriations, *Military Construction Appropriation for 1983, Part I* (Washington, D.C.: U.S. Government Printing Office, 1982), p. 842; Senate Armed Services Committee, *Military Construction Authorization Fiscal Year 1980* (Washington, D.C.: U.S. Government Printing Office, 1979); and House Armed Services Committee, *Military Construction Authorization Fiscal Year 1980* (Washington, D.C.: U.S. Government Printing Office, 1979), p. 474.

131. L.T. Peacock, *U.S. Naval Aviation Today* (Uxbridge: Cheney Press 1977), p. 25.

132. "Lockheed P-3 Orion," in *DMS Market Intelligence Report* (Greenwich, Conn.: Defense Marketing Service, 1982), pp. 1–7.

133. Peacock, *U.S. Naval Aviation Today*.

134. Ibid.

135. Owen Wilkes, "Strategic Anti-Submarine Warfare and Its Implications for a Counterforce First Strike," in *SIPRI Yearbook 1979* (London: Taylor & Francis, 1979), p. 430.

136. "Program 749," in *DMS Market Intelligence Report* (Greenwich, Conn.: Defense Marketing Service, 1977), pp. 1, 2.

137. Senate Committee on Commerce, Science and Transportation, *NASA Authorization for Fiscal Year 1980* (Washington, D.C.: U.S. Government Printing Office, 1979), p. 1723.

138. "Testimony of Admiral Metzel," in Senate Armed Services Committee, *Department of Defense Authorization for Appropriations for Fiscal Year 1980, Part 6* (Washington, D.C.: U.S. Government Printing Office, 1979), p. 2925.

139. Wilkes, "Strategic Anti-Submarine Warfare."

140. *Department of Defense Authorization for Appropriations for Fiscal Year 1980, Part 6*, pp. 2947–2949; Wilkes, "Strategic Anti-Submarine Warfare," p. 431; House Committee on International Relations, *Evaluation of Fiscal Year 1979 Arms Control Impact Statements: Toward More Informed Congressional Participation in National Security Policy Making* (Washington, D.C.: U.S. Government Printing Office, 1978), p. 112.

141. Joel S. Wit, "Advances in Anti-Submarine Warfare," *Scientific American* (February 1981): 36–37.

142. *Department of Defense Authorization for Appropriations for Fiscal Year 1980, Part 6*, pp. 2947–2949; Wilkes, "Strategic Anti-Submarine Warfare," p. 431; *Evaluation of Fiscal Year 1979 Arms Control Impact Statements*, p. 112.

143. Kosta Tsipis, "Antisubmarine Warfare: Fact and Fiction," *New Scientist,* January 16, 1975, p. 147; "ASW," in *DMS Market Intelligence Report* (Greenwich, Conn.: Defense Marketing Service, 1980).

144. Larry L. Booda, "Antisubmarine Warfare Reacts to Strategic Indicators," *Sea Technology,* November 1981, p. 12.

145. *Fiscal Year 1981 Arms Control Impact Statement* (Washington, D.C.: U.S. Government Printing Office, 1980), pp. 347–348.

146. "British Say Soviet Lags in Sub Detection," *Baltimore Sun,* December 31, 1980, p. 4.

147. NORAD/SPACECOM, *Numerical Index of Standard Publications,* Command Regulation 0-2, July 1, 1983, p. 14.

148. John Noble Wilford, "Spy Satellite Reportedly Added in Shuttle Flight," *New York Times,* October 20, 1981, p. C4. For an article questioning these assertions, see Anthony Kenden, "Was 'Columbia' Photographed by a KH-11?" *Journal of the British Interplanetary Society* 36(1983): 73–77.

149. "Washington Round-up," *Aviation Week and Space Technology,* April 18, 1983, p. 17; Jack Cushman, "Space Eyes Stretch the Limits of IR Budget and Technologies," *Defense Week,* January 24, 1983, pp. 1, 18–19.

150. House Committee on Appropriations, *Department of Defense Appropriations for 1984, Part 4* (Washington, D.C.: U.S. Government Printing Office, 1983), pp. 618–619.

151. House Committee on Appropriations, *Department of Defense Appropriations for 1984, Part 8* (Washington, D.C.: U.S. Government Printing Office, 1983), pp. 506–508.

152. "SAC Fact Sheet," August 1981, pp. 81–001, 415.

153. Ibid.

154. Owen Wilkes and Nils Peter Gleditsch, "Optimal Satellite Tracking: A Case Study of University Participation in Space Warfare," *Journal of Peace Research* 15(1978): 215–225.

155. Craig Covault, "USAF Awaits Space Defense Guidance," *Aviation Week and Space Technology,* February 22, 1982, p. 65; David Russell, "NORAD Adds Radar Optics to Increase Space Defense," *Defense Electronics,* July 1982, pp. 82–86.

156. Senate Committee on Armed Services, *Department of Defense Authorization for 1980, Part 6* (Washington, D.C.: U.S. Government Printing Office, 1979), p. 3022; "U.S. Upgrading Ground-Based Sensors," *Aviation Week and Space Technology,* June 16, 1980, pp. 239–242; Russell, "NORAD Adds Radar Optics."

157. "U.S. Upgrading Ground-Based Sensors."

158. Russell, "NORAD Adds Radar Optics."

159. "U.S. Upgrading Ground-Based Sensors."

160. "Spacetrack," in *Jane's Weapon's Systems, 1982–83* (London: Jane's, 1983), pp. 233–234; Russell, "NORAD Adds Radar Optics."

161. "The Arms Race in Space," in *SIPRI Yearbook 1978: World Disarmament and Armaments* (New York: Crane, Russak, 1978), pp. 114–124.

162. "Spacetrack"; *Department of Defense Authorization 1980, Part 6,* p. 3021; Covault, "USAF Awaits Space Defense Guidance"; *Department of Defense Appropriations for 1981, Part 8,* p. 240.

163. "Improved U.S. Warning Net Spurred," *Aviation Week and Space Technology,* June 23, 1980, pp. 38ff.

164. John Hamre, Richard Davison, and Peter H. Tarpgard, *Strategic Command, Control and Communications: Alternative Approaches for Modernization* (Washington, D.C.: Congressional Budget Office, 1981), p. 10.

165. "SLBM Detection Systems," in *Jane's Weapons Systems, 1982–83,* p. 501.

166. "U.S. Upgrading Ground-Based Sensors."

167. "SLBM Detection Systems," p. 501.

168. Hamre et al., *Strategic Command, Control and Communications,* p. 10.

169. "AN/FPS-85," in *Jane's Weapons Systems, 1982–83,* p. 506; "The Arms Race in Space," in *SIPRI Yearbook 1978,* pp. 114–124; Hamre et. al., *Strategic Command, Control and Communications.*

170. Owen Wilkes, *Spacetracking Spacewarfare* (Oslo: International Peace Research Institute, 1978), p. 27.

171. Ibid.

172. "AN/FPS-85"; Wilkes, *Spacetracking and Spacewarfare,* p. 27.

173. "SAC Fact Sheet."

174. "The Arms Race in Space," in *SIPRI Yearbook 1978,* pp. 114–124.

175. "SAC Fact Sheet."

176. *Code Name Handbook 1981* (Greenwich, Conn.: Defense Marketing Service, 1981), p. 168; House Committee on Appropriations, *Department of Defense Appropriations for 1981, Part 8* (Washington, D.C.: U.S. Government Printing Office, 1980), p. 241.

177. Senate Committee on Appropriations, *Department of Defense Appropriations Fiscal Year 1972* (Washington, D.C.: U.S. Government Printing Office, 1971), p. 672.

178. "Forum: The Explosion of October 16," *Bulletin of the Atomic Scientists,* February 1965, pp. 19–24.

179. Larry Booda, "Satellite Planned to Detect Space Blasts," *Aviation Week and Space Technology,* November 14, 1960, p. 29. Prior to that time, of course, the United States did monitor Soviet nuclear explosions; the first Soviet atomic explosion was detected by a reconnaissance aircraft outfitted with air-sampling equipment and flying a regular mission. VELA represents the beginnings of the present worldwide detection system.

180. Ibid.

181. Philip Klass, "Clandestine Nuclear Test Doubted," *Aviation Week and Space Technology,* August 11, 1980, pp. 67–72.

182. David Baker, *The Shape of Wars to Come* (New York: Stein & Day, 1982), pp. 147–148.

183. Ibid., p. 149.

184. Klass, "Clandestine Nuclear Test Doubted."

185. Sidney Singer, "The VELA Satellite Program for Detection of High Altitude Nuclear Detonations," *Proceedings of the IEEE* 53(December 1965): 1935–1948.

186. Klass, "Clandestine Nuclear Test Doubted"; Eliot Marshall, "Navy Lab Concludes VELA Saw a Bomb," *Science,* August 29, 1980, pp. 996–999.

187. "Industry Observer," *Aviation Week and Space Technology,* December 13, 1982, p. 13; "Washington Round-Up," *Aviation Week and Space Technology,* December 6, 1982, p. 19.

188. "Washington Round-Up," p. 19; House Committee on Appropriations, *Department of Defense Appropriations for 1983, Part 5* (Washington, D.C.: Government Printing Office 1982), pp. 16, 75.

189. *Department of Defense Appropriations for 1983, Part 5*, p. 16; *Department of Defense Appropriations for 1984, Part 8*, p. 337; House Committee on Armed Services, *Department of Energy National Security and Military Applications of Nuclear Energy Authorization Act of 1984* (Washington, D.C.: U.S. Government Printing Office, 1983), pp. 383–384.

190. "Navstar Bloc 2 Satellites to Have Crosslinks, Radiation Hardening," *Defense Electronics*, July 1983, p. 16.

191. *Department of Energy National Security and Military Applications*, pp. 383–384, 392; "RCA Astro-Electronics Briefing Slides," Defense Meterological Satellite Program, no date.

192. Air Force Technical Applications Center Regulations CENR 55-3, "Aerial Sampling Operations," October 22, 1982.

193. Ibid.

194. Henry R. Myers, "Extending the Nuclear Test Ban," *Scientific American* 226(January 1982): 13–23; Lynn R. Sykes and Jack F. Evernden, "The Verification of a Comprehensive Nuclear Test Ban," *Scientific American* 247(October 1982): 47–55.

195. "The Comprehensive Test Ban," in *SIPRI Yearbook 1978*, p. 335.

196. Ibid.

197. Ibid.

198. Private communication from William Arkin and Richard Fieldhouse, 1984.

199. Steven R. Taylor, "The Regional Seismic Test Network," *Energy and Technology Review*, May 1983, pp. 29–39.

200. Ibid.

201. Ibid.

202. Ibid.

203. *Department of Defense Justification of Estimates for Fiscal Year 1984*, (Washington, D.C.: Department of Defense, 1983), pp. 257–261.

204. See Jeffrey Richelson, "The Keyhole Satellite Program," *Journal of Strategic Studies* 7(1984): 121–153.

205. "Malfunction of Infrared Systems Reduces Landsat's Data Return," *Aviation Week and Space Technology*, August 28, 1978, p. 49.

206. *Los Angeles Times*, October 26, 1983, p. 16.

207. Andrew Cockburn, *The Threat: Inside the Soviet Military Machine* (New York: Random House, 1983), p. 19.

208. Philip Klass, "U.S. Scrutinizing New Soviet Radar," *Aviation Week and Space Technology*, August 22, 1983, pp. 19–20.

209. Klass, "U.S. Monitoring Capability Impaired."

210. Clarence A. Robinson, "Soviets Push Telemetry Bypass," *Aviation Week and Space Technology*, April 16, 1975, pp. 14–15.

211. Don Irwin, "Soviet Missile Data Encoded, U.S. Says," *Los Angeles Times*, February 16, 1980, p. 3.

212. Milo D. Nordyke, "The Test Ban Treaties: Verifying Compliance," *Energy and Technology Review*, May 1983, pp. 1–9.

213. Ibid.

214. Ibid.

215. Jack Anderson, "Arms Treaty Compliance Hard to Verify," *Washington Post,* September 28, 1984, p. E7.

216. Jeffrey Smith, "Scientists Fault Charges of Soviet Cheating: Experts Say That the United States Lacks Good Evidence of Soviet Dishonesty on Strategic Arms Treaties," *Science,* May 13, 1983, pp. 696–697.

217. Anderson, "Arms Treaty Compliance."

218. William J. Hannon, Jr., "Seismic Verification of a Comprehensive Test Ban," *Energy and Technology Review,* May 1983, pp. 50–65.

219. See Victor Suvorov, *Inside the Soviet Army* (New York: Macmillan, 1982), pp. 106–107.

220. Ibid.

221. Ibid.

222. Edward J. Epstein, "Disinformation: Or, Why the CIA Cannot Verify an Arms Control Agreement," *Commentary,* July 1982, pp. 21–28.

223. Ibid.

224. Hussain, *The Future of Arms Control,* p. 165.

225. Howard Stoertz, Jr., "Monitoring a Nuclear Freeze," *International Security* 8(1984): 91–110.

226. *The Merriam-Webster Dictionary* (New York: Pocket Books, 1974), p. 767.

227. Stephen M. Meyer, "Verification and Risk in Arms Control," *International Security* 8(1984): 112–126.

228. Ibid.

229. LBJ Library, "Questions and Answers on Outer Space Treaty," I-4000/67, No. 23, February 23, 1967.

230. Amrom Katz, "Verification and SALT: The State of the Art and the Art of the State," *Heritage Foundation Policy Series,* 1979.

231. Talbott, *Endgames,* pp. 194–202.

232. Robert C. Toth, "Soviets Siting New Missile, U.S. Suspects," *Los Angeles Times,* September 22, 1984, pp. 1, 18.

11

The Standing Consultative Commission: Past Performance and Future Possibilities

Dan Caldwell

At the beginning of April 1979, an epidemic of deadly anthrax broke out in the Soviet city of Sverdlovsk.[1] The epidemic lasted about six weeks, and estimates of fatalities range from 20 to 1,000. American officials became concerned that the epidemic had possibly been caused by the accidental release of biological weapons that they feared the Soviets were producing, stockpiling, and testing at a military facility in Sverdlovsk—actions prohibited by the 1972 Biological Weapons Convention (BWC). U.S. officials repeatedly raised questions about this incident with Soviet government officials but never received answers that allayed American concerns, and the Sverdlovsk incident contributed to the deterioriation in U.S.–Soviet relations.

The BWC called for the parties to the agreement to consult with one another and to cooperate in solving any problems that might arise concerning the implementation of the convention.[2] In addition, the agreement vaguely called for "consultation and cooperation...through appropriate international procedures within the framework of the United Nations." Importantly and unfortunately, the convention did not call for the establishment of a specialized consultative body to oversee implementation of the agreement and to consider questions of compliance. Had such a body been established, it is possible that the questions surrounding the Sverdlovsk incident could have been resolved satisfactorily without the negative consequences for broader U.S.–Soviet relations.

In contrast to the disappointing experience of the BWC, stands the relatively successful operation of a joint U.S.–Soviet organization—the Standing

The author would like to thank the Center for Foreign Policy Development at Brown University and Pepperdine University for supporting the writing of this chapter and Robert W. Buchheim, Ralph Earle II, Mark Garrison, Gary Guertner, Michael Krepon, Mark Lowenthal, Roger Molander, and Peter Staugaard for their comments on an earlier draft.

Consultative Commission (SCC)—which was created to work out matters related to compliance with the SALT agreements. This chapter describes the establishment and operations of the SCC since its founding and indicates possible future tasks for the SCC or similar organizations.[3]

The Establishment of the Standing Consultative Commission

The SALT I agreements of 1972 called for the formal establishment of the SCC. President Nixon and General Secretary Brezhnev signed the Antiballistic Missile (ABM) Treaty on May 26, 1972. Article XIII of this treaty called for the establishment of the Standing Consultative Commission to "promote the objectives and implementation of the provisions" of the treaty by considering questions concerning compliance; voluntarily providing information that either the United States or the USSR considers necessary to ensure compliance; agreeing on procedures for the dismantling of ABM systems and components called for in the ABM Treaty; considering questions concerning interference with national technical means (NTM)—the diplomatic euphemism for satellite reconnaissance and electronic monitoring; and considering means to increase the viability of the SALT I agreements and further limit strategic weapons.[4] Article VI of the Interim Agreement on the Limitation of Strategic Offensive Arms, signed by Nixon and Brezhnev at the same time as the ABM Treaty, calls for the SCC to promote its objectives and implementation. The provisions of the ABM Treaty concerning the SCC are of particular importance because the ABM Treaty is an agreement of unlimited duration, whereas the Interim Agreement was designed to remain in force for five years. Therefore, unless the ABM Treaty is either abrogated or amended to provide otherwise, the SCC will exist and operate in perpetuity.

In a sense, the SCC represented the "first fruit" of the SALT negotiations; during preliminary talks in November and December 1969, the United States and the Soviet Union agreed to create a special ongoing organization to deal with any questions concerning the implementation of agreements that might be achieved.[5]

Seven months after the SALT I agreements were signed, the United States and the Soviet Union concluded a Memorandum of Understanding, which officially created the SCC.[6] This agreement stipulated that in addition to its responsibilities for the SALT I agreements, the SCC should also promote the objectives and the implementation of the Agreement on Measures to Reduce the Risk of Outbreak of Nuclear War between the USA and the USSR, which was signed on September 30, 1971. The memorandum called for the SCC to meet at least twice a year in Geneva and called for each government to be represented by a commissioner, a deputy commissioner, and such staff as deemed necessary. Within the U.S. government, the president appoints the SCC commissioner and deputy commissioner on the unanimous recommendation of the secretary of state, the secretary of defense, the chairman of the Joint Chiefs of Staff, the director of central intelligence, the director of the Arms Control and Disarmament Agency (ACDA), and the president's assistant for national security affairs. There have been four U.S. commissioners to date: U. Alexis Johnson (for a brief period after the SALT I agreements entered into force), Sidney N. Graybeal (1973–1976), Robert W. Buchheim (1976–1981), and Richard D. Ellis (1982–present). In addition to the commissioner and deputy commissioner, each SCC delegation also has an executive secretary, a deputy executive secretary, and advisers from appropriate departments and agencies. For the U.S. delegation, advisers have been drawn from the Department of State, the Office of the Secretary of Defense, the Organization of the Joint Chiefs of Staff, ACDA, and the intelligence community. Both civilians and military officers serve as advisers on each side.

On May 30, 1973, U.S. and Soviet representatives signed regulations to govern the operation of the SCC.[7] Importantly, the eighth regulation states that the proceedings of the commission shall be private and that the SCC "may not make its proceedings public except with the express consent of both Commissioners." Of course, the commissioners must operate in accordance with instructions from their governments on the release of information to the public and on other matters, and they have no authority to veto decisions by their governments to release information. Even though SCC proceedings are private, in the United States the executive branch provides complete accounts of any substantive understandings reached in the SCC to six congressional committees: the Senate Committee on Foreign Relations, the House Committee on Foreign Affairs, and the armed services and intelligence committees of both houses. In addition, the executive branch responds to requests from these committees for further information.

The Operations of the SCC: The Compliance Function

Article XIII of the ABM Treaty stipulates a number of implementation tasks for the SCC. To the limited extent that the press has focused on the SCC, it has emphasized the SCC's responsibility for verifying compliance with the SALT agreements. Although the terms *monitoring, verification,* and *compliance* are often used synonymously, they refer to different processes. *Monitoring* refers to intelligence capabilities that are used to determine the existence and character of military programs that other states are pursuing. The SCC has neither the responsibility for nor the capability to monitor compliance with arms control agreements; these are tasks of the national intelligence establishments. The

United States and the Soviet Union agreed to monitor the SALT I and II agreements with national technical means of verification, which include reconnaisance satellites, aircraft-based radar and optical systems, and sea-based radars and antennas for collecting telemetry.

According to the ACDA, *verification* is "the process of determining, to the extent necessary to adequately safeguard national security, that the other side is complying with an agreement."[8] In contrast to the more technical task of monitoring, verification involves political judgment about uncertainty and ambiguity. *Compliance* refers to whether a particular party to an agreement is acquiescing to the terms of the agreement. Thus, verification of compliance refers to the political process of determining whether the behavior of the other party is consistent with the agreement at issue, and monitoring provides the technical data for making such a judgment.

In considering the compliance function of the SCC, several points are important to understand. First, the SCC is neither a "grand jury" to which a prosecutor seeking an indictment presents evidence nor a court of law in which the case is tried. Rather, the SCC is designed to be a problem-solving body in which unclear and ambiguous events and data can be clarified. Second, given the highly technical and, in some cases, ambiguous limitations contained in the SALT agreements, compliance usually cannot be determined in clear-cut, dichotomous terms. Indeed, it is precisely because of the inherent uncertainty of the data that there is a vital need for a body such as the SCC, as the Sverdlovsk incident described at the beginning of this chapter clearly illustrates.

Following its formal establishment, the SCC considered a number of compliance-related issues. The United States raised several issues, including launch control facilities, concealment measures, modern large ballistic missiles (SS-19s), possible testing of an air defense system (SA-5) radar in an ABM mode,[9] Soviet reporting of dismantling of excess ABM test launchers, Soviet ABM radar on Kamchatka Peninsula, Soviet dismantling or destruction of replaced ICBM launchers, and concealment at test ranges.[10] The Soviet Union also raised a number of questions, including shelters over Minuteman silos, the status and condition of Atlas and Titan I launchers, radar on Shemya Island, privacy of SCC proceedings, dismantling or destruction of the ABM radar under construction at Malmstrom Air Force Base, and U.S. radar deployments.[11] In all of these cases, the questioned activity either ceased or the issue was resolved. In 1979, former SCC Commissioner Sidney Graybeal testified that he was "unaware of any case where the Soviets have been in violation of the provisions of the SALT I agreements."[12] The 1982 edition of the texts and histories of U.S. arms control and disarmament agreements published by ACDA notes:

> Both the United States and the Soviet Union have raised a number of questions in the Commission relating to each side's compliance with the SALT I

agreements. In each case raised by the United States, the Soviet activity in question has either ceased or additional information has allayed U.S. concern.[13]

As these accounts demonstrate, the SCC has played a valuable role in verifying and clarifying the compliance of the United States and the USSR with the ABM Treaty and the Interim Agreement.

The Operations of the SCC: Functions Other Than Compliance

Although most public attention directed at the SCC has focused on its role in assuring compliance with the SALT agreements, it performs a number of other significant functions. For example, the SALT I agreements called for the SCC to resolve questions arising from the replacement, dismantling, and destruction of strategic offensive and defensive weapons systems. In addition, the SCC has conducted two reviews of the ABM Treaty. The Accidents Measures agreement and possible consideration of questions arising from the unratified SALT II Treaty significantly added to the responsibilities of the SCC.

An important function of the SCC that has been almost completely ignored by the public and the press is to discuss means for reducing the danger of inadvertent or accidental nuclear war. On September 30, 1971, the United States and the Soviet Union signed the Agreement on Measures to Reduce the Risk of Outbreak of Nuclear War, which called for both parties: (1) to take measures to improve organizational and technical safeguards against unauthorized or accidental use of nuclear weapons; (2) to arrange for immediate notification "in the event of an accidental, unauthorized or any other unexplained incident involving a possible detonation of a nuclear weapon which could create a risk of outbreak of nuclear war" (Article 2); and (3) to warn the other party of any planned missile launches beyond the territory of the launching party in the direction of the other party.[14] In early 1975, the SCC began discussions concerning the means by which the United States and the Soviet Union could facilitate immediate notification between the two countries. A protocol was signed in 1976 that, among other things, established a coding system designed to speed transmissions during crisis periods.[15] Thus, the SCC has played a role in developing means for avoiding and managing potential and actual crises, in addition to its more frequently cited functions.

A particularly important responsibility assigned to the SCC in the ABM Treaty and the Interim Agreement is to oversee the dismantling, replacement, and destruction of offensive and defensive weapons affected by the SALT I limitations. In June 1974, Secretary of State Kissinger and Soviet Foreign Minister Gromyko signed a protocol concerning the replacement of certain older ICBM launchers and SLBM launchers on older submarines by newer

SLBM launchers on modern submarines and the dismantling and destruction of weapons systems and components in excess of the limits set by the SALT I agreements.[16] A supplementary protocol was signed by the two SCC commissioners in October 1976. This protocol regulates the replacement of ABM systems and their components and deployment areas. The texts of these protocols have not been made public; however, the value of these agreements is clear: they serve to implement the general provisions of the ABM Treaty, the Interim Agreement, and the 1974 ABM Treaty Protocol, which limited each side to one ABM deployment area. The basic purpose of these procedures is to ensure that neither side can acquire an advantage during the process of dismantling or destruction and that the elimination of weapons can be verified confidently through national technical means. This function of the SCC could become even more important if and when further strategic arms control agreements are signed and ratified.

Article XIV of the ABM Treaty called for a review of the treaty five years after its entry into force and at five-year intervals after that. Although the treaty does not stipulate that the SCC is responsible for this review, it is permissive, and the SCC was given this responsibility in 1977 and 1982. As a practical matter, the ABM Treaty has undergone virtually continuous review by the SCC since its entry into force. During the fall of 1977, however, a special session of the SCC was convened to conduct the formal review called for by the treaty. At the conclusion of the review, the United States and the Soviet Union agreed that the treaty had operated effectively during the first five years and that it did not need amending.[17]

Prior to the 1982 review conference, there was speculation by some that the Reagan administration might either propose formal amendments to the ABM Treaty or perhaps even announce the withdrawal of the United States from the treaty. In fact, neither of these alternatives was chosen, and the review was conducted smoothly and quickly. Following the review of the ABM Treaty, however, the SCC turned its attention to a number of compliance issues, including Soviet encryption of telemetry data from missile tests.[18] The ensuing SCC sessions were very contentious and were described by one knowledgeable observer as "some of the worst SCC meetings we've had." American and Soviet members of the SCC could not even agree on the wording of a final communiqué.

Article XVII of the SALT II Treaty signed in June 1979 called for the SCC to promote the treaty's objectives and implementation. The SALT II Treaty is far more complicated than the SALT I agreements, a fact that accentuated the role and importance of the SCC in several ways. First, SALT I and II both contain quantitative limitations on SLBMs and ICBMs. However, SALT II also contains restrictions on long-range bombers and cruise missiles. Second, whereas the SALT I agreements contained primarily quantitative limitations, the SALT II Treaty contained both quantitative and qualitative restrictions, including, most importantly, limits on "fractionation"—that is, the number of multiple independently targetable reentry vehicles (MIRVs) that could be placed on various types of ICBMs and SLBMs.

The SALT II Treaty called for the SCC to perform an additional function: to maintain an agreed database on the numbers of strategic offensive weapons subject to the limitations contained in the SALT II Treaty. When the treaty was signed on June 18, 1979, the two sides submitted the number of strategic offensive weapons that they possessed in their arsenals at that time. Given the paramount importance the Soviets have traditionally placed on secrecy, the fact that they would publicly declare the numbers of strategic nuclear launch vehicles that they held was a positive step away from this traditional orientation.

An Evaluation of SCC Performance

The Standing Consultative Commission operated quietly and effectively during the Nixon, Ford, and Carter administrations. No doubt, this effectiveness was related to the businesslike, private nature of the discussions and to the less volatile political climate in which these discussions took place. Interactions among the members of the SCC were limited to the business at hand, and neither rhetoric about other aspects of U.S.-Soviet relations nor discussion of other subjects took place. This created an environment in which the SCC could be effective, and during the 1972–1981 decade, the SCC achieved significant but quiet results.

The SCC was charged with dealing with questions concerning the implementation of four agreements: the ABM Treaty, the Interim Agreement, the Accidents Measures agreement, and the SALT II Treaty. Other agreements, such as the Threshold Test Ban Treaty and the Biological Weapons Convention, are outside the purview of the SCC's responsibilities and have not been (and presumably will not be) dealt with by the SCC.

In over ten years of operation, the SCC has proved its worth as a forum in which technical issues could be addressed in a nonpolemical, businesslike manner by specialists who are knowledgeable about the issues involved. Indeed, the value of the SCC becomes evident when its history is compared with that of other arms control agreements, such as the Biological Weapons Convention, that lack an implementing organization.

Rather than covering up violations of the SALT agreements, as its critics charge, the SCC has, in fact, clarified a number of issues that could have resulted in the unravelling of the SALT agreements if they were not clarified. Such clarification often takes time, however. For example, in 1973 and 1974, the United States noted that a Soviet surface-to-air missile radar (SA-5) was used to track strategic ballistic missiles during flight.[19] Article VI of the ABM Treaty prohibited tests of SAM radars in "an ABM mode." This issue was first raised by the Ford administration and was eventually resolved to the satisfaction of the United States during the Carter administration, and much of the credit for resolving the issue goes to the SCC. It is important to note that resolution of the SA-5 issue took persistence, patience, and time.

The Reagan administration approached the verification of arms control agreements in general and the Standing Consultative Commission in particular in very different terms than the three previous presidential administrations. Many members of the Reagan administration adopted an absolute standard for compliance. However, because of the complexities of contemporary weapons systems and agreements to limit them, it is highly unlikely that the United States will ever achieve absolute confidence in its means of verification.

In 1982 and 1983, there were serious concerns about several issues, including the testing of what appeared to be two "new types" of ICBMs (the SALT II Treaty only allowed one "new type"), telemetry of missile test data, and a new radar in Siberia.[20] In April 1983, conservative senators Orrin Hatch and Steven Symms recommended that the Reagan administration publicly charge the Soviet Union with violating a number of arms control agreements.[21] President Reagan decided to pursue discussions with the Soviets on these issues through private diplomatic channels and to set up an interagency verification committee under then NSC Assistant William Clark. Reportedly, in late April, the United States raised the issue of a "new type" ICBM labeled the Plesetsk-5 (PL-5) in the SCC, and in early May, Deputy Secretary of State Dam raised the issue with Soviet Ambassador Dobrynin.[22] In July, the United States requested a special session of the SCC, which the Soviets turned down.[23] The fall 1983 meeting of the SCC lasted from late September until December and was very contentious. Not only was there much controversy between the U.S. and Soviet delegations, but there was also a great deal of dissension within the U.S. delegation. According to reports in the press, the U.S. delegation did not even have instructions during the first week of the meetings.[24]

In early October 1983, sixteen senators asked President Reagan to issue a report on Soviet violations of arms control agreements. The full Senate then voted 93–0 to require that the administration prepare a report on Soviet compliance; the report was subsequently prepared and issued in January 1984. Among its charges, it alleged Soviet "violations or probable violations" of the Biological Weapons Convention, the Helsinki Accord, the ABM Treaty, the SALT II Treaty, and the Threshold Test Ban Treaty.[25]

According to press accounts, the SALT-related issues addressed in the president's compliance report had not been brought to the SCC until 1983 because the Reagan administration did not want either to imply that it approved of the SALT II Treaty or to acknowledge that the treaty was legally binding.[26] Apparently, however, the administration eventually instructed the U.S. SCC commissioner to raise but not discuss several issues, including encryption and "new type" ICBMs.

Even with the resumption of arms control negotiations in March 1985, the status and future of the SCC were unclear. However, this should not obscure the fact that the SCC operated effectively for a decade in resolving compliance-related questions and in performing other valuable functions.

Future Tasks for the SCC or Similar Organizations

The SCC is not a panacea for the solution of U.S.–Soviet conflicts or arms-related issues, and its future operation is largely dependent on the political environment in which it will be called on to operate. Two alternative scenarios of the future can be considered: a continuation of the deterioration of U.S.–Soviet relations characteristic of the early 1980s or a reversal of these trends, leading to an improvement in relations.

Unless one concludes that the arms control agreements concluded in the 1963–1979 period are meaningless and should be abandoned (and there were some in the Reagan administration who held this view),[27] there is a clear need for the SCC. Indeed, in a hostile political climate, the case can be made that there is a great need for private, businesslike meetings between experts. Political leaders, not the technically informed members of the SCC, will determine the overall tenor of relations, but technical discussions can still continue. It is better to maintain this channel of informed communication than to do away with it, even in times of high tension.

In the tense state of U.S.–Soviet relations in the mid-1980s, it is possible that the SCC will not be able to operate effectively, much less expand its functions. However, much could be done if relations between the United States and the Soviet Union were to improve.

First, a possible future task for the SCC would be to consider measures that would strengthen existing arms control agreements. Article XII of the ABM Treaty states: "Each Party undertakes not to interfere with the national technical means of verification of the other Party." The SCC could consider an agreement to ban weapons in space that are capable of destroying satellites—so-called antisatellite (ASAT) weapons. Such a task would be within the mission of the SCC, although given the SCC's other responsibilities and the three-tiered U.S.–Soviet negotiations, it is perhaps best to leave this task to the U.S. and Soviet negotiators in Geneva.

Second, if the U.S.–Soviet negotiations result in an agreement, the SCC will be necessary to implement the details of the agreement and to deal with any compliance questions.

A third potential future task for an organization similar to the SCC would be the implementation and oversight of agreements or treaties other than those dealing with the control of intermediate or strategic nuclear weapons. For example, the Threshold Test Ban Treaty, signed by the United States and the Soviet Union in 1974 (but as yet unratified), provided for extensive exchange of data between the parties and for necessary consultations to discuss questions of compliance. However, the treaty did not specify a mechanism either for the exchange of data or for consultations. The Peaceful Nuclear Explosions Treaty—a companion treaty limiting underground nuclear explosions for peaceful purposes, signed in 1976 (but also as yet unratified)—was more specific; Article V stipulated that a Joint Consultative Commission (JCC) should be established to promote the objectives and implementation of the treaty, a charge similar to that of the SCC. Given the complexities of verifying compliance to the nuclear testing treaties and the possibility of arranging for observers of one country on the other signatory's territory, it would be advisable to establish a commission separate from the SCC for the Threshold Test Ban Treaty and the Peaceful Nuclear Explosions Treaty. Had the United States ratified these two treaties and established the JCC, it would be in a much better position to evaluate the compliance of the Soviet Union with the treaties.

A commission such as the JCC could gain experience that would be of great value in verifying compliance with a multilateral comprehensive test ban treaty, which would require some sort of multilateral SCC-type body. Similarly, an agreement limiting intermediate nuclear forces (INF) in Europe would require an SCC-like organization to consider the inevitable questions about the implementation of and compliance with any INF agreement.

A fourth category of possible tasks is the implementation of various arms control agreements limiting weapons other than nuclear weapons. The Sverdlovsk incident described in the introduction to this chapter highlights the problems encountered when questions arise concerning the implementation of an agreement such as the Biological Weapons Convention. It is worth considering whether, in negotiating such multilateral agreements, it might be useful to provide for the formal creation of a consultative body to deal with such problems. The relative success of the London Suppliers' Group, a multilateral organization of representatives from states that export civilian nuclear power plants and components, provides some hope that a multilateral arms control organization can be effective.

Finally, a fifth category of possible tasks lies in the area of crisis prevention and crisis management.[28] As noted earlier, the SCC has already taken on responsibility in this area in implementing the 1971 Accidents Measures agreement. The U.S.–Soviet Agreement on the Prevention of Nuclear War, signed in 1973, calls for the two parties to "immediately enter into urgent consultations with each other" if relations between them or countries anywhere in the world appear to involve the risk of nuclear war. Thought should be given to establishing a body operating like the SCC (but separate from the SCC) that would be in communication at all times regarding all crisis areas. The late Senator Henry Jackson and senators Sam Nunn and John Warner have proposed such an organization, and their proposal deserves further thought and study.[29]

Theoretically, normal diplomatic channels should be able to prevent and manage crises. However, it is in crisis periods that normal diplomatic channels are often least effective; when communication occurs, it tends to be stilted and formal. Ongoing discussions within a body like the SCC could provide a more flexible and effective sounding board for the two sides to make known their concerns and explore the depth of one another's concerns.

Conclusion

Competition and hostility characterized U.S.–Soviet relations during the first four years of the 1980s. This situation makes clear the need for limited cooperation—even with our foremost adversary—to lessen the risk of nuclear war, the greatest potential present danger to civilization. The SCC cannot resolve the many conflicts of interest between the United States and the Soviet Union, but it can and, since its establishment, has helped reduce uncertainties and fears. There is much that the SCC has done and much more that it and similar organizations could do to further reduce the risk of nuclear war.

Notes

1. Leslie H. Gelb, "Keeping an Eye on Russia," *New York Times Magazine*, November 29, 1981, p. 31ff.

2. "Biological Weapons Convention," in U.S. Arms Control and Disarmament Agency (ACDA), *Arms Control and Disarmament Agreements* (Washington, D.C.: U.S. Government Printing Office, 1982), pp. 124–131.

3. This chapter draws on Robert W. Buchheim and Dan Caldwell, "The U.S.–USSR Standing Consultative Commission: Description and Appraisal," Working Paper 2 (Providence, R.I.: Center for Foreign Policy Development, Brown University, May 1983).

4. U.S. Department of State, "Limitation of Anti-Ballistic Missile Systems," *United States Treaties and Other International Agreements*, TIAS 7503 (Washington, D.C.: U.S. Government Printing Office, 1973), pp. 3435–3462.

5. U.S. Arms Control and Disarmament Agency (ACDA), *Annual Report, 1979* (Washington, D.C.: U.S. Government Printing Office, 1980), p. 19.

6. U.S. Department of State, "Standing Consultative Commission on Arms Limitations: Memorandum of Understanding," *United States Treaties and Other International Agreements*, TIAS 7545 (Washington, D.C.: U.S. Government Printing Office, 1974), pp. 238–244.

7. U.S. Department of State, "Standing Consultative Commission on Arms Limitation: Regulations," *United States Treaties and Other International Agreements*, TIAS 7637 (Washington, D.C.: U.S. Government Printing Office, 1974), pp. 1124–1128.

8. U.S. Arms Control and Disarmament Agency (ACDA), *SALT II: Glossary of Terms*, ACDA Publication 99 (Washington, D.C.: U.S. Arms Control and Disarmament Agency, 1979), p. 6.

9. For the details of this case, see Buchheim and Caldwell, "The U.S.–USSR Standing Consultative Commission," pp. 8–10.

10. ACDA, *Annual Report, 1979,* pp. 20–21; and U.S. Department of State, *Compliance with SALT I Agreements,* Special Report No. 55 (Washington, D.C.: U.S. Department of State, 1979).

11. U.S. Department of State, *Compliance with SALT I Agreements,* Special Report No. 55.

12. "Testimony of Sidney Graybeal," in U.S. Congress, Senate Committee on Foreign Relations, *Briefing on SALT I Compliance* (Washington, D.C.: U.S. Government Printing Office, 1979).

13. ACDA, *Arms Control and Disarmament Agreements,* p. 138.

14. U.S. Department of State, "Measures to Reduce the Risk of Nuclear War Outbreak," *United States Treaties and Other International Agreements,* TIAS 7186 (Washington, D.C.: U.S. Government Printing Office, 1972), pp. 1590–1597.

15. ACDA, *Annual Report, 1979,* p. 20.

16. Ibid.

17. "Communiqué of the U.S.–USSR Standing Consultative Commission on the Review of the Treaty Between the United States of America and the Union of Soviet Socialist Republics on the Limitation of Anti-Ballistic Missile Systems," May 26, 1972, in U.S. Arms Control and Disarmament Agency, *Annual Report, 1977* (Washington, D.C.: U.S. Government Printing Office, 1978), p. 12.

18. *Washington Post,* January 6, 1983, p. 27.

19. See Buchheim and Caldwell, "The U.S.–USSR Standing Consultative Commission"; and Michael Krepon, "Decontrolling the Arms Race: The U.S. and the Soviets Fumble the Compliance Issues," *Arms Control Today* 14 (March/April 1984): 3.

20. Richard Halloran, "U.S. Aides Uneasy on Soviet Coding," *New York Times,* January 4, 1983, p. A3; Charles Mohr, "U.S. and Soviet Discuss Whether Moscow Violated Terms of 2 Arms Pacts," *New York Times,* October 5, 1983, p. A8. See also Strobe Talbott, *Deadly Gambits: The Reagan Administration and the Stalemate in Nuclear Arms Control* (New York: Knopf, 1984).

21. Hedrick Smith, "Panel Tells Reagan the Russians Seem to Have Broken Arms Pacts," *New York Times,* April 21, 1983, p. 1.

22. Hedrick Smith, "U.S. Sees New Soviet Arms Violation," *New York Times,* May 12, 1983, p. B9.

23. Hedrick Smith, "U.S. Seeking Soviet Parley On Arms Violation Issues," *New York Times,* August 12, 1983, p. A3.

24. Mohr, "U.S. and Soviet Discuss."

25. Bernard Gwertzman, "Reagan Is Said to Find Breaches by Soviets of Agreements on Arms," *New York Times,* January 4, 1984, p. 1.

26. Charles Mohr, "U.S. and Soviet to Discuss A-Arms Pacts," *New York Times,* January 21, 1984, p. 4.

27. See Colin Gray, "Moscow Is Cheating," *Foreign Policy* 56(Fall 1984): 141–152. See also Talbott, *Deadly Gambits,* p. 232.

28. See the stimulating article by Sidney Graybeal, "Negotiating an Accident Prevention Center: The Experience of the Standing Consultative Commission," in John W. Lewis and Coit D. Blacker, eds., *Next Steps in the Creation of an Accidental Nuclear*

War Prevention Center (Stanford, Calif.: Stanford University, Center for International Security and Arms Control, October 1983).

29. Henry M. Jackson, "Nuclear War and the Hotline," *Wall Street Journal,* September 3, 1982, p. 14; Sam Nunn, "Arms Control: What Should We Do?" *Washington Post,* November 12, 1981, p. A31; and the Nunn-Warner Working Group, "A Risk Reduction Center," *Bulletin of the Atomic Scientists* 40 (June/July 1984): 28–29.

Appendix A:
The President's Report
to the Congress on Soviet
Noncompliance with
Arms Control Agreements

The following is the text of a message to the Congress transmitting the President's Report on Soviet Noncompliance with Arms Control Agreements as required by the FY 1984 Arms Control and Disarmament Act:

To the Congress of the United States:

If the concept of arms control is to have meaning and credibility as a contribution to global or regional stability, it is essential that all parties to agreements comply with them. Because I seek genuine arms control, I am committed to ensuring that existing agreements are observed. In 1982 increasing concerns about Soviet noncompliance with arms control agreements led me to establish a senior group within the Administration to examine verification and compliance issues. For its part the Congress, in the FY 1984 Arms Control and Disarmament Act, asked me to report to it on compliance. I am herewith enclosing a Report to the Congress on Soviet Noncompliance with Arms Control Agreements.

After a careful review of many months, and numerous diplomatic exchanges with the Soviet Union, the Administration has determined that with regard to seven initial issues analyzed, violations and probable violations have occurred with respect to a number of Soviet legal obligations and political commitments in the arms control field.

The United States Government has determined that the Soviet Union is violating the Geneva Protocol on Chemical Weapons, the Biological Weapons Convention, the Helsinki Final Act, and two provisions of SALT II: telemetry encryption and a rule concerning ICBM modernization. In addition, we have determined that the Soviet Union has almost certainly violated the ABM

From The White House, Office of the Press Secretary, January 23, 1984.

Treaty, probably violated the SALT II limit on new types, probably violated the SS-16 deployment prohibition of SALT II, and is likely to have violated the nuclear testing yield limit of the Threshold Test Ban Treaty.

Soviet noncompliance is a serious matter. It calls into question important security benefits from arms control, and could create new security risks. It undermines the confidence essential to an effective arms control process in the future. It increases doubts about the reliability of the U.S.S.R. as a negotiating partner, and thus damages the chances for establishing a more constructive U.S.-Soviet relationship.

The United States will continue to press its compliance concerns with the Soviet Union through diplomatic channels, and insist upon explanations, clarifications, and corrective actions. At the same time, the United States is continuing to carry out its own obligations and commitments under relevant agreements. For the future, the United States is seeking to negotiate new arms control agreements that reduce the risk of war, enhance the security of the United States and its Allies, and contain effective verification and compliance provisions.

We should recognize, however, that ensuring compliance with arms control agreements remains a serious problem. Better verification and compliance provisions and better treaty drafting will help, and we are working toward this in ongoing negotiations. It is fundamentally important, however, that the Soviets take a constructive attitude toward compliance.

The Executive and Legislative branches of our government have long had a shared interest in supporting the arms control process. Finding effective ways to ensure compliance is central to that process. I look forward to continued close cooperation with the Congress as we seek to move forward in negotiating genuine and enduring arms control agreements.

Sincerely,

/s/   Ronald Reagan

The Fact Sheet provided to the Congress with the classified report is quoted below:

Fact Sheet: The President's Report to the Congress on Soviet Noncompliance with Arms Control Agreements

Commitment to genuine arms control requires that all parties comply with agreements. Over the last several years the U.S.S.R. has taken a number of actions that have prompted renewed concern about an expanding pattern of Soviet violations or possible violations of arms control agreements. Because of the critical importance of compliance with arms control agreements, about one year ago the President established an interagency Arms Control Verification Committee, chaired by his Assistant for National Security Affairs, to address verification and compliance issues. In addition, many members of Congress expressed their serious concerns, and the Congress mandated in the FY 84 Arms Control and Disarmament Act Authorization that "The President shall prepare and transmit to the Congress a report of the compliance or noncompliance of the Soviet Union with existing arms control agreements to which the Soviet Union is a Party."

The President's Report to Congress covers seven different matters of serious concern regarding Soviet compliance: chemical, biological, and toxin weapons, the notification of military exercises, a large new Soviet radar being deployed in the Soviet interior, encryption of data needed to verify arms control provisions, the testing of a second new intercontinental ballistic missile (ICBM), the deployment status of an existing Soviet ICBM, and the yields of underground nuclear tests. Additional issues of concern are under active study.

Soviet violations of arms control agreements could create new security risks. Such violations deprive us of the security benefits of arms control directly because of the military consequences of known violations, and indirectly by inducing suspicion about the existence of undetected violations that might have additional military consequences.

We have discussed with the Soviets all of the activities covered in the report, but the Soviets have not been willing to meet our basic concerns which we raised in the Standing Consultative Commission in Geneva and in several diplomatic demarches. Nor have they met our requests to cease these activities. We will continue to pursue these issues.

The Findings

The Report examines the evidence concerning Soviet compliance with: the 1972 Biological Weapons Convention (BWC) and the 1925 Geneva Protocol and customary international law, the 1975 Helsinki Final Act, the 1972 ABM Treaty, the unratified SALT II Treaty, and the unratified Threshold Test Ban Treaty (TTBT) signed in 1974. Preparation of the Report entailed a comprehensive review of the legal obligations, political commitments under existing arms control agreements, and documented interpretations of specific obligations, analyses of all the evidence available on applicable Soviet actions, and a review of the diplomatic exchanges on compliance issues between the U.S. and the Soviet Union.

The findings for the seven issues covered in the Report, as reviewed in terms of the agreements involved, are as follows:

1. *Chemical, Biological, and Toxin Weapons*

—*Treaty Status:* The 1972 Biological and Toxin Weapons Convention (the BWC) and the 1925 Geneva Protocol are multilateral treaties to which both the U.S. and U.S.S.R. are parties. Soviet actions not in accord with these treaties and customary international law relating to the 1925 Geneva Protocol are violations of legal obligations.

—*Obligation:* The BWC bans the development, production, stockpiling or possession, and transfer of: microbial or other biological agents or toxins except for a small quantity for prophylactic, protective or other peaceful purposes. It also bans weapons, equipment and means of delivery of agents or toxins. The 1925 Geneva Protocol and related rules of customary international law prohibit the first use in war of asphyxiating, poisonous or other gases and of all analogous liquids, materials or devices; and prohibits use of bacteriological methods of warfare.

—*Issues:* The study addressed whether the Soviets are in violation of provisions that ban the development, production, transfer, possession and use of biological and toxin weapons.

—*Finding:* The Soviets, by maintaining an offensive biological warfare program and capabilities and through their involvement in the production, transfer and use of toxins and other lethal chemical warfare agents that have been used in Laos, Kampuchea and Afghanistan, have repeatedly violated their legal obligations under the BWC and customary international law as codified in the 1925 Geneva Protocol.

2. *Helsinki Final Act—Notification of Military Exercises*

—*Legal Status:* The Final Act of the Conference on Security and Cooperation in Europe was signed in Helsinki in 1975. This document represents a political commitment and was signed by the United States and the Soviet Union, along with many other states. Soviet actions not in accord with that document are violations of their political commitment.

—*Obligation:* All signatory states of the Helsinki Final Act are committed to give prior notification of, and other details concerning, major military maneuvers, defined as those involving more than 25,000 ground troops.

—*Issues:* The study examined whether notification of the Soviet military exercise Zapad-81, which occurred on September 4–12, 1981, was inadequate and therefore a violation of their political commitment.

—*Finding:* With respect to the Helsinki Final Act, the U.S.S.R. by its inadequate notification of the Zapad-81 military exercise, violated its political commitment under this Act to observe the Confidence-Building Measure requiring appropriate prior notification of certain military exercises.

3. *ABM Treaty—Krasnoyarsk Radar*

—*Treaty Status:* The 1972 ABM Treaty and its subsequent Protocol ban deployment of ABM systems except that each party can deploy one ABM system around the national capital or at a single ICBM deployment area. The ABM Treaty is in force and is of indefinite duration. Soviet actions not in accord with the ABM Treaty are therefore a violation of a legal obligation.

—*Obligation:* In an effort to preclude a territorial ABM defense, the Treaty limited the deployment of ballistic missile early warning radars, including large phased-array radars used for that purpose, to locations along the national periphery of each party and required that they be oriented outward. The Treaty permits deployment (without regard to location or orientation) of large phased-array radars for purposes of tracking objects in outer space or for use as national technical means of verification of compliance with arms control agreements.

—*Issue:* The study examined the evidence on whether the Soviet deployment of a large phased-array radar near Krasnoyarsk in central Siberia is in violation of the legal obligation to limit the location and orientation of such radars.

—*Finding:* The new radar under construction at Krasnoyarsk almost certainly constitutes a violation of legal obligations under the Anti-Ballistic Missile Treaty of 1972 in that in its associated siting, orientation, and capability, it is prohibited by this Treaty.

SALT II

—*Treaty Status:* SALT II was signed in June 1979. It has not been ratified. In 1981 the United States made clear its intention not to ratify the Treaty. Prior to 1981 both nations were obligated under international law not to take actions which would "defeat the object and purpose" of the signed but unratified Treaty; such Soviet actions before 1981 are violations of legal obligations. Since 1981 the U.S. has observed a political commitment to refrain from actions that undercut SALT II as long as the Soviet Union does likewise. The Soviets have told us they would abide by these provisions also. Soviet actions contrary to SALT II after 1981 are therefore violations of their political commitment.

Three SALT II concerns are addressed: encryption, SS-X-25, and SS-16.

4. *Encryption—Impeding Verification*

—*Obligation:* The provisions of SALT II ban deliberate concealment measures that impede verification by national technical means. The agreement permits each party to use various methods of transmitting telemetric information during testing, including encryption, but bans deliberate denial of telemetry, such as through encryption, whenever such denial impedes verification.

—*Issue:* The study examined the evidence whether the Soviets have engaged in encryption of missile test telemetry (radio signals) so as to impede verification.

—*Finding:* Soviet encryption practices constitute a violation of a legal obligation prior to 1981 and a violation of their political commitment subsequent to 1981. The nature and extent of encryption of telemetry on new ballistic missiles is an example of deliberate impeding of verification of compliance in violation of this Soviet political commitment.

5. SS-X-25—2nd New Type, RV Weight to Throw-weight Ratio, Encryption

—*Obligation:* In an attempt to constrain the modernization and the proliferation of new, more capable types of ICBMs, the provisions of SALT II permit each side to "flight test and deploy" just one new type of "light" ICBM. A new type is defined as one that differs from an existing type by more than 5 percent in length, largest diameter, launch-weight and throw-weight or differs in number of stages or propellant type. In addition, it was agreed that no single reentry vehicle ICBM of an existing type with a post-boost vehicle would be flight-tested or deployed whose reentry vehicle weight is less than 50 percent of the throw-weight of that ICBM. This latter provision was intended to prohibit the possibility that single warhead ICBMs could quickly be converted to MIRVed systems.

—*Issue:* The study examined the evidence: whether the Soviets have tested a second new type of ICBM (the SS-X-25) which is prohibited (the Soviets have declared the SS-X-24 to be their allowed one new type ICBM); whether the reentry vehicle (RV) on that missile, if it is not a new type, is in compliance with the provision that for existing types of single RV missiles, the weight of the RV be equal to at least 50 percent of total throw-weight; and whether encryption of its tests impedes verification.

—*Finding:* While the evidence is somewhat ambiguous, the SS-X-25 is a probable violation of the Soviets' political commitment to observe the SALT II provision limiting each party to one new type of ICBM. Furthermore, even if we were to accept the Soviet argument that the SS-X-25 is not a prohibited new type of ICBM, based on the one test for which data are available, it would be a violation of their political commitment to observe the SALT II provision which prohibits (for existing types of single reentry vehicle ICBMs) the testing of such an ICBM with a reentry vehicle whose weight is less than 50 percent of the throw-weight of that ICBM. Encryption on this missile is illustrative of the impeding of verification problem cited earlier.

6. SS-16 ICBM—Banned Deployment

—*Obligation:* The Soviet Union agreed in SALT II not to produce, test or deploy ICBMs of the SS-16 type and, in particular, not to produce the SS-16 third stage, the reentry vehicle of that missile.

—*Issue:* The study examined the evidence whether the Soviets have deployed the SS-16 ICBM in spite of the ban on its deployment.

—*Finding:* While the evidence is somewhat ambiguous and we cannot reach a definitive conclusion, the available evidence indicates that the activities at Plesetsk are a probable violation of their legal obligation not to defeat the object and purpose of SALT II prior to 1981 during the period when the Treaty was pending ratification, and a probable violation of a political commitment subsequent to 1981.

7. *TTBT—150 kt Test Limit*

—*Treaty Status:* The Threshold Test Ban Treaty was signed in 1974. The Treaty has not been ratified but neither Party has indicated an intention not to ratify. Therefore, both Parties are subject to the obligation under international law to refrain from acts which would "defeat the object and purpose" of the TTBT. Soviet actions that would defeat the object and purpose of the TTBT are therefore violations of their obligation. The U.S. is seeking to negotiate improved verification measures for the Treaty. Both Parties have each separately stated they would observe the 150 kt threshold of the TTBT.

—*Obligation:* The Treaty prohibits any underground nuclear weapon test having a yield exceeding 150 kilotons at any place under the jurisdiction or control of the Parties, beginning March 31, 1976. In view of the technical uncertainties associated with predicting the precise yield of nuclear weapons tests, the sides agreed that one or two slight unintended breaches per year would not be considered a violation.

—*Issue:* The study examined whether the Soviets have conducted nuclear tests in excess of 150 kilotons.

—*Finding:* While the available evidence is ambiguous, in view of ambiguities in the pattern of Soviet testing and in view of verification uncertainties, and we have been unable to reach a definitive conclusion, this evidence indicates that Soviet nuclear testing activities for a number of tests constitute a likely violation of legal obligations under the TTBT.

Conclusions

The President has said that the U.S. will continue to press compliance issues with the Soviets through confidential diplomatic channels, and to insist upon explanations, clarifications, and corrective actions. At the same time we are continuing to carry out our obligations and commitments under relevant agreements. We should recognize, however, that ensuring compliance with arms control agreements remains a serious problem. Improved verification and compliance provisions and better treaty drafting will help, and we are working toward this in ongoing negotiations. It is fundamentally important, however, that the Soviets take a constructive attitude toward compliance.

Appendix B:
A Quarter Century of Soviet Compliance Practices Under Arms Control Commitments: 1958–1983

The General Advisory Committee on Arms Control and Disarmament (GAC) is a Presidential advisory committee established by the Arms Control and Disarmament Act of 1961. The members are private citizens appointed by the President with the advice and consent of the Senate. Its duties are to advise the President, the Secretary of State, and the Director of the Arms Control and Disarmament Agency on matters affecting arms control and disarmament and world peace. The current General Advisory Committee is bipartisan, and its members have been drawn from the scientific, academic, business, and national security communities. A number of its members have held high government positions in previous administrations. The General Advisory Committee provides advice and analysis that is independent from the bureaucratic process, with a point of view not tied to any particular institution.

Introduction

In response to President Reagan's request and in accord with its statutory mandate,[a] the President's General Advisory Committee on Arms Control and Disarmament has conducted an independent, comprehensive, one-year study of the long-term pattern of Soviet performance pertaining to arms control obligations arising from agreements and Soviet unilateral commitments. The classified report of that study, entitled *A Quarter Century of Soviet Compliance Practices Under Arms Control Commitments: 1958–1983,* was submitted to the President on December 2, 1983, with the Committee's unanimous endorsement, and has since been presented to senior administration officials and briefed to congressional committees and members upon their request. In

From General Advisory Committee on Arms Control and Disarmament, *Summary,* October 1984.

[a]As specified in Section 26 of the Arms Control and Disarmament Act of 1961 as amended. A list of members is attached.

accordance with Congressional Amendments to the Fiscal Year 1985 Defense Authorization Bill and in response to instruction from the White House, the General Advisory Committee has prepared this unclassified summary for transmittal to the Congress.

Using all available data concerning Soviet actions pertinent to such obligations, the Committee has determined that the Soviet Union's practices related to about half of its documentary arms control commitments have raised no questions regarding compliance. Soviet practices related to the other half, however, show material breaches—violations, probable violations, or circumventions —of contractual obligations.

Many of the compliance issues considered in the report have been reviewed by the U.S. Government, raised by the U.S. in the U.S.-Soviet Standing Consultative Commission, or brought to Soviet attention through diplomatic channels. The prevailing practice has been to consider each instance as an isolated event. The General Advisory Committee report is the first comprehensive U.S. study of all Soviet practices under arms control obligations since World War II and explores the cumulative pattern of pertinent Soviet conduct. Such a study, based on wide access to official information, has never before been done within the U.S. Government.

Twenty-six documentary agreements were examined, along with numerous unilateral Soviet commitments. The sources of information included previous U.S. Government studies and documents, Soviet statements, and briefings by a wide range of U.S. Government officials and non-government experts. While the Committee is grateful for assistance from many quarters, the Committee acknowledges full responsibility for the content of its report and this summary.

The report used a conceptual framework based upon the norms of international law.[b] According to these norms, treaty violations, circumventions which defeat the object and purpose of the treaty, and breaches of authoritative unilateral commitments all constitute material breaches and justify appropriate corrective measures. All types of material breaches are considered in the report, and the distinctions among them are noted.

The Committee has found that in most cases of alleged Soviet violations, the Soviets readily could have shown that the allegations were false—if they had been false. This the Soviets have repeatedly failed to do, even though diplomatic and other channels have been used by the U.S. in seeking to clarify possible misconceptions.

---

[b]The Committee used the 1969 Vienna Convention on the Law of Treaties and decisions of the International Court of Justice as the principal legal bases for analyzing Soviet compliance behavior. (The United States is a signatory of the Vienna Convention; the Soviet Union is not. Neither nation has ratified it, but the Vienna Convention is regarded by both the U.S. and the Soviet Union as a codification of customary international law on treaty obligations, applicable to parties and non-parties alike.)

Past analyses (other than the President's report to the Congress of Janury 23, 1984) have tended to invoke standards of proof applicable only when powers to collect and to inspect evidence, to subpoena witnesses, to take testimony under oath, to prosecute for perjury, etc., are available as legal tools.

The General Advisory Committee's report distinguishes between instances for which the evidence supports high confidence that material Soviet breaches have occurred, and those cases for which the evidence gives substantial reason for suspicion but is short of being conclusive.

Categories used in the report are:

Areas of Apparent Soviet Compliance as determined within the limitations of U.S. verification capabilities.

Material Breaches ranging from highly probable to certain, including:
—*violations* of an international obligation involving conduct contrary to a treaty or other binding international agreement;
—*breaches of authoritative unilateral commitments,* whether written or oral, as well as unilateral commitments reciprocally negotiated; and
—*circumventions,* or practices incompatible with the essential objects or purposes of agreements though not in explicit violation of their terms.

Suspicious Events indicative of possible material breaches.

Breaches of the Duty of Good Faith incumbent upon all national states.

The following summarizes areas of apparent Soviet compliance:

Areas of Apparent Soviet Compliance

Accident Avoidance

Direct Communications Link/Hot Line Agreement of 1963, amended 1971

USSR–US Accidents Agreement of 1971 (one violation, judged to be inadvertent)

USSR–United Kingdom Accidents Agreement of 1973

USSR–France Accidents Agreement of 1976

Nonproliferation

Nonproliferation Treaty of 1968

Guidelines for Nuclear Transfers, IAEA INFCIRC/209 of 1974

Guidelines for Nuclear Transfers, IAEA INFCIRC/254 of 1978

Protocol II of the Treaty of Tlatelolco (Latin American Nuclear Free Zone), USSR Ratification of 1979

Convention on the Physical Protection of Nuclear Material, USSR Ratification 1983

Other

Antarctic Treaty of 1959

Outer Space Treaty of 1967

Seabed Treaty of 1971

Convention on Environmental Modification of 1977

The following summarizes specific instances of probable to certain Soviet non-compliance, as determined by the Committee's study:

Soviet Violations, Breaches of Unilateral Commitments, and Circumventions Defeating the Object or Purpose of Arms Control Agreements: High Confidence in Reliability of Data Interpretation:

A. *Non-SALT Matters*

1. Nuclear Test Moratorium: *breach of unilateral commitment* to suspend all nuclear testing—by resuming and continuing atmospheric nuclear testing, 1961–1962.

In September 1961, the Soviet Union breached its unilateral commitment to the nuclear test moratorium upon giving three days of notice and while conducting related treaty negotiations with the U.S. This breach resulted in the Soviet Union testing a total explosive yield of more than 300 megatons in the ensuing 13 months.

2. Offensive Weapons in Cuba: *breach of unilateral commitment* not to send offensive weapons to Cuba—by the covert shipment and deployment of offensive weapons, 1962.

The Cuban missile crisis was caused by the breach of the Soviets' unilateral commitment not to send offensive weapons to Cuba, 1962.

3. Limited Test Ban Treaty of 1963: numerous *violations* of the prohibition on conducting nuclear tests that cause extraterritorial venting of radioactive

debris—by testing nuclear devices that vent radioactive debris beyond the borders of the Soviet Union, 1965 to present.

The Limited Test Ban Treaty not only prohibits testing of nuclear weapons under water, in the atmosphere, and in space, but also bans the venting of underground explosions that cause radioactive debris to cross national boundaries. Since 1965, the Soviet Union has repeatedly allowed such radioactivity to vent in connection with many of its nuclear weapon tests. U.S. experience has shown that care can prevent such venting, and that Soviet violations of this treaty could reasonably have been prevented.

4. Offensive Weapons in Cuba: *breach of unilateral commitments* of 1962 and 1970 not to place offensive weapons in Cuba—by deploying and tending Soviet nuclear missile-carrying submarines in Cuban territorial waters, 1970–1974.

After the termination of the Cuban missile crisis, the record shows the Soviets did commit themselves not to base offensive weapons in Cuba if the U.S. refrained from invading Cuba. Soviet tending and operation of nuclear weapons submarines in Cuban territorial waters from 1970 to 1974 breached this unilateral commitment.

5. Biological Weapons Convention of 1972: *violations* of provisions requiring the destruction or diversion to peaceful purposes of all biological agents, toxins, weapons, equipment, and means of delivery—by the retention of facilities, continued biological munitions production, storage, transfer, and use, 1972 to present.

The Soviets' biological weapons program continued during the negotiating, signing, ratification, and entry into force of this treaty.

6. Geneva Protocol of 1925: *circumventions defeating the object and purpose* of treaty provisions (a) by the transfer of chemical weapons and toxin weapons to their Vietnamese clients with subsequent use in Southeast Asia, 1975–1982; and (b) by Soviet use of lethal agents in Afghanistan, 1980–1982.

The Soviet reservations relative to the ratification of the Geneva Protocol of 1925, claiming exemption for first use against protocol Non-parties, might be put forward to explain the Soviet use of chemical and toxin weapons in Afghanistan, Laos, and Kampuchea. Such circumventions nevertheless defeat the object and purpose of banning first use of lethal chemical or toxin weapons. The Soviets have not asserted this or other legal defense of their actions, but rather they have denied the facts of the matter, falsely claiming no such use.

7. Montreux Convention of 1936: *violations* of the prohibition on the transit of aircraft carriers through the Turkish Straits—by the recurring transit of Soviet KIEV-class aircraft carriers, 1976 to present.

The Soviets additionally have under construction at their Black Sea shipyards an even larger aircraft carrier that will also violate the Montreux Convention upon passage to the open seas.

8. Helsinki Final Act of 1975: *violations* of the commitment to notify Final Act Parties and provide specified data 21 days before conducting exercises of more than 25,000 troops—by undertaking major military troop maneuvers without providing specified information concerning the maneuvers, March and September 1981, and June 1983.

9. Conventional Weapons Convention of 1981: *violations of customary international law*—by failing to observe the Treaty between signing and ratification—by the use of booby-trap mines and incendiary weapons against civilians in Afghanistan, 1981–1982.

10. The March 16, 1982, Brezhnev-declared Moratorium (further clarified in May 1982) on the completion of SS-20 ballistic missile launchers in the European part of the U.S.S.R.: *breach of unilateral commitment*—by the continued construction of SS-20 bases and facilities in the European part of the Soviet Union, March 1982 to November 1983.

On March 16, 1982, President Brezhnev committed the Soviet Union to a moratorium on the completion of SS-20 launch facilities in the European part of the Soviet Union. In May 1982, President Brezhnev specified "an end to the construction of launching positions" as a part of the moratorium. The continued construction and completion of SS-20 sites in 1982 and 1983 violated that unilateral commitment.

B. *SALT Matters*

1. The SALT I Interim Agreement on Offensive Arms, 1972: *circumvention defeating the stated U.S. object and purpose* of limiting the throwweight of Soviet ICBMs *and breach of the 1972 Principles Agreement*—by the deployment of the large throwweight SS-19 and SS-17 ICBMs, 1972 to present.

The SALT I Interim Agreement prohibits the conversion of launchers for light ICBMs into launchers for heavy ICBMs. The intent of this provision was to limit the growth of ICBM throwweight and its resultant potential counterforce capability. The Soviet conversion of launchers for the light SS-11 into launchers for the SS-17 and SS-19 ICBMs circumvents this provision, thereby defeating an essential stated U.S. object and purpose in entering into the agreement. This action widened the disparity between Soviet and U.S. strategic missile throwweight and increased significantly the threat to U.S. ICBMs.

2. The SALT I Interim Agreement on Offensive Arms, 1972, Article V(3); ABM Treaty of 1972, Article XII(3); SALT II Treaty of 1979, Article XV(3): *violation* of the provisions not to use deliberate concealment measures which impede verification of compliance by national technical means—by numerous deliberate concealment activities that impede verification of SALT Agreements, 1972 to present.

The SALT I agreements and the exchange of commitments made concerning SALT II bind the U.S. and the Soviet Union not to use deliberate concealment measures which impede verification, by national technical means, of compliance with provisions of these agreements. However, during the decade of the 1970s, there has been a substantial increase in Soviet arms control-related concealment activities. An example of Soviet concealment activities that clearly impede U.S. verification efforts is the encryption of the SS-X-25 missile telemetry, which impedes the U.S. ability to determine the characteristics of this missile, including characteristics controlled by SALT II. (This issue is further discussed below.) A second example of prohibited deliberate Soviet concealment activity is connected with the probable continued deployment of the SS-16 ICBM at Plesetsk. The present Soviet concealment activities constitute a continuing violation of binding commitments.

3. The ABM Treaty of 1972: *violation* of the prohibition on the development and deployment of non-permanently fixed ABM radar [Article V(1) Common Understanding C]—by the development and deployment of such a radar on the Kamchatka Peninsula in 1975, and by continuing developmental activities between 1975 and the present.

The ABM Treaty prohibits the development, testing and deployment of mobile ABM components. During the negotiations the U.S. and the Soviet delegations agreed (on January 29, 1972 and April 13, 1972 respectively) that this provision would rule out deployment of ABM launchers and radars which "were not permanent fixed types." This agreement constitutes a binding interpretation of the treaty.

4. SALT I Interim Agreement of 1972, Protocol: *violations* of the numerical launcher limits—by the deployment of DELTA submarines exceeding the limit of 740 launch tubes on modern ballistic missile submarines without dismantling sufficient older ICBM or SLBM launchers, March 1976 to October 1977.

The SALT I Interim Agreement required the Soviets to dismantle ICBM launchers to compensate for modern SLBM launchers in excess of 740. Following the sea trials of new DELTA-class submarines in 1976 and 1977, the Soviets did not dismantle a sufficient number of launchers to compensate for deployments of their new submarine ballistic missile launchers. Upon U.S. inquiry, the Soviets admitted this excess, but failed to accelerate their dismantling activities.

The Committee has reviewed the data relative to this matter, and has concluded that the violation was probably not inadvertent, but rather was part of a deliberate Soviet effort to challenge U.S. arms control verification capabilities.

5. SALT II Treaty of 1979: *probable violations* of the provision banning the production, testing, and deployment of the SS-16 mobile ICBM—by the probable continued deployment of SS-16 ICBMs at Plesetsk, and by falsifying the

SALT II data base identifying specific systems and their numbers covered by the Treaty, 1979 to present.

The SALT II Treaty prohibits the deployment of the SS-16 ICBM (Soviet designation—RS-14). Deliberate Soviet concealment which impedes verification of compliance by U.S. national technical means has been associated with the probable SS-16 deployment. Nevertheless, the SS-16 apparently has been maintained at Plesetsk since the signing of the Treaty, in violation of Soviet commitments relative to that treaty. The probable existence of the SS-16 at Plesetsk also shows that the Soviets deliberately falsified the SALT II data base concerning the number of ICBM launchers. This data base was to be corrected semi-annually; however, the Soviets have not corrected it.

6. SALT II Treaty of 1979: *probable violation* of Article IV (9) which limits each side to one new type ICBM—by the testing of a second new type ICBM, February 1983 to present; *violation* of the anti-MIRV provision of Article IV(10)—by testing a lighter warhead than the Treaty allows; and *violation* by the deliberate concealment (encryption) of data, contrary to Article XV(3), May 1983 to present.

SALT II allows each party to develop only one new type of ICBM. Since the Soviets have designated the SS-X-24 as that one new type, the SS-X-25, which appears to be another new type of ICBM, violates the Treaty. The Soviets, however, claim that this missile is a modification of the SS-13, an ICBM developed in the mid-60s. While common sense judgment would hold a 1980's high technology missile to be new, the extensive encryption on the flight telemetry impedes U.S. understanding of the missile. U.S. analyses, however, indicate that it is very likely that the missile fits the Treaty definition of a new type of ICBM.

7. The SALT I ABM Treaty of 1972: *violation* of Article VI(b) limiting the location and orientation of radar deployment—by the construction of a large, phased array radar not located on the periphery of the Soviet Union and not oriented outward, 1981 to present.

The ABM Treaty restricts the deployment of early warning radars to sites on the periphery of the national territory; such radars must also be oriented outward. The construction and orientation of such a radar near the city of Krasnoyarsk, an interior site, violate this provision. The design of the facility is substantially identical to another radar declared by the Soviets to be an early warning radar. The Soviets, however, have stated that the Krasnoyarsk radar is a "space tracking" radar. All early warning radars can also perform limited "space tracking" functions, and while this radar is no exception, its location and geometry are inappropriate for a dedicated space tracking radar.

Suspicious Soviet Activities Related to Arms Control Commitments

The Committee also reviewed fifteen areas of Soviet activity that raise suspicion of further material breaches of arms control agreements. In these cases the data neither confirm that a material breach has occurred nor eliminate suspicion concerning non-compliance. Most of these suspicious activities have been connected with Soviet offensive forces and may indicate the existence of either an offensive force structure in excess of that allowed by various agreements, or offensive weapons with greater capability than allowed by agreements. In addition, several events are indicative of further violations or circumventions of the ABM Treaty, and a review of Soviet testing of nuclear explosives strongly suggests that the Soviets may have repeatedly violated the Threshold Test Ban Treaty. Moreover, other Soviet activities may relate to obligations under the provisions of one or more accords addressing non-interference with national technical means of verification of compliance. Each of these activities may indicate Soviet plans and efforts to develop further military capabilities of considerable significance.

Breaches of the Duty of Good Faith

Customary international law, as codified by the Vienna Convention of the Law of Treaties and by decisions of the International Court of Justice, obligates nations to act in good faith in their dealings with other nations. The Committee reviewed a number of Soviet actions which, while not material breaches of binding agreements, were breaches of that duty of good faith. Some Soviet actions in this category have been misrepresentations made during arms control negotiations or after binding agreements came into effect. An example of such misrepresentation concerns the erroneous data provided by Soviet negotiators at the Mutual Balanced Force Reduction negotiations in Vienna concerning Warsaw Pact troop numbers. This material misrepresentation has been a major barrier in these negotiations.

The Soviets have also disregarded all six unilateral declarations made by the U.S. in SALT I to clarify constraints upon Soviet forces under that agreement. While unilateral declarations do not bind the other party, Soviet unwillingness either to concur promptly or to take exception to such U.S. statements constitutes a breach of the duty of good faith in negotiations.

Further, the Soviets have demonstrated a lack of good faith by their largely non-responsive posture concerning compliance concerns brought to their attention by the U.S. Government over a span of nearly two decades.

Patterns in Soviet Compliance Practices

The Soviet Union's actions since 1958 concerning arms control agreements demonstrate a pattern of pursuing military advantage through selective disregard for its international arms control duties and commitments.

The Committee found recurring instances of Soviet conduct involving deliberate deception, misdirection, and falsification of data during negotiations. In addition to the military value accruing to the Soviets from individual violations, the overall pattern of Soviet practices could have several possible motivations:

(1) The Soviets may be indifferent to U.S. objections and responses to their non-compliance with arms control treaties.

(2) The Soviets may be attempting to weigh the effectiveness of U.S. verification capabilities.

(3) The Soviets may be testing U.S. willingness to reach definitive conclusions concerning Soviet arms control compliance.

(4) The Soviets may be testing U.S. and international resolve and responses to their arms control behavior.

(5) These activities, as well as the other concealment activities, may be intended to raise the level of U.S. confusion in order to hide more serious covert activities, such as development and deployment of a ballistic missile defense system.

Soviet denial activities significantly increased over the last quarter century and today are challenging U.S. verification capabilities despite improvements in U.S. verification technology. Deliberate Soviet efforts to counter U.S. national technical means of verification strongly indicate a Soviet intention to persevere in circumventing and violating agreements.

U.S. verification capabilities have not deterred the Soviets from violating arms control commitments. Furthermore, the near total reliance on secret diplomacy in seeking to restore Soviet compliance has been largely ineffective. The U.S. record of raising its concerns about Soviet non-compliance exclusively in the Standing Consultative Commission and through various high level diplomatic demarches demonstrates the ineffectiveness of this process. In contrast, the international participation in verifying the use of chemical and toxin weapons and the disclosure to the public of such use may have contributed to limiting the extent of these prohibited Soviet activities.

The United States has never had a long-range, comprehensive strategy to deter and if necessary initiate measures to offset Soviet arms control compliance. Development of a U.S. arms control policy that anticipates Soviet behavior in light of the historical compliance record was beyond the scope of the Committee's review. Nevertheless, the development of means to safeguard the U.S. against Soviet non-compliance is essential if the arms control process is to avoid being further undermined, if it is to have favorable long-term prospects, if it is to build trust among nations, and if it is to contribute to U.S. national security and the cause of peace.

U.S. efforts to obtain Soviet compliance have been most effective when reliable information about compliance has been presented to the American people and to the world. The strength of America's democracy lies in an informed citizenry. Fundamental to this nation's effort to negotiate equitable and verifiable arms control agreements is an American public informed on the critical issue of arms control compliance.

Members of the General Advisory Committee on Arms Control and Disarmament

Chairman, *William R. Graham* of California. A founder and Senior Associate, R&D Associates, Marina del Rey, California. Served as a consultant to the Office of the Secretary of Defense and the National Research Council in 1968–1981.

Colin Spencer Gray. President of the National Institute for Public Policy in Virginia. Formerly the Director of National Security Studies at the Hudson Institute in New York.

Roland F. Herbst has been with R&D Associates, Marina del Rey, California since 1971. Formerly Deputy Director, Defense Research and Engineering (Space and Strategic Systems), Office of the Secretary of Defense, 1969–1971.

Francis P. Hoeber. President of Hoeber Corp, Arlington, Virginia since 1974. Formerly with the Rand Corporation (1968–1974) and the Stanford Research Institute (1960–1968).

Robert B. Hotz. Senior Editorial Consultant, McGraw-Hill Publications. He is also an author and lecturer. Formerly editor-in-chief and publisher of *Aviation Week and Space Technology* magazine.

Eli S. Jacobs, a private businessman in Los Angeles, California.

Charles Burton Marshall. Resident consultant, System Planning Corporation, Arlington, Virginia. Formerly staff consultant to House Committee on Foreign Affairs, member of State Department Policy Planning staff, Professor of International Politics at Johns Hopkins School of Advanced International Studies, Washington, D.C.

Jaime Oaxaca. President, Wilcox Electric, Incorporated, Kansas City, Missouri.

John P. Roche. Academic Dean and Professor of Civilization and Foreign Affairs, Fletcher School of Law and Diplomacy, Tufts University, Medford, Massachusetts. Formerly consultant to the Vice President and the Department of State (1964–1966), and Special Consultant to the President (1966–1968).

Donald Rumsfeld. President and Chief Executive Officer, G. D. Searle and Company, Skokie, Illinois. Formerly Secretary of Defense (1975–1976), U.S. Permanent Representative to NATO (1973–1974), member of U.S. Congress (1963–1969).

Harriet Fast Scott. Author and lecturer. She serves as a consultant on Soviet military and political-military affairs to various research institutions and government organizations. Formerly with Stanford Research Institute.

Laurence Hirsch Silberman. Partner, Morrison and Foerster, Washington, D.C. Also a visiting fellow of the American Enterprise Institute and member of the Council on Foreign Relations. Formerly Ambassador to Yugoslavia 1975–1977. Deputy Attorney General of the United States 1974–1975, Under Secretary of Labor, 1970–1973.

Index

List of Contributors

Dan Caldwell is associate professor of political science at Pepperdine University.

F.R. Cleminson heads the Department of Verification Program in the Canadian Department of External Affairs.

William J. Durch is a doctoral student in political science at the Massachusetts Institute of Technology and an adjunct research fellow at the Center for Science and International Affairs, Harvard University.

Warren Heckrotte is a physicist at Lawrence Livermore National Laboratory and has served as a member of the U.S. delegation during the TTBT, PNET, and CTBT negotiations.

Allan S. Krass is professor of physics and science policy at Hampshire College.

Michael Krepon is a senior associate at the Carnegie Endowment for International Peace.

Mark M. Lowenthal is an analyst in national defense with the Congressional Research Service, Library of Congress.

Jeffrey Richelson is associate professor at the School of Government and Public Administration, American University.

James A. Schear is on the research staff of the Center for Science and International Affairs, Harvard University.

Dean A. Wilkening is a physicist and research associate at the Rand Corporation.

Joel S. Wit is a defense consultant currently working on a congressional staff.

About the Editor

William C. Potter is executive director of the Center for International and Strategic Affairs, University of California, Los Angeles, and program coordinator for the Rand/UCLA Center for the Study of Soviet International Behavior. He is the author of *Nuclear Power and Nonproliferation: An Interdisciplinary Perspective* (1982), the editor of *Verification and SALT: the Challenge of Strategic Deception* (1980), and the co-editor of *Soviet Decisionmaking for National Security* (1984). He also has contributed to numerous scholarly books and journals. His current research focuses on Soviet nuclear export policy and verification of arms control agreements.

Studies in International and Strategic Affairs

**Center for International and Strategic Affairs
University of California, Los Angeles**

List of Publications

William C. Potter, ed., *Verification and SALT* (Westview Press, 1980).

Bennett Ramberg, *Destruction of Nuclear Energy Facilities in War: The Problem and Implications* (Lexington Books, 1980); revised and reissued as *Nuclear Power Plants as Weapons for the Enemy: An Unrecognized Military Peril* (University of California Press, 1984).

Paul Jabber, *Not by War Alone: Security and Arms Control in the Middle East* (University of California Press, 1981).

Roman Kolkowicz and Andrzej Korbonski, eds., *Soldiers, Peasants, and Bureaucrats* (Allen & Unwin, 1982).

William C. Potter, *Nuclear Power and Nonproliferation: An Interdisciplinary Perspective* (Oelgeschlager, Gunn, and Hain, 1982).

Steven L. Spiegel, ed., *The Middle East and the Western Alliance* (Allen & Unwin, 1982).

Dagobert L. Brito, Michael D. Intriligator, and Adele E. Wick, eds., *Strategies for Managing Nuclear Proliferation—Economic and Political Issues* (Lexington Books, 1983).

Bernard Brodie, Michael D. Intriligator, and Roman Kolkowicz, eds., *National Security and International Stability* (Oelgeschlager, Gunn, and Hain, 1983).

Raju G. C. Thomas, ed., *The Great Power Triangle and Asian Security* (Lexington Books, 1983).

R.D. Tschirgi, *The Politics of Indecision: Origins and Implications of American Involvement with the Palestine Problem* (Praeger, 1983).

Giacomo Luciani, ed., *The Mediterranean Region: Economic Interdependence and the Future of Society* (Croom Helm, St. Martin's Press, 1984).

Roman Kolkowicz and Neil Joeck, eds., *Arms Control and International Security* (Westview Press, 1984).

Jiri Valenta and William C. Potter, eds., *Soviet Decisionmaking for National Security* (Allen & Unwin, 1984).

Rodney W. Jones, Cesare Merlini, Joseph F. Pilat, and William C. Potter, eds., *The Nuclear Suppliers and Nonproliferation: International Policy Choices* (Lexington Books, 1985).